WINCHESTER'S 30-30, MODEL 94

WINCHESTER'S 30-30, MODEL 94

The Rifle America Loves

Sam Fadala

STACKPOLE BOOKS
Essex, Connecticut
Blue Ridge Summit, Pennsylvania

STACKPOLE BOOKS
An imprint of Globe Pequot, the trade division of
The Rowman & Littlefield Publishing Group, Inc.
4501 Forbes Blvd., Ste. 200
Lanham, MD 20706
www.rowman.com

Distributed by NATIONAL BOOK NETWORK

Copyright © 1986 by Stackpole Books
First Stackpole Books paperback edition, 2022

Photos by Sam Fadala and Nancy Fadala unless otherwise credited.

All rights reserved. No part of this book may be reproduced in any form or by any electronic or mechanical means, including information storage and retrieval systems, without written permission from the publisher, except by a reviewer who may quote passages in a review.

British Library Cataloguing in Publication Information available

Library of Congress Cataloging-in-Publication Data

Fadala, Sam, 1939-
    Winchester's 30-30, model 94.
    Includes index.
    1. Winchester rifle.   I. Title.   II. Title:
Winchester's thirty-thirty, Model ninety-four.
TS536.4.F33   1986   683.4'22   85-14806
ISBN 0-8117-1905-7 (cloth)

ISBN 978-0-8117-7176-4 (paper)
ISBN 978-0-8117-7179-5 (electronic)

Contents

	Preface	7
	Foreword	11
1	America Meets the 30-30	15
2	Commercial Loads for the 30-30	25
3	Handloading the 30-30	38
4	The 30-30 Improved	57
5	Sights, Sighting, and Trajectory	66
6	Small-Game Hunting with the 30-30	78
7	Varmints and the 30-30	85
8	Best Deer Rifle in the Woods	94
9	The 30-30 on the Plains	104
10	Larger-than-Deer Game	112
11	The 30-30 and the Bear	120
12	Tuning Your Model 94	130
13	Mastering the 94	140

14	Accoutrements for the Model 94	150
15	Maintaining Your Model 94	164
16	The 94 Goes to the Movies	173
17	The Model 94 in Your Life	178
18	Commemorative 94s	185
19	The Model 94 Today and Tomorrow	194
20	A Year of Modern Hunting with My 94	208
	Index	220

Preface

I was interwoven into the thickets along the riverbottom, slowly working my way along the banks of a stream that snaked in and out of the lowland trees and brush. Close to the stream I stayed, for the busy water's constant gurgling covered the cracking of splintery twigs beneath my boots. I placed one foot firmly before lifting the other, raising my boots only high enough to clear the brush, walking Indian-style with toes pointed straight ahead. In slow motion I observed the thickets ahead, sometimes with unaided eye, sometimes with the compact binoculars which hung at my neck

Through a tunnel in the maze I spotted a small whitetailed buck feeding away from the stream — a "meat buck," we would call him. Through that little passage I held the bead of my Model 94 on the target about 70 to 80 yards in front of me. I depressed the trigger while maintaining my sight picture, knowing any tendency to "snapshoot" would probably cause a miss.

Crack! The tumbling water of the stream seemed to go silent at the bark of my rifle as the 170-grain handloaded bullet dropped my deer. There was nothing spectacular about the harvest. I had a fine piece of venison for family and self, and had probably helped the lowland whitetail herd, which was not being harvested at proper management levels, so I felt useful as a hunter there. The little 30-30 had come through again, and in such workmanlike fashion that I could not help being impressed.

No fanfare. No scintillating ray gun zapping the buck with overwhelming force. Just a cleanly dispatched game animal. The little 30-30 had done it again—not with flare, but with its usual reliability, the kind of reliability I had counted on for almost 33 years of deer hunting. I have faith in the "little 30," and I have learned how to strain the most from the round and its rifle. Though I own a closetful of guns, the 30-30 in one of my three models still comes forth when meat is the object of the chase, too, for it does its work without undue spoilage and loss of food, and yet the game is dropped cleanly and quickly.

You couldn't ask for much more.

There are well over eight million 30-30s in this land, and close to five million of these are the Model 94 Winchester. You see, the Model 94 Winchester in 30-30 caliber is still America's rifle and round. And this combination has been a favorite for a long time. Sure, faster cartridges in bolt-action rifles have surpassed the old 30-30 lever-action. And in many situations, these modern arms are indeed a better choice than the 94 in 30-30. I know that. I also know that there are plenty of other theaters in which the Model 94 in some form with its old 30-30 chambering is just right. Not "also ran," but just right. I was awakened to this fact when an editor of mine wrote me saying, "I'm not sure you have the old 30-30 straight in your own head, Sam. There are times and places when the 30-30 is the *best* choice, not merely good enough."

Of course. Why else would the 30-30 and its lever-action firearm last from 1895 to the present day? Because of good luck? No, because of service. The American shooter knows what he's doing. He buys what works. Yes, there have been other reasons for selecting the 30-30, such as low-cost ammo and arms, as well as virtually worldwide distribution of ammo. But nothing could have saved the 30-30 if in the final analysis it did not perform properly and with dispatch.

Obstinacy was no doubt part of my reason for writing this book. I became tired of hearing many of my contemporaries berating the little 30-30 and its lever-action rifle. When one fellow gunwriter said the 30-30 was useless on deer beyond 45 yards, my pen began moving as if an invisible force were guiding it. Why, my own handloads for the 30-30 were more powerful at 200 yards than *anything* loaded in a 243 Winchester or 6mm Remington, both considered good deer calibers by this same writer. I couldn't put up with it anymore. I had to say something.

And as I said something in print, my mind wandered back over years of hunting with the little caliber. I had my first Model 94 in 1955. I wasn't any good with it. I used it as a snapshooter, something you pulled up and banged away with in some sort of attempt to guide a bullet from muzzle to target with wishful thinking. I hunted with the 30-30 four seasons in a row, 1955, '56, '57 and '58. It was in 1958 that I decided to abandon both round and rifle for something better. I had missed, as I recall now, four good bucks that season, and I blamed the little carbine for it.

By 1959, I told myself, I'd have a "good gun." I did. I had a Model 70 Winchester with a 4X Bear Cub scope attached. The rifle was chambered in 270 caliber. And that outfit did make a difference. On my first hunt using it I bagged a then-record Coues deer (Arizona whitetail) with my new rifle—at a distance of about 30

Preface

steps! The buck left his bed like a ball of fur fired from a huge slingshot, and I put up the rifle, saw some brown hide in the 4X scope and fired, the 140-grain MCS bullet going through the buck lengthwise.

For years I stayed away from the 94. I had bought mine for $40 used, refinished the stock beautifully with linseed oil and, when offered $50 for it, took the money and ran. But at times I wished I had it back. There were times when I wanted to carry a little slab-sided carbine into the brushpockets with me, times when I desired to work through the live oaks down in Sonora with a handmate rifle along, a good friend tucked under my arm, a rough little rifle I could take overnight on the backtrail without having to treat it as if it were made out of glass.

I got another Model 94, another 30-30. I still carried my 270 in long-range country, or when I felt I needed an edge when hunting for special trophies. But I had learned what escaped me the first time. I had learned to master the 30-30, and I found out that the Model 94 is not a beginner's rifle, not a "good gun for a woman," as I had read so often. Not so much a gun for the now and then hunter, but rather a tool for someone willing to work toward being an expert or near expert in the outdoors.

Anyone can learn to master the Model 94, and certainly thousands — no, millions — of hunters had done so. They learned how to handle her, and how to *aim* her. The 30-30 is the most famous sporting round ever developed in the history of firearms. The reason? I already said it — it works. But it does take presence of mind to strain the most from the little lever-action and its celebrity round.

The cognoscenti of the day may consider the 30-30 caliber to be no good past 45 or 50 yards, but the shooting public at large simply goes on putting venison in the pot without heeding the word of these experts. Of course, there are ways to make the Model 94 and its 30-30 round more proficient, and these ways will be discussed in this book. Today I often carry one of my Model 94s on the hunting trail because I have learned how to handload powerful ammo for them, and my 94s are tuned to shoot with good accuracy. I still have that reliable action, as well as the slab-sided profile which allows me to pack the rifle so easily. And I still have a 30-30, of course, which is fine, because, as Warren Page said, the round is "balanced," a factor we go into later in the book. It's just that my 30-30 handloads are a bit zippier (though totally safe) than factory fodder.

The little 30-30 has made up for lack of range by allowing me an easy carry. She has made up for lack of punch by being easy to stalk with. And she has taught me many lessons in ballistic effectiveness, for the 30-30 fires bullets of superb design — though we may often fail to take note of the fact. I found the 30-30 to be my "middle ground gun."

My love for muzzleloaders has kept me using a round-ball rifle for much hunting. This rifle, my primitive hunting piece, would be on one end of my hunting continuum. On the other end, I use modern, high-intensity, low-trajectory rounds fired from excellent scope-sighted bolt-action rifles. The 30-30 takes up the middle ground for me, between the old and the new as it were.

And the 30-30 apparently holds a middle ground for a good many other hunters in this land, as well as casual shooters, ranchers, farmers, cowboys and others who work in the outback as well as enjoying the outdoors. This is their book. This book belongs to just about all shooters across the country, because most of us have owned a 30-30, still own one or will have one someday. And at the very least, the rifle and round are much too famous to be less than familiar to every serious shooter. There simply are no shooters who don't recognize the Model 94 Winchester.

Foreword

This book is dedicated to the eight million 30-30s which have served shooters and hunters since 1895, and especially to the famous Model 94 Winchester which first chambered this round and which has grown to five million strong in manufactured numbers. The book is also dedicated to the shooter who owns a 30-30, has owned one or will own a Model 94. The 30-30 has been a milestone in American shooting, and as such is an important part of the history of firearms.

When the Model 94 appeared in 1895, it was an immediate success. In Chapter One we discuss briefly this amazing story of the first sporting round in the world to be loaded with smokeless powder, its 165-grain bullet propelled at a muzzle velocity of 1,970 feet per second with 30 grains of the new fuel. Here is the grassroots rifle, the workhorse, Everyman's gun, capable of putting food on the table today as it did yesterday, when the little rifle served also for protection in the undeveloped West where the law was not yet fully a part of society.

More venison has been harvested with the 30-30 than with any other round in the world of smokeless-powder shooting. Its detractors today say more deer have been wounded with the 30-30 as well. If so, it was through misuse of the round, for no deer properly targeted with correct 30-30 loads gets away. In my recent hunting, I have taken several game animals with the venerable 30-30 out of different Model 94 firearms: a standard carbine manufactured in the middle 1950s, a 26-inch octagon-barreled Model 94 made in 1899, a little Trapper's Model of today's manufacture and my constant companion—a customized Model 94 with a

24-inch octagon barrel. All of this game has been harvested cleanly and honorably.

The Model 94 is light in weight. It is fast-pointing, too, and I enjoy carrying my 94s because they feel good in the hand. They are well-balanced, and they are flat-sided. There is plenty of power in a factory 30-30 load for deer and similar game within range, and that power is enhanced by handloading. Almost amazing versatility results when the little round is handloaded. Then the fast-swinging 94, with its natural carrying ease and balance, becomes a rather powerful hunting tool as well.

She's an expert's rifle, and I call her a rifle even when she wears the 20-inch barrel. Carbine may be the more correct term, but just as the Model 7 Remington with its 18-inch barrel is a rifle, so the Model 94 with its 20-inch barrel is a rifle—or a carbine. Take your choice. Managing the Model 94 takes definite concentration and knowledge, and an entire chapter of the book is devoted to handling this superb shooting instrument. Anyone can master the 94, of course. It requires only a desire to do so.

America and Canada are not the only countries to employ the Model 94 30-30, though certainly this is America's rifle and caliber. In Europe, the 30-30 round is known as the 7.62x51R—7.62mm in caliber with a rimmed case 51mm long. And in Mexico—well, that's a story by itself. The little round and rifle made history south of the border. They were used by Pancho Villa's men as well as by countless hunters. Called the *"treinta y treinta"* in Mexico, the round and its 94 rifle are an institution. No *vaquero* would turn down a chance to own a 94 30-30.

There is *challenge* here. No doubt about it. Compared with the hotrock numbers of our day, the 30-30 is limited in range and power. But the reliable 94 and equally reliable 30-30 load are both a match for big game when the hunter accepts the challenge and hunts in accord with the ability of the cartridge. I accept the challenge of the 30-30, and so do millions of other hunters. The reward is plenty of quickly and cleanly harvested big game. Especially with handloads, the little 30 is up to many tasks. It's a plinker, a turkey rifle and load, even a varmint rifle and small-game taker. The 94 30-30 is also a wild-boar rifle with handloads, a close-range black bear gun and a "brush rifle," and of course it's a premium deer-harvester, even at 200 yards with the loads I will recommend.

Knowing the limits and capabilities of a firearm and its round allows us to increase those capabilities and reduce the limitations. This book works from beginning to end to do just that—increase the effectiveness of the 94 and its famous round. My own 94s have never balked, never jammed, never misfired. They have been true at all times, like old and trusted friends.

"I've owned three rifles," the man told me. I was in the Yukon. The year was 1966. And the man before me was a trapper of many years, having been born 60 years earlier at Whitehorse. "Three rifles," he continued, "all of them in 30 caliber. I started with a 30-40 Krag. Good round. I still have the rifle. Then I went to a 30-06. Got one cheap, and it was a good rifle, but I don't have it now. And I traded some furs for a little Model 94 carbine 30-30. I like my 30-40 real well still, but when it comes to getting my winter moose meat, I just grab the old 30-30. It's all I ever need."

Foreword

A lot of hunters have felt just this way, and this book quotes a few of these successful outdoorsmen. Part of the 30-30's fame rests in the hands of the expert outdoorsmen who learned to use that rifle and round in a professional fashion. They gave these little rifles names. There was Novia, a 30-30 of the Mexican countryside owned by a well-known American bear hunter. There was Little Eva, an Arizona 30-30 which put a lot of meat on the table of one hunter during the Depression. There was Turkey Track, a little carbine which inhabited a ranchhouse in Arizona in such a fashion that the rifle seemed to belong to the home more than to its occupants. There was Meatmaker, another 30-30 of the Arizona-Mexico border which lived up to its name in the hands of an old miner.

Guns Annual Book of Hunting, Fall 1979, Volume 18, page 29, says this of the 30-30: ".30-30 Winchester — Without question the greatest commercial success of the cartridges, thanks in great measure to the Model 94 Winchester." Yes, thanks to the Model 94 Winchester, and thanks also to that balance of round spoken of earlier, a balance which gives properly constructed bullets sufficient velocity for expansion and penetration without bullet "bustup" or separation of core and jacket, as can happen with some bullets of the day.

The 30-30 is no doubt a part of another era. And I am not trying to breathe life back into it, for it needs no resuscitation. The old round is alive and well and apt to remain that way for a long time to come. This book is not aimed at hard-selling the 30-30 or Old Slab-side. Neither needs my help. The book is intended solely to be a study of round and rifle, with hardrock information, not sentiment, filling its pages.

1

America Meets the 30-30

The year—1895. The world of shooting was about to have its very foundations shaken by an earthquake of 6.0 on the Richter Scale, the epicenter being a small (for the times) 30-caliber projectile of 160 to 165 grains in weight, driven by a relatively minuscule powder charge weighing only 30 grains. The cartridge case was also small—it would be eclipsed in the shadow of the ponderous blackpowder metallics of the day, such as the 50-110 Winchester or even the 45-70 Springfield, whose big brass sides would all but hide this modest case. But the 30-caliber bullet would leave the muzzle at about 1,970 feet per second with that little powder charge pushing on it. And the propellant would not be the familiar black powder of the day, but rather a relatively new fuel—smokeless powder, they called it. Yes, it was the 30 WCF, or 30 caliber Winchester Center Fire, a round which would soon be known around campfires from the eastern seaboard to the high Rockies as the 30-30.

The 30-30 was not the first smokeless cartridge. But it was the first smokeless *sporting* cartridge of the day. In about 1885 the military ballisticians had smokeless powder on the drawing board, soon to be used in a metallic cartridge case. Actually, smokeless powder formulas had existed for several years, but it was 1886 when the French 8mm Lebel appeared, a military round loaded with smokeless powder. And in our own country, the military would offer a good cartridge to be adapted to the Krag rifle. This was the 30-40 Krag round, 30 caliber, loaded with 40 grains of smokeless powder, and available prior to 1892.

But the 30-30 was the first American

15

round to be offered to the shooting public at large, along with its sister round, the 25-35, of course. It made history. Boy, did it make history! The experts argue about it now, but the round was offered with either a 160-grain or 165-grain bullet. Nobody seems to know which for sure, or at least, no one I contacted could prove which weight was the first to be loaded into the 30-30 case. There is even some argument concerning the smokeless powder load. Some sources suggest that the 30-30 was actually a blackpowder round first: 30 caliber with 30 grains of FFg or similar black powder.

I don't believe that for a moment. The 30 WCF was called a 30-30 because it was popular in the late 19th century to name rounds based upon the average powder charge used in that round. Sure, the 44-40 was a blackpowder number: 44 caliber (actually more like 43 caliber) loaded with 40 grains of black powder. The 50-110 was 50 caliber loaded with

The author shows an original Model 94 Winchester rifle with a 26-inch octagon barrel. It's a take-down type, and the rifle literally breaks in two at the receiver.

The modern Model 94 Angle-Eject XTR with its 20-inch barrel looks much like the original, but a Model 94 fan can easily tell the difference between the old and the new.

110 grains of black powder. And so forth. But there was also the 30-40 Krag, and it used smokeless powder. No, the 30-30 was designed to be smokeless from the start, in my opinion, and note that it was called the 30 WCF by Winchester. The 30-30 name came later, after it was recognized that 30 grains of powder — smokeless powder — happened to be the nominal load for the round at the time.

That the 30-30 was fast for its day and that it used smokeless powder were two big factors, all right, but the bullet itself was another interesting particular from the sportsman's point of view. It was not the common lead or lead alloy bullet, but rather a jacketed bullet. That is, it had a lead core, but the core was covered by a metallic skin. This combination allowed that high velocity figure without leading of the bore, which would have occurred, most likely, with the lead alloys of the day if the bullet had worn no jacket.

Today, with 3,000-foot-per-second muzzle velocity being ho-hum to us, and over 4,000 feet per second being available to any shooter who wants to buy a hot 22 centerfire round, we may fail to understand what was achieved for hunters and shooters with the little 30-30 and its then-exciting exit velocity of 1,970 feet per second. I have personally chronographed quite a number of oldtime blackpowder cartridge loads, and I go on record now as saying that 1,500 feet per second was just about all a shooter of that time could expect. I fired some 44-40 blackpowder loads recently, with fresh black powder, and the 1,200-foot-per-second mark was about all I could muster over my chronograph screens. About the fastest blackpowder round I have personally fired happened to be a 45-120 Sharps. That round gained a muzzle velocity of 1,500 feet per second in my tests.

Two factors, at the very least, were at work on the side of the 30-30, helping the rancher, the explorer, the hunter and any shooter. First, the higher muzzle velocity of the 30-30 meant flat shooting. The trajectory, as compared with that of the blackpowder "punkin tossers" of the day, was very level. If a shooter sighted the 30-30 for 150 yards, it would be no trick at all to make a good hit out of 200 yards without undue guesswork or "Arkansas elevation." For those hunters who lived with their firearms on a daily basis, I will bet that learning to place the bullet out to 250 yards was no trick.

And there was a second factor at work in favor of the little 30 — recoil was much reduced as compared with the big-bore blackpowder rounds, and yet the 30-30's

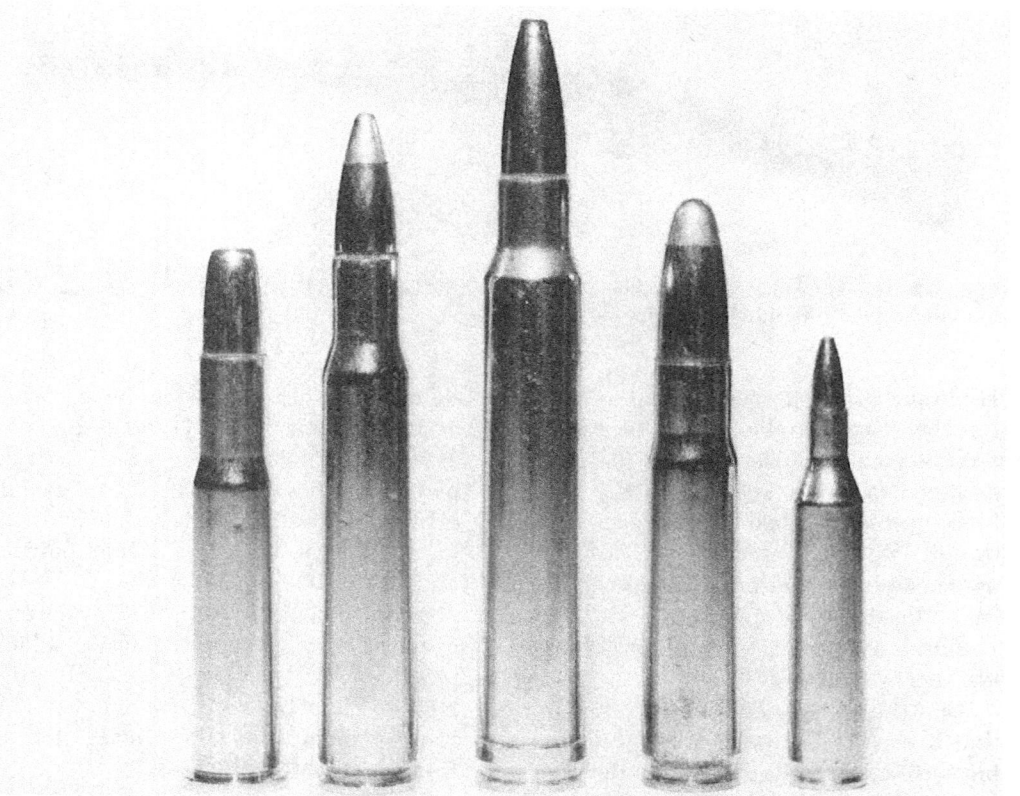

The power of the 30-30 is often impugned these days, but for its intended game, the little 30 still does a fine job at modest range. Here's the old 30-30 as compared with a few other interesting factory rounds. The 30-30 is on the far left, and the super popular 30-06 is to its right. Next is an 8mm Remington Magnum, a specialized round for long-range work on big game, never destined to be popular. The fine 358 Winchester round is next, and then, just for comparison, take a look at the little 17 Remington with its tiny 25-grain bullet.

effectiveness on game was excellent. In short, hunters found that they could manage their 30-30s quite well.

Recoil is a condition of Newton's Third Law of Motion, stating that every action has an opposite and equal reaction. Momentum is zero before the gun is fired; at firing, the gun is trying to head backward as fast as the bullet goes forward, but because the mass of the firearm is far greater than the mass of the bullet, there is not equal velocity in both directions — fortunately for us. However, the gun does recoil, of course, dependent upon several factors. One of these factors is the actual weight of the powder charge. In a 45-70, we are dealing with 70 grains of fuel, and the big 50-110 used 110 grains of black powder. But the 30-30 was working with only 30 grains of fuel, and that lighter powder charge was one of the factors in favor of the round's light recoil.

Sooner than you could say "Winchester, the gun that won the West," everyone was carrying a newfangled 30-30. Not only were the advantages of flat trajectory and light recoil in the round's favor, but smokeless powder was comparatively clean-burning. The blackpowder shooter had to scrub his firearm to get rid of the fouling. That fouling was not so terribly corrosive in and of itself, but it was hygroscopic — that is, the residue attracted moisture like a bathing beauty on the beach attracts attention. With the use of hot water, usually, the blackpowder fouling had to be removed not only from the bore, but also from the cartridge cases. Although the first 30-30 rounds were not totally clean in terms of non-corrosive primers, they were certainly a lot cleaner than the blackpowder rounds.

Also, there was no cloud of smoke to contend with. This element, however, was not all-important. I have taken big game as well as winged game with front-loaders, and though it is disconcerting to have to wait for the self-created smokescreen to disappear before the shooter can see what he got, the smoke can be lived with. Nonetheless, the lack of smoke was a favorable dimension of the new 30-30.

What about actual power? Let's be fair about it and look at this from both sides of the fence — the 30-30 and its blackpowder predecessors. A 44-40 could push a 200-grain bullet from the muzzle at about 1,200 feet per second, in actual chronographed velocity. The energy level, using Newton's formula, would be about 640 foot-pounds. But the 45-70 drove a 500-grain that fast, so its energy level was about 1,600 foot-pounds. The new 30-30 with a 165-grain bullet — I'll assume that was the actual weight of the first 30-30 bullet — at 1,970 feet per second would earn a muzzle velocity of 1,422 foot-pounds.

At the muzzle, using Newtonian data, the 45-70 would be more powerful than the 30-30 back in 1895 when both could be purchased freely over the gun counter. But the 30-30's velocity held up quite well. At 150 yards from the muzzle, the 30-30 bullet would still be doing about 1,400 feet per second. The 45-70 would be down to maybe 950 feet per second. The 30-30 would have about 720 foot-pounds remaining and the 45-70 about 1,000 foot-pounds left, but you would probably have to hold at least a foot high with the 45-70 at 150 yards, while the little 30-30 was *right on the money* at 150 yards.

What about the rifle for the 30-30? Actually, the design started out in the fertile mind of John Browning a good long while before 1895. U.S. Patent Number 524704, dated August 1894, gave us the Winchester Model 1894 rifle, which we now call the Winchester Model 94. In November of 1894, Winchester's catalogue showed the 1894 rifle, but not, of course, with the 30-30 smokeless round. Instead, two good blackpowder cartridges were chambered in this lever-action rifle, the 32-40 and 38-55. Those blackpowder rifles did not have to contain the pressure developed by smokeless powder, and the steel in their manufacture was commensurate with the rounds used in them. Hence, the blackpowder version of the 1894 rifle was not strong enough to withstand the rigors of smokeless powder.

Winchester took care of this. In August of 1895, the Model 1894 rifle was available in a new steel. It was called Nickel Steel, and this barrel *would* withstand the higher pressures developed by smokeless powder. Now we had the 30-30, for this 1895 introduction of the 1894 rifle model carried two chamberings, the famous 30-30 and the 25-35 round. The rifle wore a barrel 26 inches long, and there was also a carbine with a barrel of 20 inches in length. The rifle weighed about eight pounds, the carbine about 6½ pounds. You had to pay $18 for a new 1894 Winchester rifle in 1895.

The 25-35 was an interesting one. It lasted for quite some time in the lineup, firing its 117-grain bullet, and I believe the rate of twist in that Model 1894 rifle for the 25-35 was the fastest in a commercial rifle, perhaps even to date—being 1:8, one turn of the bullet in every eight inches of barrel. Of course, barrel length has nothing to do with actual RPS, or revolutions per second of the bullet, since RPS is a factor of the *rate* of twist and the exit velocity. A one-inch barrel with a 1:8 twist imparts the same RPS value as a 30-inch barrel with 1:8 twist, provided the muzzle velocity of the bullet is the same.

There was also the 32 Winchester Special, a 30-30 in case shape firing a bullet of 32 caliber instead of 30 caliber. Its actual purpose is still questioned by experts, but some feel that the 32 Winchester Special was introduced as a slightly better blackpowder round for those who preferred to handload with black powder. One thing is certain—the 32 Winchester Special was not chambered in any rifle to the level enjoyed by the 30-30, nor was the 25-35. It was the 30-30 that lived on and is still with us in force to this day.

In our study of the Model 94 30-30, it is important to understand the *force*—and I think that is the right word—which this round and rifle had on the shooting fraternity. As Browning and Gentry said in the 1964 Doubleday book, *John M. Browning, American Gunmaker*, pages 130 to 131:

There has never been so sudden and complete a change in the gun world as was occasioned by the advent of the Model 94 .30/30. Few, if any, rifles made specifically for black powder appeared after the 94 came on the market. For years, if you met a rider in the mountains with a rifle in his saddle scabbard, you could lay long odds on its being a .30/30. That model, especially the carbine, was a favorite arm of Mexican rebels, in the days when uprisings were frequent in Mexico. Older jobbers can remember bonuses above retail for the carbines and cartridges, coming from all points along the border. The .30/30 is still widely used, preferred by many as a deer gun, and a special favorite of ranchers and sheepmen. With them it is an old habit, hard to break. Winchester's 1958 advertisements represented it as 'the most popular hunting rifle ever built—bar none!' and their catalogue of the same year states that 'probably more deer have fallen to this old favorite in the past six decades than to all other rifles combined.'

Harold F. Williamson, in his A. S. Barnes book of 1952 entitled, *Winchester: The Gun That Won the West*, says that over 700,000 Model 94s were manufactured by Winchester by the year 1914. And Williamson states that in 1927 a very special engraved Winchester Model 94 with the serial number 1,000,000 was presented to Calvin Coolidge, then President of the United States. Furthermore, on May 8, 1948, President Harry Truman was presented with a Model 94 Winchester bearing the serial number 1,500,000. I understand that by 1966 the figure was 3,000,000 and that today it is 5,000,000 copies strong.

Indeed, there have been other 30-30 chamberings besides the Model 94 Winchester. The Models 55 and 64 Winchesters were variations of the 94, using essentially the same action. Winchester's single-shot Model 85 was briefly chambered in 30-30 caliber, as was the Remington Rolling Block single-shot. The Savage Model 99 was chambered in 30-30, too. So was the Marlin Model 93, which became the Model 36, which became the famous Model 336. In this last model, about 3,000,000 copies have been made, most of them in 30-30.

A modern-day single shot, the Savage Model 219, has been chambered in 30-30 caliber. And the Europeans have made a number of drillings and combination guns in 30-30, too. Even the bolt-action has been chambered in 30-30, to include the well-known Savage Model 340 and Winchester's Model 54, forerunner of the Model 70 Winchester. Savage's Model 40 bolt-action was also a 30-30 chambering.

Actually, when you consider that the Savage 99 was also chambered for the 303 Savage, this fact gives more impetus to the thrust of the 30-30; the 303 Savage is in fact very much like the 30-30 round, though the two will *not* interchange, and the 303 Savage was loaded with a 190-grain bullet for much of its life. You can still buy 303 Savage ammo with the 190-grain Silvertip bullet, and I do buy this load, but only to get the 190-grain bullet, which I pull and load into my 30-30 Winchester cases. The 30 Remington was a rimless version of the 30-30, and for all practical purposes the 32 Winchester Special was a 30-30 with a bullet of larger diameter. So the 30-30 round had its imitators.

Even when I was a youth, the 30-30 was so widely used that to say "Get your 30-30" meant the same as saying "Get your rifle." Larger rounds, in fact, did not supplant the 30-30. Think it over. The fine 30-06 was on the scene very early in the 20th century, but it did not send the 30-30 to the showers. In 1925, the excellent 270 Winchester hit the gun world like a tornado, but in spite of its whirlwind force, it did not blow the little 30-30 off the map. The good 300 Savage didn't, either. No, the old 30-30 M94 hung on. I enumerated the reasons earlier: its light weight in the carbine, good balance, sufficient power of the round, good firepower, good bullet penetration, fine handling aspects of the gun itself. These and others were and are the reasons for the 94's continuing popularity.

"The fact of the matter is that Winchester's .30-30 is and always has been a big seller because it does the job!" So said Al Miller in Rifle Number 37, page 43 of the January-February 1975 issue. H. V. Stent cited another interesting and, on the surface, somewhat amazing point concerning our little 30-30. He wrote in the *Gun Digest*, page 13 of the 34th 1980 edition, "In a whitetail deer survey taken by *The American Rifleman* in 1947, the 32 Special scored slightly better than the 30-06/220 gr. when it came to dropping a deer in its tracks with a hit in the heart area. The 30-30 170-grain scored about 15% less. What were the only two calibers which scored 100% when all the others made only about 50%? The 300 Magnum and — wait for it — the 30-30/150-gr!"

Sounds far out on the face of it, but as we go into the ballistics end of this story, you will see some underlying factors which make the above statement clearer. Make no mistake — the 30-30 is not as powerful as the 30-06, and nobody is suggesting any such thing. But I say again what Warren Page stated a long time ago, that the 30-30 is a balanced round. And it is that balance which makes it effective within its sphere, where it belongs — up to medium range on game of medium size.

Oh yes, the popularity of this round

and its Model 94 were amazing, and that popularity has been analyzed by many shooters over the years. Even in the 1950s, and probably well into the 1960s, the 30-30 was king in the West. As I grew up in Arizona, I doubt that I had a deer-hunting friend who didn't own a 30-30, and the ranches I visited, and even worked on in two cases, were veritable strongholds for Model 94s. Everyone raised "out West" knew this. Jack O'Connor said on page 117 of his book *The Hunting Rifle*, Winchester Press 1970:

> The best testimonial evidence I ever got on the impact of the .30/30 on the Western hunter, however, was from an interesting old character who lived just across the Arizona border in Sonora [Mexico]. I used to hunt sheep, antelope, and deer with him. He had been born in Jackson Hole, Wyoming, and he had hunted for the market in Wyoming, Montana, Arizona, and the Yukon. He said that when he got his first .30/30, along about 1896, it was a revelation to him that he could kill much better with it than with his black-powder rifles because he had to do less guessing on where he should hold on shots over 125 yards. He told me that he never had any trouble killing elk with a .30/30 and that if he didn't get seventeen or eighteen elk with a box of cartridges, he felt he was doing poorly.

O'Connor goes on to tell of this old hunter and his exploits on moose and caribou in the Yukon with the 30-30. And his story reminds me of Sweetwater John Bradsher, who lived for years in Patagonia, Arizona, on the Mexican border. I had the good fortune of living in Mr. Bradsher's home for a time, being best friends with his son, Robert, and when I came along, the only deer rifle around was a Model 94 30-30, which had brought in plenty of meat in its time.

None of this is meant to convince anyone to rush out and latch onto a Model 94 30-30. I already said neither the round nor its rifle need any promotion from me. Also, there are rifles and loads more surefire across a canyon than the 30-30 is, and I admit to using the 30-30 because I accept and enjoy the added challenge. However, that old 30-30 certainly has a history, a story to tell, and Al Miller in the aforementioned article says, "To the best of my knowledge, no sporting arm in the world has ever come close to its [Model 94's] sales record, and from all indications its popularity shows no sign of diminishing."

No sign of diminishing, even in the face of a "bad press," which is often the fate of the 30-30 today. One of the criticisms tossed against the Model 94 and the 30-30 round is lack of accuracy. To be sure, I doubt that the Model 94, out of the box, will shoot along with a Model 70 Winchester or a Model 700 Remington or any of the other fine bolt-action arms of the day. But watch out. A tuned Model 94 will maintain hunting accuracy in fine style. Let me turn once again to Al Miller's comments: "With a bit of practice, it's no trick at all to put all six or seven rounds in an 8-inch bull at 100 yards in 20-25 seconds [with the Model 94 30-30]." (Page 44, Rifle Number 37.) And furthermore, specially barreled Model 94s have proved highly accurate. Al Barr, one of the most respected arms experts in our century, obtained groups of only one-half inch at 100 yards with a specially barreled Model 94 30-30. (*Gun Digest*, 1980 34th edition, page 16.)

With my own handloads, I can sight in to strike the target about three inches above the center of the bull at 100 yards, and the bullet will drop into the dead

There's more power available to Model 94 fans today. John Fadala tries a shot with the Big Bore Model 94 in 356 Winchester, a potent round for big-game hunting.

center of the bull's-eye at 200 yards. At 200 yards, more energy is delivered from my 30-30 handloads than anything that can be put through a 6mm Remington or 243 Winchester, though these last two are great rounds. My statement is made to prove a point. Game departments in various places tried to get rid of the 30-30 for game larger than deer, and they probably had a point. An elk is big and tough, and I'd rather see a 30-06 or bigger used for it than a 30-30.

But should such a rule be applied to the fellow who has trained himself to hunt, *truly hunt?* No, he should be given some slack, and even more so if he handloads, because he's likely to do better work with his old 30-30 on just about any game than a less experienced hunter.

I was looking through a book entitled *Chips From a Wilderness Log* by Calvin Rutstrum, parts of which expounded on hunting, and on page 42 was a picture showing some snowshoes, a Peterborough toboggan of the "wilderness" type, some packs and provisions and a sheathed Model 94 Winchester carbine. The scene made me nostalgic. I thought to myself that if I were going to live in the backcountry for a while during the hunting season, and I wanted to pack along a rugged little firearm, it would very likely be a Model 94 30-30, just like Calvin's.

She's an old gal, but she has aged gracefully and well, and she has also been updated from time to time, especially in the ammo department. The ballistics of the 30-30 in factory form have been mildly improved over those of 1895, and it's not unusual to find a 170-grain bullet leaving the muzzle of the carbine at about 2,100 feet per second. My handloaded ballistics are a bit better yet, as we shall see as we travel the path of the 30-30 together.

The Model 94 has been updated, too, with an Angle-Eject model which has an excellent action, and with calibers of more punch than any 30-30 ever had, such as the 307 Winchester, the 356 Winchester and the 375 Winchester. There is also the fine 7-30 Waters, a 7mm based somewhat on the 30-30 case and chambered into the Model 94 in a rifle with a 24-inch barrel, not terribly unlike the very first Model 94s, which were *rifles* instead of carbines, having longer-than-20-inch barrels.

As you slip in and out of the brush or forest with that little Model 94 in hand, its flat sides hanging up on nothing at all, balanced like a piece of bamboo, light in the palm of the hand, you feel that you are up to the task of harvesting deer-sized game even though your weapon is a 30-30 and nothing more. If you have handloaded, your confidence may be even deeper-seated. She's going to come fast to the shoulder and point pretty well, though a veteran hunter will *aim* that shot — he won't simply toss a bullet out there like a hand-thrown rock in hopes of intercepting his game. And when that well-aimed shot is home, an honorable harvest will follow swiftly. I've known the experience many times.

2

Commercial Loads for the 30-30

The year—1916. The 30-30 has been on the scene for 21 years, and the Model 94 is on its way to selling one million copies. Winchester's extensive 1916 catalogue of its arms and ammo is a good starting place for those of us who are 30-30 fans, and who want to know what was happening to the 30 WCF and its Model 94 firearm at the time. Our central theme here is commercial ammunition for the 30-30, an important topic. After all, 30-30 ammunition could be—still can be—bought at just about any well-stocked crossroads sporting goods store and plenty of gas stations as well.

This fact was one of the reasons for the continued growth of the 30-30, I'm sure. It was an interesting self-perpetuation. The 30-30 was popular with new buyers because ammo could be found just about anywhere, and ammo could be found just about anywhere because the 30-30 was so popular. There was something else, too. The ammo was always excellent. To be sure, American ammunition makers have always turned out a fine product, but I have tested no ammunition which proved superior in loading over 30-30 fodder.

I have taken batches of various ammo and tested each for excellence. One of the major tests is ascertaining the standard deviation from the mean velocity, or the average discrepancy a box of ammo will have inherent in it. Standard deviations of 25 to 50 feet per second are certainly within permissible parameters, and most of our ammo from the great firms such as Winchester, Remington and Federal have managed this range and better.

An interesting old box of 30-30 ammo came my way one day. It had been found in an attic and was given to me for dis-

25

Thirty-thirty ammo has always been excellent. The author used some of these 170-grain Remington loads to harvest game. The ammo goes way back in time, but it is still good.

posal. I wish I had kept the container, but an expert on the matter told me that the old Winchester ammo was dated in the middle 1940s. I tested it in the late 1970s, and standard deviation from the mean velocity averaged around 10 feet per second. I was amazed at the fine results.

Today those results are still possible, and I am no longer surprised when I fire five or 10 rounds through my chronograph and learn that the standard deviation figure is 10 to 20 feet per second. That's good ammo. Not all factory fodder, or even handloads, will do as well. So 30-30 ammo, as far as I can detect, was always well-loaded. And there is something more — the bullets were always matched to the velocity. You could count on the bullet penetrating well, and yet the projectiles out of 30-30s "mushroomed," or expanded. Seldom did 30-30 bullets blow apart, sending bits of jacket this way and that while the lead core took its own course.

The bullet in most instances does not actually create the exit hole in game. Remember that last buck you got? You may have harvested that deer with a 30 caliber bullet, but the exit hole could have been the size of a teacup. No 30 caliber bullet flattens out to the size of a teacup, so something else made that big exit hole, and that something is a shock wave.

Shadowgraphs show us these shock waves emanating from the bullet at various angles. Special cameras managing speeds in the area of one three-millionths of one second photographically "stop" bullets in flight. The shock wave of the bullet makes a big crater in a block of gelatin.

The shape of the shock wave and its direction are dictated by the bullet, of course. So it is the bullet's ability to disrupt tissue that produces the quick harvest of game. In my hunting experiences over the past three decades plus, I have autopsied a great number of game animals, studying recovered bullets as well as wound channels. Truths have repeated themselves. The bullet which retains jacket and core in one unit is going to produce a consistent and effective wound channel. If a bullet totally blows up in the lung area, its effect may be dramatic, but that same bullet going to pieces in a shoulder or hip may be another story, and not a happy one at that.

The 30-30 bullet, it seems, has always been superb in mushrooming back with sufficient shape change to affect a good, wide shock wave, while at the same time hanging together to create a long wound channel. There is no magic in the 30-30 round which brings this fact about—it's simply a matter of modest velocity. And this modest velocity is one of the factors Warren Page was thinking of when he spoke of the 30-30 as "balanced." This part of the balance was between bullet and velocity.

Suppose we have a big 300 Magnum round. The bullet from that round—say a 150 grain at 3,400 fps, which is exactly what the 300 Winchester Magnum realizes from my custom Bishop rifle with a 24-inch barrel—must hang together when it smacks the terrible brick wall called the atmosphere. It must hold together under fantastic centrifugal force, for the revolutions per second (RPS) are very high. It must then make its way to the target and open up some, but not blow up.

It's just a lot easier to make a bullet behave at modest velocity than it is at high velocity, so there's no magic in the effectiveness of the ammo for the 30-30. The 30-30's velocity made it easier to build a bullet which would hold together well while still offering a good shock wave via mushrooming. By the way, today's fine big game or premium bullets—such as the Nosler Partition, Hornady Interlock, Speer Grand Slam or Mag-Tip and Sierras, as well as bullets loaded in commercial ammo—are so well designed

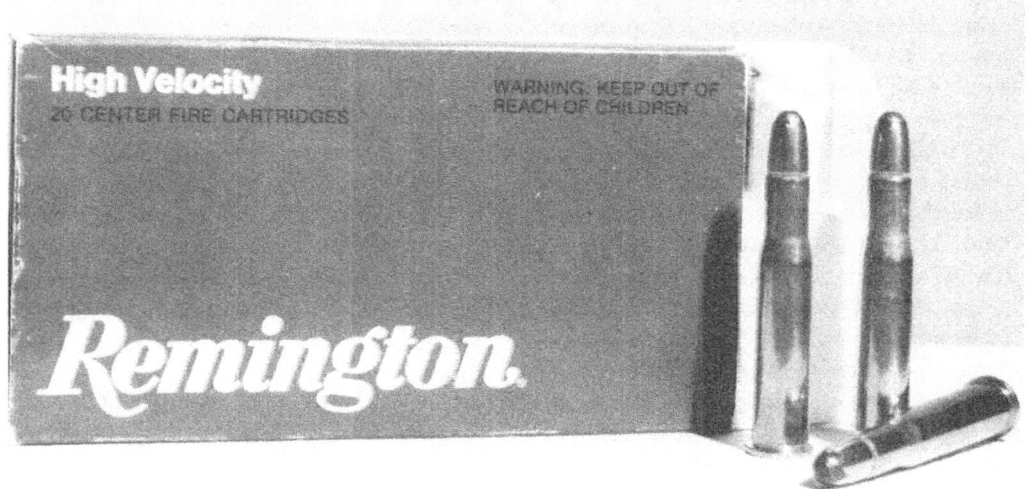

Today's Remington 170-grain Core-Lokt is generally the same excellent factory load, though the box is changed and Remington no longer takes the space to say "20 Center Fire Smokeless Cartridges."

that they tend to work very well at high velocity, even out of magnum calibers.

I have researched bullets for many years, and have asked hunters in many areas to relate various harvests to me, and quite often I've been able to learn much from their information. After much consideration and a reasonable number of personal experiences, I can safely say that with factory ammunition in the 30-30, a deer-sized game animal taken in or behind the shoulder will be harvested cleanly within the ranges commensurate with the 30-30's "power," that being up to 200 yards.

Something else—the old soft-point bullet with quite a bit of lead exposed at the tip is truly excellent as a reliable 30-30 bullet. One cannot go wrong in selecting a Winchester 170-grain Power-Point, Remington 170-grain Core-Lokt, Federal 170-grain Soft Point Hi-Shok and so forth. The Winchester Silvertip and Remington Hollow-Point Core-Lokt are beautiful bullets, too, though I think of these as more specialized in the 30-30, the Silvertip being excellent for deep penetration and the Hollow-Point Core-Lokt superior with the chest strike. I have found that the Silvertip tends to hold together very well in the 30-30, creating a long wound channel that is somewhat narrower than that of Winchester's Power-Point. The Hollow-Point Core-Lokt Remington bullet in the 30-30 is not explosive in the same way a varmint bullet will "blow up," but it does offer a wide wound channel. I have both of these bullets on hand right now in factory ammo because I like them in the 30-30. But if we're talking averages, that "old fashioned" soft-point bullet such as the Frontier 170-grain Flat-Point Interlock is hard to beat for deer hunting with the 30-30.

Incidentally, when I say "old-fashioned," I'm referring to chronology here, not implying any lack of sophistication in the soft-point bullet. Make a lengthwise cut in a modern 170-grain 30 caliber Hornady Interlock, a soft-point design, and you'll see a very advanced design.

Time and again, it is the 150-grain bullet out of the 30-30 which is the real knockout artist. I have spoken with hunters who could cite upwards of a dozen one-shot kills with any of the 150-grain commercial loads. Is the 150-grain bullet better in the 30-30 than the 170-grain bullet? Not really. What tends to happen is a bit more expansion of the lighter bullet, which creates quite a disruption in the chest cavity. Therefore a chest-hit deer will usually drop faster from a factory 150-grain bullet than from a factory 170 grain.

But for a shot *through* the shoulder, or for that matter just about anyplace other than the chest cavity, the 170-grain bullet is really a good one, perhaps a bit better than the 150 grain day in and day out in the 30-30.

The 150-grain bullet seems faster-acting than the 170-grain bullet on deer because the former is often of lighter construction, meaning more bullet upset and greater tissue disruption. Added velocity for the 150 bullet also promotes bullet upset. However, the 170-grain bullet with plenty of lead exposed at the nose is also superb, and probably better than the 150-grain bullet when greater penetration is desired.

Let's journey back to 1916, where this chapter began, and take a look at the Model 94 and its ammunition from the factory. In 1916 the extensive Winchester catalogue listed on page 39 the "Winchester Repeating Rifle Model 1894." The information states that this model was available "For .25-35 And .30 Winchester Smokeless, .32-40 And .38-55 Cartridges." Note that nothing is said here about a 30-30. In fact, 30 WCF, Winchester Center Fire, is also left out here.

By 1916 the 20-inch barrel was standard. The 26-inch barrel was still available, however. You could still buy the take-down model at this time, too, in the longer-barreled rifle. There was an Extra Light model weighing 7.5 pounds in the 26-inch-barrel version, and an Extra Light Take Down Model 94, too. And on page 40, all by itself, is a notice for ".32 Winchester Special Caliber" for smokeless powder. The Winchester people called the 32 Winchester Special a "new" round here, though it was probably introduced at least as early as 1902 or 1903.

The 32 Winchester Special is still a mystery cartridge in some ways. I have read it was available in 1895, while other sources say 1902 and yet others 1903. This is the story of the 30-30, of course, but also of the Model 94, so taking a brief glance at the 32 Winchester Special is worth the time. In the 1916 catalogue, Winchester explains that:

> The .32 Winchester Special cartridge, which we have perfected, is offered to meet the demand of many sportsmen for a smokeless powder cartridge of larger caliber than the .30 Winchester and yet not so powerful as the .30 Army [30-40 Krag]. The .32 Winchester Special cartridge meets these requirements. Loaded with smokeless powder and a 170-grain bullet, it develops a muzzle velocity of 2,112 foot seconds [actually feet per second], thereby generating a muzzle energy of 1,684.2 foot pounds. At the standard testing distance of 15 feet from the muzzle, this cartridge, with a full patch bullet, will give a penetration of 45 ⅞-inch pine boards.

Actually, the slightly larger hole in the barrel did offer more volume for the powder gases, and the base of the slightly larger bullet did allow more surface for the gas to expand upon, so the 32 Winchester Special could obtain slightly more velocity, hence energy, with the same bullet weight as fired from the 30-30; but the gain is academic. Also, a 30 caliber 170-grain bullet would have a greater sectional density than a 170-grain 32 caliber bullet, so the gain at the muzzle would probably be given up somewhat down-range anyway. So be it. The 32 Winchester Special hung on for quite some time. It also created a lot of controversy.

I recall cracker-barrel "discussions," some of them heated, in which a 30-30 fan and a 32 Winchester Special fan literally screamed at each other. The 30-30 lover was convinced that his was the more accurate and the more deadly round, while the 32 Winchester Special lover shouted that his round was better than the 30-30 in every way. The main reason the argument never got anywhere is that the two rounds were so much alike as to be in the same ballistic ballpark anyway.

But the 32 Winchester Special went on to be chambered in the Marlin 1893 rifle, and Marlin's 36 and 336 as well. It was imitated in the 32 Remington, a rimless version, and it was later loaded with a 180-grain bullet at an advertised 2,200 feet per second muzzle velocity, no doubt in a 26-inch barrel. It was also loaded with bullets from 110 grains in weight up to 180 grains. Today we have a 170-grain bullet advertised at 2,250 feet per second in Winchester and Remington loads.

In 1916 that Model 94 rifle would cost a buyer a full $21 in the carbine version, and in 25-35 or 30-30 caliber. It ran $17.50 in 32-40 or 38-55.

Ammunition was very cheap. You could buy 1,000 loaded rounds of 30-30 soft-point for $38. Or the handloader could purchase 1,000 primed cases for $18. The bullets were $6 for 1,000. Commercial ammo from Winchester included a 170-grain soft-point bullet or a 170-grain full patch (full metal jacket) bullet, same price. Winchester advised, "The cartridges described below are adapted to the Model 94 Winchester Repeating Rifles. For shooting big game, soft point bullets should always be used in preference to full patch bullets, as the effect of the former on animal tissues is much more deadly."

You could also buy a 30 Winchester Smokeless Soft Point in a "Short Range" version. These, with lead bullets, cost $30 per thousand rounds, loaded, soft-point bullet only, or $35 for the Short Range with a full metal jacket bullet. These bullets weighed 117 grains, and Winchester warned, "These cartridges require a different adjustment of sights from regular cartridges."

As for the naming of the 30-30, a 1903 catalogue from Schoverling, Daly & Gales, a New York–based company, called the cartridge the "30, W.C.F.," and the rifle was still the Model 1894, not Model 94, at that time and for some time to come. Incidentally, this 1903 catalogue did have the "Model 1894, 32 Special. Made for the .32 calibre 'special' cartridge, smokeless or black powder. Fitted with special sight, graduated for both black powder and smokeless powder. Twenty-six inch, octagon nickel steel barrel, weight about 7¾ pounds, number of shots 9." Ah, some light is shed on the 32 Winchester Special, indicating that those who feel the round was introduced for blackpowder shooting as well as smokeless could have a point.

By 1932 the ammunition was being called "30-30." The A.F. Stoeger catalogue of that year, page 56, calls the 1894 model the "Winchester Model 94 Take Down and Solid Frame." And in calibers it lists the "30 Win., (30-30)." In that year, the 30-30 devotee could buy a 170-grain full metal jacket bullet in factory-loaded form. Possibly this was more a law-enforcement measure than some-

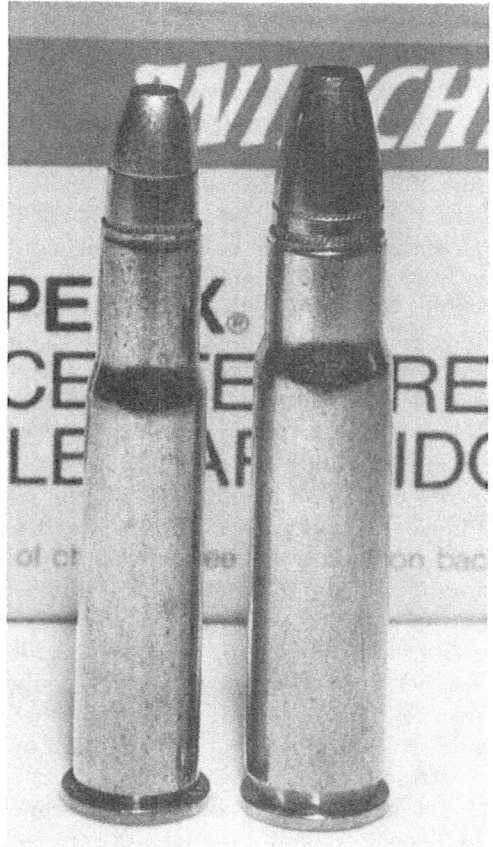

Factory ammo for the Model 94 is crimped, as shown by the 30-30 round on the left and the 356 round on the right. The handloader must also crimp his bullets in place because they can become loose in the tubular magazine.

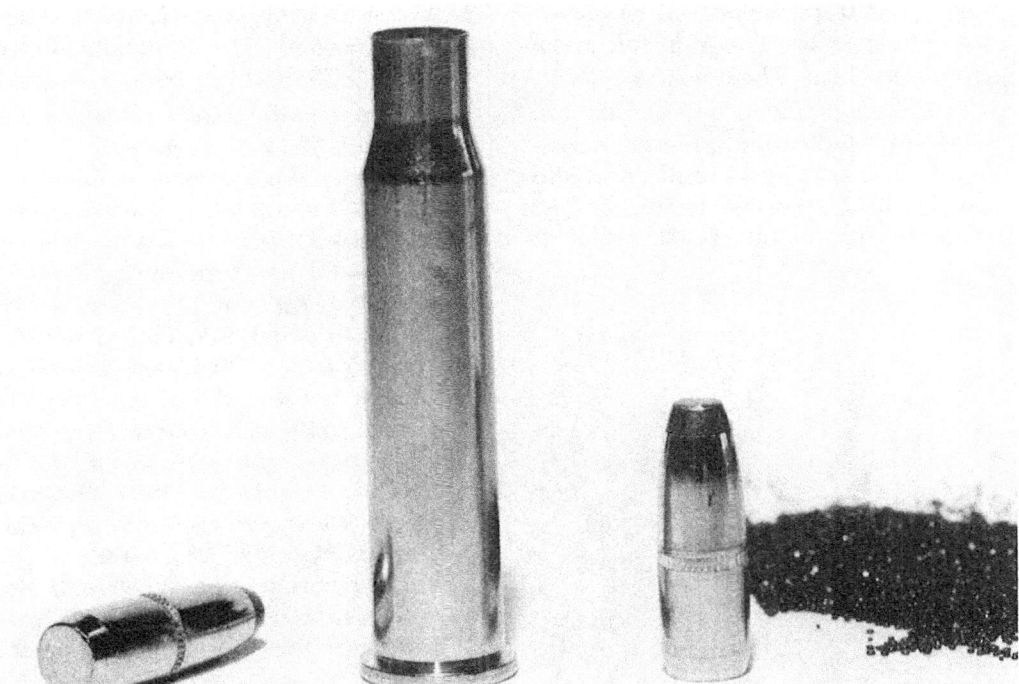
The modern factory load is a precise product. This Federal 7-30 Waters round uses a Nosler 120-grain boat-tail bullet. Note the spherical powder.

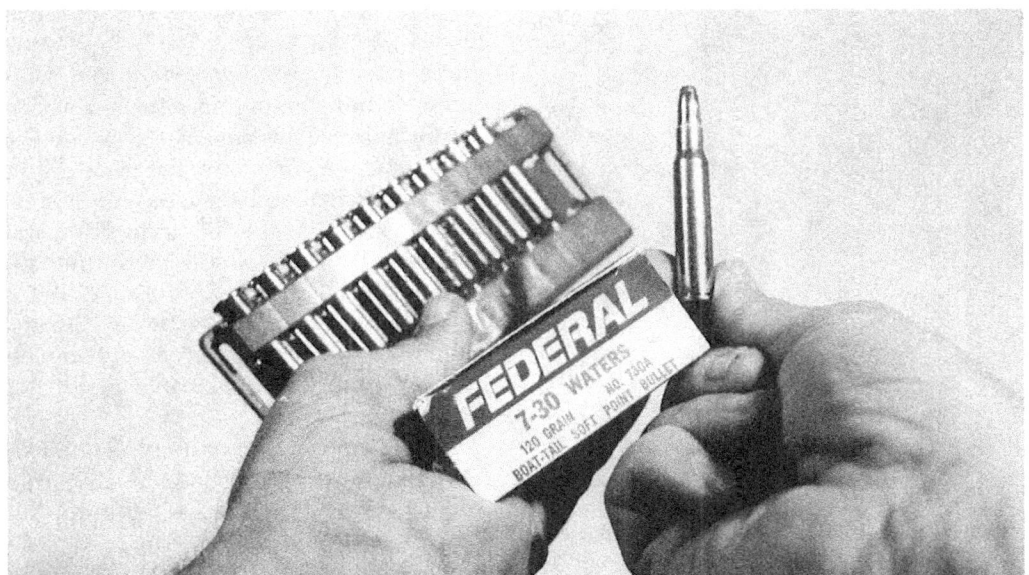
The Model 94 has been made in many different calibers. This Federal factory ammo is 7-30 Waters caliber.

thing aimed at sportsmen, but sportsmen could purchase the 170-grain full metal jacket bullet load. There was also a soft-point 170-grain bullet, a 160-grain full metal jacket bullet and a 165-grain soft-point bullet. A 125-grain bullet was also loaded in 1932, according to Stoeger. The 160-grain full metal jacket bullet is

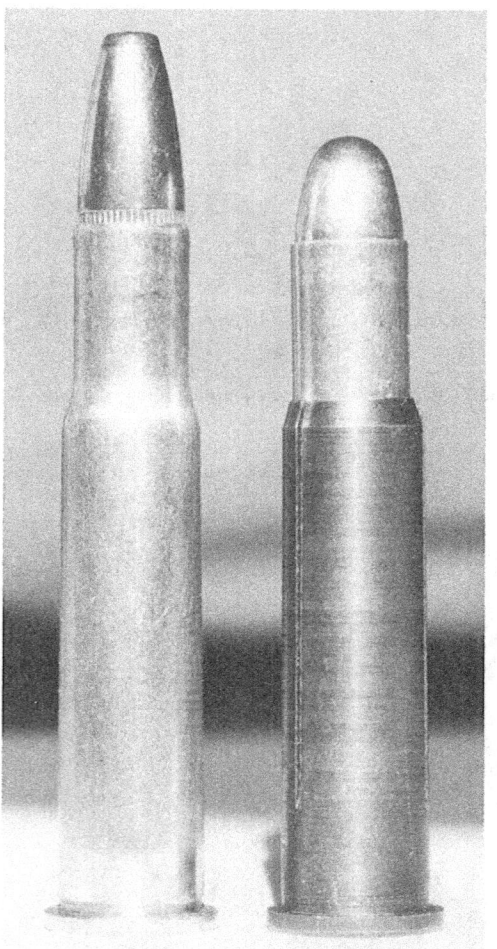

The 30-30 is using a factory round here which is not a 30-30. On the right, the 32 ACP round is fitted into an Alex Auxiliary Cartridge (Alex, Inc., POB 3034, Bozeman, MT 59715).

shown with a muzzle velocity of 2,200 feet per second. The 165-grain load is listed at 2,250 feet per second. And the 125-grain bullet is shown leaving the muzzle at 2,550 feet per second.

There was also a jacketed bullet of 170 grains in hollow-point configuration, much like our modern 170-grain Remington Hollow-Point Core-Lokt, I would imagine. Stoeger's for 1939 shows a 180-grain belted bullet at 2,100 feet per second, along with a 170-grain soft-point at 2,200 feet per second and the 160-grain full metal jacket at 2,250 feet per second. The 165-grain soft-point is still offered at 2,250 feet per second, as is the 125 grain at 2,550. These velocities, it is my opinion, are all from a 26-inch barrel.

But in the same year, Winchester factory loads had a different look from the aforementioned Peters (Remington) rounds. Winchester had a 170-grain bullet at 2,200, a 150-grain bullet at 2,370 and a 110-grain bullet at 2,750 feet per second. In the 1951 *Gun Digest*, there was a 150-grain Open Point Expanding bullet at 2,380 feet per second from Winchester, and Remington also had a 150-grain bullet at the same speed but in the soft-point version. The 150-grain Winchester Silvertip is listed, too, at the same muzzle velocity. The 160-grain full metal jacket bullet load is still in the lineup, too, at 2,200. And the 170-grain bullet is available in the full metal jacket, the soft-point and the Silvertip. Again, all velocities are from 26-inch barrels as far as I can tell.

The *Western Ammunition Handbook*, 19th edition, 1954, shows a 150-grain Open Point Expanding, a 160-grain Silvertip, a 170-grain Silvertip, 170-grain soft-point and a 170-grain full metal jacket. The 150-grain bullet is listed at

Commercial Loads for the 30-30

The fine Premium line of ammo from Federal is offered with a special 170-grain Nosler Partition bullet. Spherical powder is used to propel it.

2,410 feet per second, with that velocity dropping to 2,020 at 100 yards, 1,700 at 200 yards, and 1,430 feet per second at 300 yards. Listed energies are 1,930 foot-pounds at the muzzle, 1,360 at 100 yards, 960 at 200 yards and 680 foot-pounds at 300 yards.

The same book shows the 170-grain bullet at 2,220-feet-per-second muzzle velocity, dropping to 1,890 feet per second at 100 yards, 1,630 at 200 yards and 1,410 feet per second at 300 yards. Listed energy figures show 1,860 foot-pounds at the muzzle for the 170-grain bullet, dropping to 1,350 at 100 yards, 1,000 flat at 200 yards and 750 foot-pounds at 300 yards.

Remember the original load? That was the 160- or 165-grain bullet at 1,970 feet per second at the muzzle for a muzzle

One of the most interesting factory loads for the 30-30 is not even in 30 caliber. It's the Remington 30-30 Winchester Accelerator Cartridge, firing a 55-grain 22 caliber bullet.

energy of 1,422 foot-pounds. Because of the way the Newtonian formula for energy works out, that added velocity boosts the energy quite a bit when the 170-grain bullet takes off at 2,220 feet per second. Soon we'll show a handload with a 170-grain bullet at about 2,300 feet per second, for a muzzle energy of very close to a full ton—2,000 foot-pounds.

In 1965 the *Shooter's Bible* listed a Remington 150-grain Core-Lokt, a 160-grain Express load (Express was used originally to denote a load of greater force) with a full metal jacket bullet, a 170-grain Express with a "Mushroom, Core-Lokt" and a 170-grain Express with a soft-point Core-Lokt. Winchester had a 150-grain bullet and a 170-grain, and the Peters branch of duPont showed some "Inner Belted" bullets, including hollow-points.

The important point here is the sophistication of the bullets. In 1979 Remington introduced its "Accelerator," a 55-grain 22 caliber bullet (.224-inch diameter) in soft-point style and encased in a plastic sabot (pronounced sah-bow) weighing seven grains. The idea was to give high velocity to the little 30-30 with an under-caliber projectile. The sabot drops away from the bullet, which speeds toward the target at a muzzle velocity of 3,400 feet per second.

By 1985 the *Gun Digest* shows several 30-30 loads from the factory, starting with the 55-grain 22 caliber Accelerator and going to a 125-grain bullet at a listed 2,570 feet per second. The 150-grain bullet is shown at 2,390 feet per second now, less than in the 1950s, but still taken, I believe, in a 26-inch barrel. The 170-grain bullet is still with us, too, at 2,200 feet per second, and in many styles.

The moon has been reached. Movies are contained on little discs and whole albums of music on even smaller discs. Space probes wander farther from earth than anyone a few decades ago may have dreamed they would. The computer is spewing out data faster than 50 college professors could if they were mentally linked together, and fast food is really fast. And yet, the fuddy duddy 30-30 and its little Model 94 still thump along, doing in the hands of the practiced and careful shooter everything that was ever expected of either of them.

Francis Sell, who has been writing outdoor material for quite a number of years, made a little summary statement in the *Gun Digest* of 1985 which seems fitting as we close our brief glance at factory 30-30 ammo over the years. He said, on page 177:

> First, I doubt if 10 out of 100 deer hunters can handle the recoil of the 30-06. This opinion, it seems to me, is endorsed afield by the persistent popularity of such old-time favorites as the 30-30, which has been condemned by all the experts punditing on rifle shooting. But despite all of this missionary effort, the 30-30 is still the top choice of the majority of deer hunters, along with the 35 Remington caliber—mostly in lever actions.

Commercial Loads for the 30-30

BALLISTICS FOR SELECTED MODERN DAY 30-30 FACTORY AMMUNITION

Chronograph: Oehler Model 33 with Skyscreens, two machines

(All velocities instrumental at five feet from baffled screens) 40°F to 50°F in most tests, elevation 5,700 feet

WINCHESTER

150 grain
Power-Point (soft-point)
No. X30306

Barrel	Low	High	Extreme Spread	Average	Standard Deviation
20"	2,283 fps	2,305 fps	22 fps	2,294 fps	15 fps
26"	2,422 fps	2,452 fps	30 fps	2,437 fps	21 fps

170 grain
Power-Point (soft-point)
No. X30303

Barrel	Low	High	Extreme Spread	Average	Standard Deviation
20"	2,146 fps	2,150 fps	4 fps	2,148 fps	2 fps
26"	2,202 fps	2,237 fps	35 fps	2,224 fps	19 fps

170 grain
Silvertip
No. 30304

Barrel	Low	High	Extreme Spread	Average	Standard Deviation
20"	2,035 fps	2,039 fps	4 fps	2,037 fps	2 fps
26"	2,097 fps	2,108 fps	11 fps	2,102 fps	7 fps

FRONTIER CARTRIDGE COMPANY

150 grain
Interlock Round-Nose
No. 8080

Barrel	Low	High	Extreme Spread	Average	Standard Deviation
20"	2,266 fps	2,275 fps	9 fps	2,270 fps	6 fps
26"	2,365 fps	2,382 fps	17 fps	2,371 fps	9 fps

**170 grain
Interlock Flat Point
No. 8085**

Barrel	Low	High	Extreme Spread	Average	Standard Deviation
20"	2,058 fps	2,072 fps	14 fps	2,065 fps	9 fps
26"	2,126 fps	2,152 fps	26 fps	2,139 fps	13 fps

FEDERAL CARTRIDGE COMPANY

**125 grain
Hollow Point
No. 3030C**

Barrel	Low	High	Extreme Spread	Average	Standard Deviation
20"	2,388 fps	2,417 fps	29 fps	2,408 fps	20 fps
26"	2,517 fps	2,529 fps	12 fps	2,531 fps	8 fps

**150 grain
Soft Point Hi-Shok
No. 3030A**

Barrel	Low	High	Extreme Spread	Average	Standard Deviation
20"	2,199 fps	2,203 fps	4 fps	2,201 fps	2 fps
26"	2,281 fps	2,296 fps	15 fps	2,288 fps	10 fps

**170 grain
Soft-Point Hi-Shok
No. 3030B**

Barrel	Low	High	Extreme Spread	Average	Standard Deviation
20"	2,041 fps	2,064 fps	23 fps	2,052 fps	11 fps
26"	2,107 fps	2,124 fps	17 fps	2,116 fps	8 fps

REMINGTON ARMS COMPANY

**170 grain
Core-Lokt Soft Point
No. 30302**

Barrel	Low	High	Extreme Spread	Average	Standard Deviation
20"	2,055 fps	2,073 fps	18 fps	2,064 fps	5 fps
26"	2,162 fps	2,206 fps	44 fps	2,184 fps	31 fps

How To Select a 30-30 Factory Load

Never choose ammo based upon muzzle velocity alone. The minor variations in muzzle velocity here, brand to brand, may well prove different in different test firearms. All of the factory ammo tested showed excellent results. Instead, choose the ammunition based upon accuracy in your personal 30-30 rifle, and upon experience with a given bullet. For example, you may wish to use a 125-grain bullet on varmints, a strongly constructed 170-grain bullet for big mule deer and a faster-opening 150 grain for smaller deer or antelope.

3

Handloading for the 30-30

Versatility out of the old 30-30? You'd better believe it. But depth and breadth in its use come only for those shooters who handload. Factory ammunition for the 30-30 is excellent, as proved earlier through tests. But the factories see the 30-30 as a "deer cartridge," which it most certainly is, and they load it mainly for deer-sized game. True, we do have a 125-grain hollow-point factory load, and a good one, but those old squib loads listed in the 1916 catalogues, with all-lead bullets at modest velocity, are no longer to be found. And the 30-30 devotee will not find loads intended for game larger than deer.

Once again, we find the banners of the anti-30-30 writers waving in the wind as they march along singing the tune: "You can't get any more out of a 30-30 than the factory puts into it." I have read this statement many times. It simply isn't true, and the American shooter typically takes these admonitions as seriously as a heavyweight boxing champ would take threats from a flyweight boxer. RCBS, the famous reloading-tool outfit of Omark Industries, keeps a list of die sales, and over the years the 30-30 has always been way up toward the top of that list. In short, plenty of shooters reload for the 30-30.

A reloader can turn his 30-30 into a modest-range varmint rifle, as we shall investigate in a chapter on that subject. He can also hunt small game with a properly loaded 30-30. I have taken many cottontails and some squirrels with a downloaded 30-30, as well as mountain grouse and snowshoes, which are legal during my state's big game season. Load a 30-30 down to 25-20 or 32-20 ballistics, and you

Handloading for the 30-30

have a fine wild-turkey rifle. Of course, there are many loads suited for deer-sized game, but the reloader has a big edge here, too, because he can select bullets which will greatly increase the effective range of his firearm, or he can choose bullets for hard-hitting close-range work. He can even load according to the type of harvest he wants.

For example, I have used the strongly constructed 150-grain Speer Mag-Tip bullet, *in single-shot fashion only,* as it cannot be loaded in the tubular magazine, as we shall soon discuss. That bullet, however, will leave the muzzle at well over 2,500 feet per second with a safe handload from the loading manuals, and I have never known it to ruin much meat. Certainly, to harvest game, tissue must be disrupted, but I want to do that without mutilation, and this 150-grain bullet — truly meant for velocities in the 3,000-foot-per-second domain — holds together perfectly when started at 2,500 + feet per second, expands sufficiently and yet drops game with workmanlike efficiency. And the 30-30 fan can also load for a bit more range, too. The above-mentioned 150-grain handload shoots flat enough to allow a sight-in of three inches high at 100 yards, with the bullet being right on target at a full 200 yards.

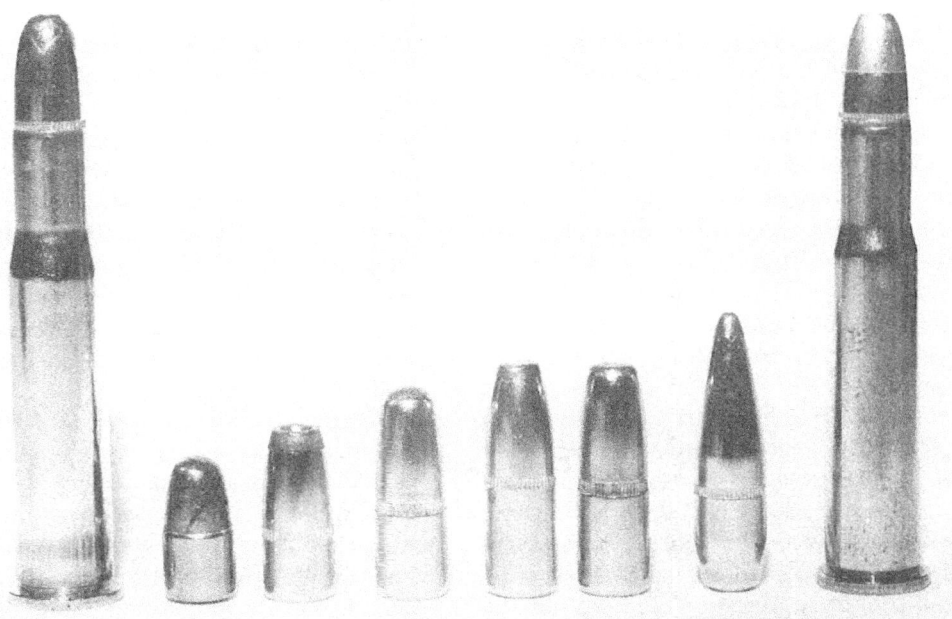

The versatility of the handloaded 30-30 round is amazing, especially when coupled with factory fodder. A fine 170-grain Core-Lokt soft-point factory load on the left is shown with a 170-grain Silvertip factory load on the right, with an array of bullets for handloading, including, from left to right, 100-grain Speer Half-Jacket, Sierra 125-grain hollow-point, 150-grain Hornady round-nose, 170-grain Sierra flat-point, 170-grain Hornady flat-point, and a 165-grain Hornady boat-tail bullet which can be loaded *SINGLY ONLY. Never use pointed bullets in the tubular magazine,* for the pointed bullet could detonate the primer of the round in front of it.

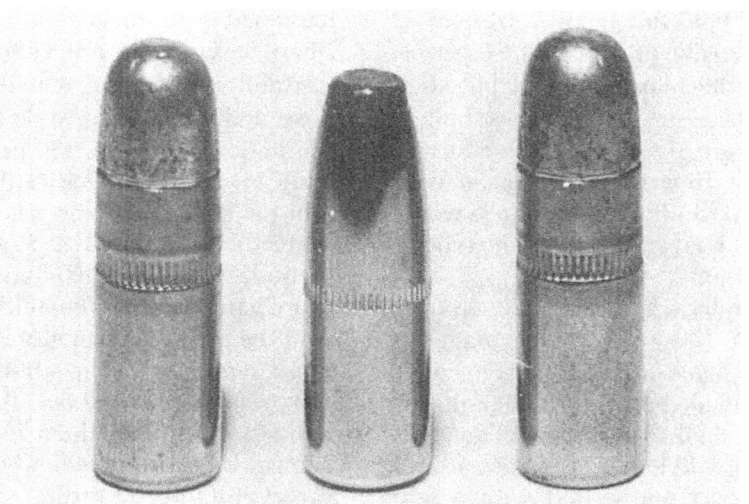

The .307-inch 170-grain Sierra bullet for the 30-30 is flanked by two 190-grain Winchester Silvertip bullets withdrawn from factory 303 Savage loads. Only the handloader can now use the 190-grain Silvertip in the 30-30, for the bullet is no longer available as a reloading item.

A 130-grain Speer bullet can be pushed along with an approved powder charge which develops a muzzle velocity in the 2,600–2,650-foot-per-second area. This is another flat-shooting load, and generally very accurate to boot. I have used it on the Plains in some rifles. However, I feel the heavier 150-grain bullet pushed out at about 2,500 feet per second is fine for antelope and other game which might be harvested at about 200 yards from the muzzle.

Finally, if a shooter lives where he can get close to larger-than-deer game, and if he is truly expert with his 30-30, he can build loads which will drop such game with assurance. Of course, shot placement is the name of the game when using ballistic force that is minimal for the game being hunted. I do not advocate the use of the 30-30 on game larger than deer, but there are experts who have cleanly taken some pretty big animals with the 30-30. A 180-grain bullet at 2,100 to 2,200 feet per second is pretty formidable in the hands of the expert shot, as is a 190-grain bullet at 2,000 to 2,100. At one time, it was safe to say that more moose were taken with a 30-30 in Alaska than with any other round. Those were serious hunters who needed the meat for survival. They got close to their game, and they *placed* their shots. They did all right, and would have done even better with our handloads for the 180- and 190-grain bullets.

Those who always have to have the fastest and the sleekest won't understand it when some of us say there are many days when we much prefer to have old Slab-side along than one of the modern long-range rifles, even though the latter are, in hard terms, better. These gentlemen may not understand, either, why we handicap ourselves, why we sometimes hunt with a muzzleloader or why we may select that middle-of-the-road lever-action 30-30, in between the muzzle-

Handloading for the 30-30

loader and the hotrock modern high-intensity round. We carry the little 30-30 for the challenge, yes, but we want it to do the job honorably for us, too, and as handloaders that work can be accomplished by the 30-30 with good *hunting*, and not simply by counting on long-range shooting to fill the tag.

One season I had the privilege of hunting the Apache Indian Reservation in central Arizona. Talk about wild country! I had been given permission to hunt squirrels, as well as fill my Coues deer (Arizona whitetail) tag. My rifle for both squirrels and deer was one and the same, the old 30. It was handloads which made that 30-30 into two distinctly different firearms in one. I had a load with a 110-grain bullet at near 22 Long Rifle muzzle velocity and a load with a 150-grain bullet at close to 2,600-feet-per-second muzzle velocity, both from the 24-inch barrel of my Model 94 custom rifle. That's what I mean by versatility. And this brand of versatility is realized through handloading. Aside from the usual reasons for reloading ammo—savings and increased performance—I say that the 30-30 is reloaded for versatility, a major reason RCBS shows the round ranked about fourth to sixth in popularity.

The Bullets

The Model 94 Winchester barrel has a 1:12 rate of twist. A 1:10 rate of twist is employed in the Marlin 336 and the Remington 788. In the 30-30, either 1:10 or 1:12 seems to work out well, The reason is that there is a *range* of RPS, or revolutions per second, to consider. The RPS of a bullet dictates its stability. But there is a range to work with here. I have gotten fine accuracy with a 170-grain bullet from a 1:10 twist, and from a 1:12. So in selecting bullets, I choose weights all the way from a mere 100 grains to a full 190 grains. All shoot well from the 30-30s I have personally tested. When I had a custom barrel built for a special Model 94

Bullets make the 30-30 versatile, and the handloader has a wide selection to choose from, including the 110-grain round-nose all the way up to a 190-grain Silvertip. *Pointed bullets must never be used in the tubular magazine of the Model 94.*

rifle (24-inch), I went with the 1:10 rate of twist and am happy with it.

Handloading for Accuracy

Since so many bullet weights work well from the 30 caliber bore with a 1:10 to 1:12 rate of twist, a shooter can select his bullet based upon what he needs to accomplish with the handload. He may also try various bullets in order to see which work best for his personal rifle. Even though barrels come through the same manufacturing process in the same manufacturing plant, they vary. Handpicking bullets for given loads and rifles can bring about better accuracy.

Another accuracy factor in handloading is powder selection. The little 30-30 case must use powders of medium to fast burning rates if decent velocity is to be achieved. Therefore, I choose my powders in accord with the work I want the 30-30 to do, from small game to big game, but it is very true that some powders will give better accuracy with given load combinations. At the close of this chapter, I'll give a few results of some very careful accuracy tests. For what it is worth, IMR 3031 powder has always proved to be very accurate in my own tests.

Care in reloading also aids accuracy. A careful handloader uses carefully controlled powder charges, weighed or at the very least spot-checked on a scale if a powder measure is used. I use a powder measure for my 30-30 loads, but I do check each tossed volumetric charge on my scale before dropping that charge into the case. It takes more time this way, but I think accuracy is somewhat improved by keeping the powder charges uniform from one case to the next. When loading plinking rounds, however, I don't spot-check with a scale, as these loads are very light to begin with and I do not fear that a miscue on the powder measure will bring me over my maximum. As long as accuracy is good, I'm satisfied with the plinkers.

Accuracy with underloads—in my tests, at least—has often been disappointing. My custom 30-30 Model 94 will keep three-shot groups within an inch at 100 yards, but the cluster gets broader than a Mexican sombrero with some squib loads. In fact, I have come across only a few underloads which have given me truly fine accuracy out of either 1:12 or 1:10 barrels. I urge the 30-30 buff to target-test underloads before calling them accurate. Again, firearms are individuals.

The handloader can create a fine product. This reload is ready for the seating of the bullet. It will then become another custom round.

Handloading for the 30-30

Your 30-30 may digest loads which my 30-30 gets sick on.

Handloading Problems

Another black mark cited against the 30-30 is that it is a difficult round to load for. I'll concede this point a bit. This case is somewhat thin and fragile as compared with 30-06 or 7mm Remington Magnum brass. Also, 30-30 loads must be crimped, and because these cases are bottlenecked rather than straight-walled, there is always the chance of crunching one during this operation. In the step-by-step description of reloading the 30-30, which follows later in this chapter, the shooter will see a crimping method which has worked for me and many others.

Another problem one must deal with in reloading the 30-30 is the fact that the Model 94 action does not enjoy the lockup that belongs to the bolt-action. Although it's pure poppycock to think of that action as "springing" way back during firing, which it certainly does not do, on the other hand, case stretch is possible, and we are dealing with an action which works best when the loads are kept under 40,000 PSI (pounds per square inch) pressure. I have no data on the new Angle-Eject Model 94 action as far as strength goes, but it must be quite a bit stronger than the old design, for its rounds do develop over 40,000 PSI. Also, in one test of the Angle-Eject, ejection with certain test handloads was perfect, whereas these same loads "hung up" in the older Model 94 test rifles.

Handloading Variations

We try to keep everything as constant as possible in handloading—the cases, bullets, powder and powder weight, primers, even the way we crimp the neck of the case on the bullet. However, perfection is not possible. And, of course, we are always dealing with the "extraneous variable," that little gremlin which seems to creep in like Mr. Tooth Decay, trying to foul things up.

Because of variables, it is highly unlikely that two Model 94s or two of any rifle will deliver precisely the same velocity, even if the same ammo is used in both arms. The information listed below was set down only after careful testing. And the testing was extensive. Some loads were brought to the range many times so that I could seek out a reliable average velocity and standard deviation. Even so, however, it's doubtful that the exact velocity will repeat in another set of test firearms. But the results should be very close, and therefore the listed loads are quite reliable and useful for the shooter. He can expect very much the same results as offered here.

All of the loads given were initially taken from the pages of reloading manuals such as Speer's, Hornady's, Lyman's, Sierra's and so forth. No load given here is an off-the-wall prescription. These companies have pressure-testing apparatus, and therefore the loads have been deemed safe in the Model 94 Winchester; that is why only loading-manual loads have been used in this book. But each load has been chronographed in barrels of 20, 24 or 26 inches. You have two important figures to work with here, the *average* muzzle velocity obtained with the load, and the *standard deviation from the mean velocity*, a figure which gives an indication of the reliability of the load.

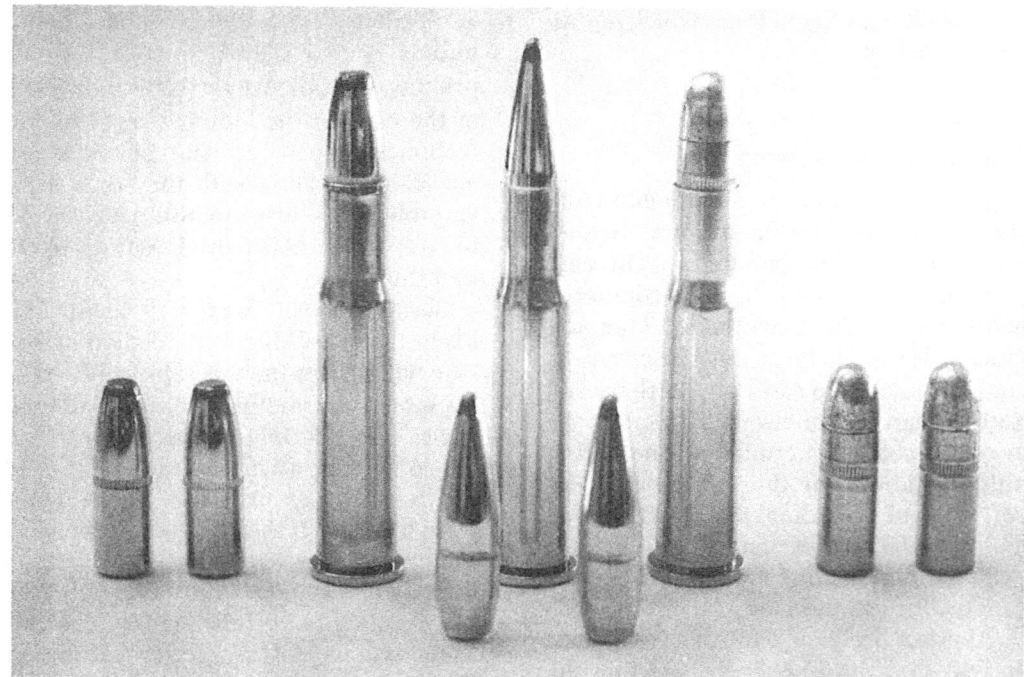

The 165-grain Hornady load in the center is for *single-load only*, and cannot be used in the magazine of the rifle. However, the .307-inch 170-grain Sierra, left, and the 190-grain Silvertip round-nose on the right can be used in the tubular magazine.

Pointed Bullets

Warning! Never use a pointed bullet of any type in the magazine of the Model 94 Winchester or any other firearm that has a tubular magazine. This warning has been sounded like a fog horn from the top of a lighthouse. It has been shouted so many times in so many places that a shooter not heeding it will gain little sympathy, not even from a court of law. To reinforce the point even further, here is a quote from Al Miller, editor of *The Rifle Magazine*, that prestigious periodical on firearms: "As everyone knows — or should, by this time — the idea of a spitzer's point resting against the primer of the round ahead of it is a worrisome thing." (*Rifle No. 37*, page 44.)

On page 43 of the same magazine, Al Miller goes on to say: "Pointed bullets such as the spire point should not be loaded ahead of each other in the '94's tubular magazine [or any tubular magazine], but can safely be used with one round in the chamber and one in the magazine, which is adequate for most hunting." The whole point here is that the pointed bullet resting upon the primer ahead of it could detonate that primer when the firearm recoils. Has it ever happened? I have sought out documented cases and have not found one, but this may be because shooters know better than to load pointed bullets in tubular magazines. *They just don't do it*; therefore, there are no rampant cases of damage from pointed bullets in tubular magazines.

Though I personally could not find a documented case of the pointed bullet blowing up in the Model 94 tubular magazine, I think it can indeed happen! Furthermore, there is documentation of full metal jacket bullets of the *round-nose* type blowing up in a tubular magazine. Hornady company has this data. In fact, four rounds detonated in a tubular magazine when a round-nose full metal jacket bullet was used. Though the rifle was not a Model 94, this is not the point. The fact is that a hard bullet, even though it was not a pointed bullet, did set off the primer of the round in front of it in a tubular magazine. Any full metal jacket bullet, Hornady warns, must be loaded in such a manner that only *one round* is in the magazine and one in the chamber when a tubular magazine of any type is used.

But as Al Miller points out, one may safely load the pointed bullet in the chamber with only one round in the magazine. I will go on record now as saying that I load a pointed projectile in single-shot fashion only, and that I never even carry loads with pointed projectiles in my pocket. I have a Cobra sling from Michaels of Oregon on my pet Storey Conversion, a custom Model 94 30-30, and that sling has a pouch which holds two rounds. These can be pointed because I will never use them except to single-load them directly into the chamber. I state again—do not even carry cartridges with pointed bullets when you are hunting.

But why would a 30-30 fan want a pointed bullet in the first place? Most of the time the pointed projectile is totally unnecessary. Hunting the brush? You don't need a pointed projectile, though pointed bullets do work OK in the brush.

The forest? No pointed bullet needed here. Get out on the Plains or into the big mountains, where I often hunt, and then a pointed bullet makes some difference in trajectory. It shoots flatter than a blunt-nose bullet. But it harvests close-range game no better. Blunt bullets do fine on game.

I personally tested two 150-grain bullets with loads which gave them an almost identical muzzle velocity. One was a load with a flat-point 150-grain bullet, and the other round was fitted with a 150-grain spitzer bullet. Here are the results of this test:

150-grain flat-point bullet
MUZZLE	200 YARDS	
2,327 fps	1,691 fps	– 8"

VS.

150-grain spitzer bullet
MUZZLE	200 YARDS	
2,317 fps	1,911 fps	– 6.5"

The sectional density of these two 30 caliber 150-grain bullets is identical. But the ballistic coefficients, which have to do with the shape of the missile, are not at all alike. For example, taking two Hornady bullets of 30 caliber and 150 grains weight, we find that the Round Nose has a sectional density of .226 and the 150-grain Hornady 30 caliber Spire Point has the very same .226 figure. But the 150-grain Round Nose is only worth a figure of .185 in terms of ballistic coefficient, while the 150-grain Spire Point is worth .358, a much better figure.

Now it is clear why, though both 150-grain bullets leave the muzzle at about the same velocity, the pointed bullet is going much faster at 200 yards than the round-nose bullet. The pointed 150-grain

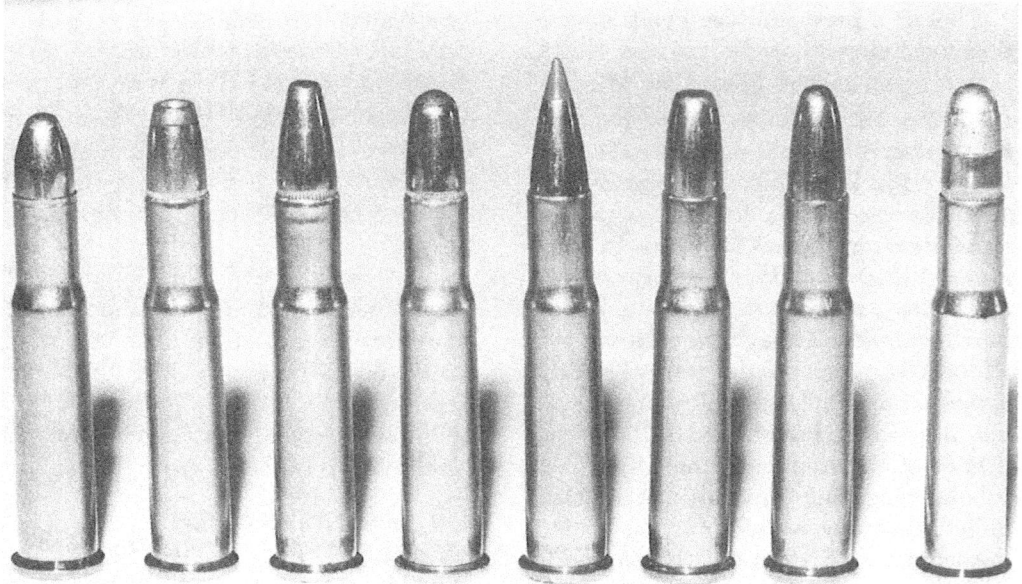

This array of 30-30 handloads shows versatility plus. On the far left is a 110-grain underloaded round-nose, with a faster 125-grain Sierra hollow-point for varmints next to it. Then comes a 150-grain bullet for deer and similar game, and a 150-grain bullet for the same work but with a blunter design. The pointed bullet is a 165-grain Nosler Ballistictip, but it was intended for single-shot use only—*never load a pointed bullet in a tubular magazine!* Next is a 170-grain Hornady flat-point for general use, and then a 180-grain round-nose for deep penetration, but this last bullet is *not allowable* in the tubular magazine. On the far right is the big 190-grain Silvertip load.

bullet drops 6.5 inches at 200, and the round-nose drops eight inches. As for energy, at 200 yards the pointed bullet has retained a lot more authority. It has 1,217 foot-pounds of energy left, but the round-nose only has 953 foot-pounds of energy remaining.

Furthermore, the spitzer-pointed bullet could be sighted in for 200 yards, while the blunt-nose bullet would be better sighted at about 150 yards. Meaningful? Not in the brush, so much, and not in the thick woods. But in the open spaces and some mountain settings, sure. The sharper bullet would be better. But . . . load it in single-shot fashion only, please. As for trajectories, several will be offered in Chapter 5 of this book.

The pointed bullet is going to win hands-down in terms of retained velocity. Hence it will also have more retained energy as well as a flatter trajectory. Frank Marshall Jr., in his *Handloader's Digest* article in the 5th edition of that publication, compares a 170-grain Sierra Flat-Point at 2,100-feet-per-second muzzle velocity with a 165-grain Sierra at the very same muzzle velocity. At 200 yards the blunt bullet has dropped to 1,300 feet per second, with only 680 foot-pounds of energy left. Marshall also shows a group size of eight inches at 200 yards for this bullet. Meanwhile, at 200 yards the pointed bullet is still going along at 1,760 feet per second for a retained energy of 1,200 foot-pounds, and Marshall shows a

Handloading for the 30-30

A case tumbler makes the finished product professional-looking.

three-inch group for it out of the same rifle (page 97). The title of Marshall's article, "Upgrading the 30-30 with Handloads," is amplified by an introductory remark which says, "Woefully retarded as a ready rolled, no cartridge responds more readily to the reload route than the all-time renegade favorite 30-30" (page 96).

Cast Bullets

Cast bullets work extremely well in the 30-30. You can get full power with the heavier cast bullets, and the lighter ones are good for small game hunting, plinking, practice in general and so forth. Since there is no mystery in casting bullets for the 30-30, and the usual procedures and tools are used, we won't belabor the issue here. All a 30-30 handloader needs to know is that cast bullets do very well in the 30-30, enhancing its versatility. I use standard Alloy No. 2 for my own 30-30 cast bullets, and I have found fine accuracy with those bullets

because they provide a lot of *bearing surface*. The more-pointed bullets are no good for the magazine anyway, and the long-shank bullet seems to be a lot more accurate in the 30-30, so this is the one to select. With a 180-grain cast bullet out of the 30-30, I have gotten groups measuring only an inch center to center. I use an RCBS Auto-Lube for sizing my cast bullets, as well as lubing them and applying a gas check. Instructions for casting are available in Lyman's *Cast Bullet Handbook*, and from other sources such as RCBS.

Handloading Procedures

This is not a handloading book; however, a few important points should be broached when considering the reloading of the 30-30 Winchester round. Here they are.

A casting furnace is used to produce lead cast bullets.

1. Inspect the Case

This step is always important, but perhaps more so with the 30-30 than with some other rounds. As I suggested earlier, the 30-30 case is not the strongest ever made, so it's wise to check that there are no splits and that the entire case, but especially the neck, is intact. Also, forget old cases. Many millions of 30-30 rounds have been manufactured over the years, and a person can still locate older cases now and then. Do *not* reload them. Some of those old mercuric primers caused structural damage to the case itself.

2. Clean the Case

I use a tumbler to clean all my cartridge cases, but I especially insist upon turning 30-30 cases shiny bright—for two main reasons. First, a clean case is easy to inspect. I know, the cases were already inspected in Step 1, but I like to clean and inspect again for cracks. Second, a clean case works well through the action and extracts better than a dirty case. Also—I'll admit it—I like clean and shiny reloaded ammo that looks brand new.

3. Trim the Case

Trimming is vital. An over-long case can mean a rise in pressure. I use a trim die for my standard 30-30 and a rotary trimmer for my 30-30 Improved cases. If the over-long case gets pinched in the throat of the chamber, it can retard the escape of the bullet and pressures then rise, so always trim cases to length. I went to the 30-30 Improved with my own custom Model 94 mainly to improve case life, to avoid having to trim so much and to gain powder capacity to make handloading easier, but not for ballistic improvements.

4. Full-Length Resize

Take the lubed case and full-length resize it. I know of no neck-size-only 30-30 dies anyway, but you can stop short of full-length resizing if you want to. Don't. Due to case stretch and other factors, a full-length resized case is a must in the Model 94.

5. Prime the Case

I have tried many different primers in the 30-30 and have yet to find a bad one. Therefore, I have no suggestion to offer as to a primer. Standard primers work well, but the Winchester large rifle primer, which is considered a magnum/standard, works very well in the 30-30 with no change in standard deviation of velocity.

6. Charge the Case

Never overload the 30-30 or any other cartridge. Use the loads found in the loading manuals. One potential problem with the powder charge for the 30-30, however, is that full cases of powder can mean crushing a case while attempting to seat the bullet. As the powder charge is poured through the funnel, gently tap the case to settle the powder and leave room to seat the bullet. Never bang anything which contains powder of any type, of course. Just tap the case lightly to settle the charge.

7. Seat the Bullet

Do this job carefully. I say "carefully" because of the case-crunching problem. Slow is the way to go.

8. Crimping

One way to set the die so that the crimp will be correct is to take a correctly *trimmed* and *empty* 30-30 case and use it as a model. Insert the seating/crimping die in the press, but leave the base of the die up off the ram's head. Now, enter the case into the die and screw the die downward a little at a time, continually checking the case to see if it is being crimped. Soon the empty case will show a crimp, and at that point the seating die is no longer screwed downward. It is set with the locking ring. This will ensure that the die is the correct distance from the ram to put a crimp on the mouth of the case only. Then the bullet-seating depth is altered until the bullet's cannelure is aligned with the neck of the case so that the crimp is placed on the cannelure with the mouth of the case folding into that cannelure slightly.

9. Try Your Loads

In a safe manner and in a safe place, work the reloads through the magazine and action of the firearm, as well as into the chamber. The rounds should feed perfectly, and the lever should close without force. Also, of course, the round should not stick in the chamber. It's a real blow for a shooter to get to his destination and find out that his reloads don't fit!

There are so many good handloads for the 30-30 that it is impossible to list them all here. Those few covered below are designed to make that old 30-30 quite a versatile and lethal round—given that a hunter will truly hunt for his game, get close and place those shots just right.

100-grain bullet (Half-Jacket design)

33.0 grains of H-4198 powder
20" barrel	2,672 fps MV	19 fps standard deviation
26" barrel	2,878 fps MV	9 fps standard deviation

43.0 grains of H-335 powder
20" barrel	2,659 fps MV	11 fps standard deviation
26" barrel	2,853 fps MV	21 fps standard deviation

Comments

Squib loads were tested with the 100-grain Speer Plinker Half-Jacket bullet, but were not as satisfactory as the loads listed above. Furthermore, it might be well to use the half-jacket design with full-power loads in order to ensure that the jacket does not strip. Although I know of no documented cases of this happening, loads I researched always showed this bullet at over 1,900 fps MV.

WARNING! Never use pointed bullets in a tubular magazine.

110-grain bullet

37.0 grain of BALL-C-2 powder
20" barrel	2,609 fps MV	12 fps standard deviation
26" barrel	2,671 fps MV	17 fps standard deviation

30.0 grains of RE-7 powder
20" barrel   2,752 fps MV   22 fps standard deviation
26" barrel   2,811 fps MV   24 fps standard deviation

16.0 grains of Accurate Arms Company No. 5744 powder
20" barrel   not tested
26" barrel   1,505 fps MV   25 fps standard deviation

Comments

    Many 110-grain bullets exist which will work in the 30-30. Speer lists its 110-grain Varminter hollow-point as correct for the 30-30. Light loads are sometimes less accurate with these 110-grain bullets in the 30-30, but good accuracy was obtained using Accurate Arms Company's 5744. With some of the harder 110-grain bullets, the latter load would be good for small game or wild turkey hunting.

WARNING! Never use pointed bullets in a tubular magazine.

125-grain bullet (flat nose)

38.0 grains of H-335 powder
20" barrel   not tested
26" barrel   2,709 fps MV   14 fps standard deviation

Comments

    Although this bullet and load was not chronographed in the 20-inch barrel, you can expect a loss of no more than 100 to 125 fps in that barrel length. This is a good varmint bullet and load.

WARNING! Never use pointed bullets in a tubular magazine.

130-grain bullet (flat nose)

31.0 grains of RE-7 powder
20" barrel   2,451 fps MV   11 fps standard deviation
26" barrel   2,593 fps MV   14 fps standard deviation

37.0 grains of H-335 powder
20" barrel   2,614 fps MV   17 fps standard deviation
26" barrel   2,683 fps MV   20 fps standard deviation

Handloading for the 30-30

Comments

The Speer flat-nose 130-grain bullet has proved very accurate from the 30-30 and certainly adequate in weight for deer at modest ranges with decent bullet placement. Construction of the bullet is more in the big-game domain than in the varmint class; however, for larger varmints this 130-grain bullet and load would certainly prove worthwhile.

WARNING! Never use pointed bullets in a tubular magazine.

150-grain bullet

38.5 grains of W-748 powder
20" barrel	2,371 fps MV	17 fps standard deviation
26" barrel	2,425 fps MV	16 fps standard deviation

38.0 grains of H-335 powder
20" barrel	2,570 fps MV	2 fps standard deviation
26" barrel	2,636 fps MV	10 fps standard deviation

Comments

The H-335 load of 38.0 grains of H-335 powder makes the 30-30 quite a potent number using the 150-grain bullet. The load was originally located in the *Lyman Reloading Handbook, 46th Edition*. In that manual on page 283, however, Lyman lists 39.0 grains of powder. My load is one grain lighter as I stopped at this point in testing since accuracy was excellent, as was muzzle velocity. From the 26-inch barrel, the muzzle energy with this load is 2,315 foot-pounds — much, much higher than the old original 30-30 load and also much more than today's factory 150-grain load.

WARNING! Never use pointed bullets in a tubular magazine.

165-grain bullet

39.0 grains of W-748 powder
20" barrel	2,358 fps MV	8 fps standard deviation
26" barrel	2,522 fps MV	23 fps standard deviation

37.0 grains of W-748 powder
20" barrel	2,367 fps MV	11 fps standard deviation
26" barrel	2,400 fps MV	13 fps standard deviation

Comments

Interestingly, repeated tests showed that with the 20-inch barrel, 37.0 grains of W-748 seemed to peak out in our test arms. While the 39.0-grain charge did offer over 2,500 fps

MV in the 26-inch barrel, we found better accuracy with 37.0 grains and decided on that load. Originally, this load came from the *Hornady Handbook of Cartridge Reloading, Third Edition*, page 211, as 39.0 grains of W-748 with a 170-grain bullet. The 37.0-grain load is my recommendation. Energy at 2,400 fps equals 2,111 foot-pounds.

WARNING! Never use pointed bullets in a tubular magazine.

170-grain bullet

37.0 grains of W-748 powder

20" barrel	2,295 fps MV	9 fps standard deviation
26" barrel	2,368 fps MV	15 fps standard deviation

36.5 grains of W-748 powder

20" barrel	2,318 fps MV	14 fps standard deviation
26" barrel	2,350 fps MV	16 fps standard deviation

Comments

This load, too, was found in the 3rd edition Hornday manual as 39.0 grains, but I reduced it because of high velocity with less powder. You will notice a higher velocity for the 36.5-grain load than the 37.0-grain load in the 20-inch barrel. This is one of those testing variables that are a fact of life. The 36.5-grain charge is strongly recommended for the 170-grain bullet. Most of these 170-grain bullets will be the standard .308-inch diameter, but Sierra offers a .307-inch bullet in an attempt to reduce pressure, and it is worth trying.

WARNING! Never use pointed bullets in a tubular magazine.

180-grain bullet

29.0 grains of IMR-4064 powder

20" barrel	2,009 fps MV	22 fps standard deviation
26" barrel	2,111 fps MV	26 fps standard deviation

Comments

This bullet was extracted from Winchester factory 307 Winchester ammunition. It is a strong bullet and a good choice for those wishing to hunt large game at close range. The load comes from Lyman's 45th edition handbook for the 190-grain Silvertip bullet.

WARNING! Never use pointed bullets in a tubular magazine.

190-grain bullet

29.0 grains of IMR-4064 powder
20" barrel	1,987 fps MV	6 fps standard deviation
26" barrel	2,005 fps MV	16 fps standard deviation

Comments

This load was listed for the 190-grain Silvertip bullet, which is still loaded in 303 Savage factory ammunition today. The handloader, using the appropriate commercial bullet puller, extracts the 190-grain bullet from the Savage 303 load and reloads it into the 30-30 — an acceptable practice. At close range, this hefty bullet with its strong jacket is a good penetrator. In a personal load in the 30-30 Improved, I have realized 2,150 fps MV with this bullet.

112-grain bullet (CAST, No. 2 Alloy) Lyman Mold No. 311316 with Gas Check

13.0 grains of Unique powder
20" barrel	1,292 fps MV	9 fps standard deviation
26" barrel	1,333 fps MV	11 fps standard deviation

Comments

In spite of a very good standard deviation, this bullet fell into groups of about two inches center to center at 50 yards. However, accuracy was adequate for plinking or small game. If lead can be obtained at a reasonable cost, economy is excellent with this load due to the low powder charge — over 500 shots from a one-pound can.

180-grain bullet (CAST, No. 2 Alloy) RCBS No. 30-180-F.N.

30 grains of H-380 powder
(Not tested in the 20" barrel.)
26" barrel	1,911 fps MV	16 fps standard deviation

Comments

This cast bullet load was very accurate, with five-shot groups of less than an inch at 50 yards consistently. Also, this load and bullet would serve for deer hunting, especially close-range work. The double-cavity RCBS mold allowed for rapid casting of bullets. Lead was purchased at 50 cents a pound for a bullet cost of about 1¼ cents each.

This book belongs to the shooter who finds that the 30-30, outdated to some people, is still quite a round, and one made even better with handcrafted ammunition. I'm aware that the 30-30 is not considered a reloader's special pet, but it's a fact that a lot of shooters have discovered that they can do much more than just save money when they load for this round. They can turn the simple little cartridge into many things all at once — a round that changes its posture and punch like a chameleon changes its color. The 30-30 is small-game getter, turkey-taker, deer-harvester and antelope-procurer, all in one case, with a lot of different loads.

Accuracy Chart

My friend Bob Anderson called me one morning with a range report on a pre-WW II Model 94 carbine he had recently acquired. He had consistently produced five-shot groups of 1.75 inches at 100 yards with that little firearm, using open sights. He had allowed the little barrel to cool between shots. Other than that, he'd simply fired 150-grain factory ammo and let the chips fall as they would. They fell into a good group.

A number of shooters have found — either by tuning their own Model 94s or by finding the correct handload — that accuracy was not the hit-or-miss proposition which the anti-30-30 boys would have us believe. Sure, a bull-barrel 308 match rifle is going to whip the little two-piece-stock 30-30. I imagine just about any good bolt-action rifle out of the box will, too. But this isn't a contest. The fact remains that 30-30 owners can obtain good hunting accuracy. Sometimes the first box of factory ammo they try will be the right fodder to feed the little 30. Other times it takes a little research in the form of shooting various loads until the right one is found.

This following report is only a sample of what happened with one 30-30 rifle. As such, its statistical validity is nil, but the shooter can go forth with his own 30-30 and do his own shooting and compare his groups with those obtained by my test rifle. The test rifle in this instance wore iron sights, though I have tested other 30-30s using a high-power scope. Because of the iron sights, all shooting was done at 50 yards, not 100 yards. Therefore, these are actual group sizes at 50 yards off the bench. The barrel was allowed to cool between shots. The rifle was a Model 94 Winchester made about 1899, and it wore a 26-inch octagon barrel.

The shooting went like this: Three three-shot groups were fired with each load, and an average was taken of the two best groups. This helped to create a "weighted average." In other words, if a group had fliers, that group was tossed out and the two better groups were averaged. A three-shot group was used because our interest is in *hunting* accuracy, not benchrest accuracy. While only six shots per average is again a small sample, it's enough to see that this particular 30-30 could shoot with hunting accuracy, and it also pointed out that this rifle did prefer certain loads over others. The latter finding has proved true in most of our 30-30 testing, as well as testing of other arms.

100-grain Speer Half-Jacket at 2,878 fps average MV

smallest group	largest group	average group
.80 inch	1.12 inches	.96 inch

100-grain Speer Half-Jacket at 2,727 fps average MV

smallest group	largest group	average group
.86 inch	1.05 inches	.96 inch

110-grain Hornady Round Nose at 2,671 fps average MV

smallest group	largest group	average group
.83 inch	1.09 inches	.96 inch

110-grain Hornady Round Nose at 1,700 fps average MV

smallest group	largest group	average group
1.06 inches	1.12 inches	1.09 inches

125-grain Sierra Flat Nose at 2,709 fps average MV

smallest group	largest group	average group
.89 inch	.99 inch	.94 inch

130-grain Speer Flat Point at 2,683 fps average MV

smallest group	largest group	average group
.57 inch	.59 inch	.58 inch

150-grain Hornady Round Nose at 2,425 fps average MV

smallest group	largest group	average group
1.22 inches	1.31 inches	1.27 inches

165-grain Hornady BT at 2,522 fps average MV

smallest group	largest group	average group
.92 inch	.97 inch	.95 inch

170-grain Sierra Flat Nose (.307-inch) at 2,105 fps average MV

smallest group	largest group	average group
.66 inch	.87 inch	.77 inch

190-grain Winchester Silvertip at 2,012 fps average MV

smallest group	largest group	average group
.67 inch	.71 inch	.69 inch

Conclusion

Remember, these scores are from one rifle only. They do not indicate that a particular bullet at a particular muzzle velocity is better than another brand of bullet. The very accurate load with the 170-grain Sierra bullet, using 28.0 grains of IMR-3031 powder, did repeat itself in three other 30-30s. However, as an example of how rifles vary, the

Hornady Round Nose 150-grain bullet, which did not deliver the best accuracy from this old Model 94, achieved half-inch groups at 50 yards from my custom 30-30 while the Sierra bullet and load, still supremely accurate of course, did not shrink in group size. Again, each rifle is a law unto itself. Feed it the diet that it wants. Find out what that diet is by shooting various loads, be they factory-made or home-rolled.

4

The 30-30 Improved

When the Storey Conversion, my custom Model 94 Winchester, was on the drawing board, its maker, Dale Storey, came up with a suggestion. "Why not chamber it for the 30-30 Improved?" he asked. "You can still use standard factory 30-30 ammo whenever you want, and you'll have better case life." So that's what we did. Since there are virtually millions of good Model 94 Winchester 30-30 rifles on the scene today, I'd be remiss in not reporting some facts concerning the 30-30 Improved round, because this option is available from several gunsmiths at a very nominal cost. Storey converted another Model 94 to 30-30 Improved for me at a cost of $45.

The 30-30 Improved is merely the standard 30-30 Winchester round with the case "blown out." In other words, when a standard 30-30 is fired in this improved chamber, the brass fills out to the dimensions of the chamber itself to make the "fireformed" round. The beauty here is that a shooter need not worry about looking for special ammo for the 30-30 Improved. Forget your ammo at home? Go to the nearest sporting goods shop and buy some standard 30-30 factory stuff. It will work perfectly through the action of the Improved. It will shoot with the same accuracy always provided by that rifle before it was improved, or perhaps better. So nothing is lost. But is anything gained? Yes and no.

There is no great improvement in raw ballistics that I can uncover. Using standard 30-30 loads—loads which can be and were found in reloading manuals—the 30-30 is boosted considerably over the factory ammo's authority. And that seems to be about it. In my 30-30 Im-

The 30-30 Improved is an interesting conversion for the standard 30-30 round, for which millions of rifles have been chambered. The author does not use hotter loads in his 30-30 Improved. Rather, he likes the fact that case stretch is lessened in the Improved round. Standard 30-30, center, is compared with two 30-30 Improved rounds.

have the Ackley design myself, but could not duplicate the ballistics Mr. Ackley found when he tested. This is not a slam at Mr. Ackley, who has forgotten more about cartridges than most of us will ever know. I cannot say why our ballistics differ. His rifle must have been different in some respect from the four Improved rifles I have tested and owned.

Ackley, in his *Handbook for Shooters and Reloaders*, Volume I, 1980 edition, says, "The Improved .30/30 in its various versions, all of which are quite similar to the one illustrated, is quite decidedly a surprising cartridge. With its minimum body taper design it can be loaded relatively 'hot' and still work fine in lever action rifles. It is an easy cartridge to handload and can be highly recommended."

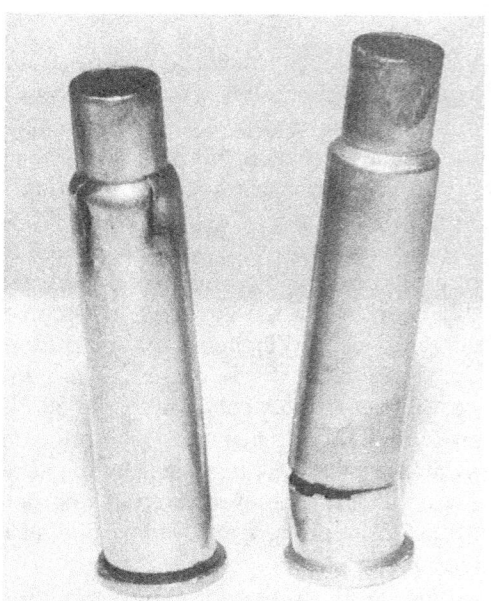

Improved rounds do have some attrition. These cases failed in the transition from 30-30 to the Improved dimensions.

proved, I have ended up using the same loads I've always used in my handloaded 30-30 ammunition. Recently, one of the anti-30-30 clan, a fellow writer, stated that he had a 30-30 Improved, only to find that there was no improvement. He concluded that improving the 30-30 was of no worth and that both the 30-30 and the 30-30 Improved were about as valuable as dirt. He's entitled to his own opinion, wrong though it is.

So the gain with the 30-30 Improved does not fall in the realm of increased power. P.O. Ackley, the renowned wildcat-cartridge designer, lists some super ballistics for his own 30-30 Improved. I

The 30-30 Improved

110	30	4227	3280 fs
	36	4198	3175
125	39	3031	2940
	35	4198	2940
150	34	4198	2700
	36	3031	2535
	37	HiVel #2	2700
	38	3031	2700
	40	4320	2500
	43	H375	2535

Standard twist: 10"

The above loads are from page 412 of the above-mentioned book. Though I have not gained quite the velocities shown here, by using the data presented, I have gotten 2,660 fps with H-335 powder in my 26-inch barrel 30-30 rifle with easy case extraction. But accuracy was not up to par, so I moved down two grains in the load, using 37.0 grains of H-335 with the 150-grain bullet and realizing 2,550 fps average muzzle velocity in the 24-inch barrel of my custom 30-30 with the Improved chamber. Make no

Fadala's custom Model 94 is in the 30-30 Improved caliber. Of course, the rifle shoots standard 30-30 ammo perfectly as well as the Improved ammo. Also, author uses standard 30-30 data for his Improved. The Storey Conversion, shown here, has accounted for many one-shot harvests with handloads.

mistake: nearly 2,600 fps with a 150-grain bullet is pretty good ballistics, about equal to the *original* 30-06 loads we had in this country. (My current 30-06 handload, however, pushes a 150-grain bullet at 3,100 fps MV.) In testing some very old 30-06 ammo, I got about 2,650 fps with the 150-grain bullet, and old

Properly constructed bullets are a must for all rounds. This fine Hornady Interlock bullet shows perfect mushrooming effect with minimal weight loss. Such bullets from the 30-30 with handloads prove extremely effective on game.

loading data show that to be pretty close to expected velocity.

The point is that the 150-grain bullet at almost 2,600 fps MV is quite adequate for medium-sized game up to 200 yards and perhaps farther. But I can get this velocity out of the standard 30-30 case and using data provided by a reloading manual. So I don't have to turn to a 30-30 Improved in order to achieve very zippy hunting loads out of the Model 94 Winchester.

As long as we are talking about the 30-30 Improved in the arena of power, it might be a good time to list the loads I use in my own Storey Conversion Model 94 Winchester with its 24-inch barrel. They are:

130-grain bullet	40.0 grains H-335	2,780 fps MV
150-grain bullet	37.0 grains H-335	2,550 fps MV
165-grain bullet	34.0 grains H-4895	2,400 fps MV
170-grain bullet	37.0 grains W-748	2,350 fps MV
180-grain bullet	33.0 grains IMR-3031	2,222 fps MV
190-grain bullet	32.0 grains IMR-3031	2,100 fps MV

These are all out of the Improved case, but I have tested them all in the standard case and they work fine. However, the value of the 30-30 Improved shows itself in areas other than gain in power. But before I go into them, I'm sure the 30-30 fan is interested in seeing the above loads with energy data attached. Here is that information:

	ENERGY	
	MUZZLE	200 YARDS
130-grain bullet/2,780 fps MV	2,231 foot-pounds	2,100 fps/1,273 f-p
150-grain bullet/2,550 fps MV	2,166 foot-pounds	1,999 fps/1,331 f-p
165-grain bullet/2,400 fps MV	2,111 foot-pounds	2,041 fps/1,527 f-p
170-grain bullet/2,350 fps MV	2,085 foot-pounds	1,804 fps/1,229 f-p
180-grain bullet/2,222 fps MV	1,974 foot-pounds	1,701 fps/1,157 f-p
190-grain bullet/2,100 fps MV	1,861 foot-pounds	1,611 fps/1,095 f-p

Interestingly, the ballistic coefficient of the Speer 170-grain bullet, which was used for the 170-grain-bullet test above, turns out to be .304, or better than that of a 150-grain Mag-Tip bullet, which was my 150-grain test bullet. It is also better than a 165-grain round nose and about the same as a Speer 180-grain round-nose bullet. So the profile of the Speer 170-grain bullet, in spite of the flat nose, is rather streamlined after all.

I had some fun with the 165-grain handload. I chronographed it with a shooting friend who told me that the 30-30 should have followed in the footsteps of the dinosaur and the dodo bird—become extinct, in other words. He had to believe his own eyes, and he saw the cases flicking out of the little 94 slick as a steel ball bearing rolling on ice, but he had not quite fathomed the upshot of the 200-yard remaining velocity and energy of that 165-grain bullet starting out at 2,400 fps MV.

He used a 243 Winchester, which I certainly admire as a fine deer/antelope

The 30-30 Improved

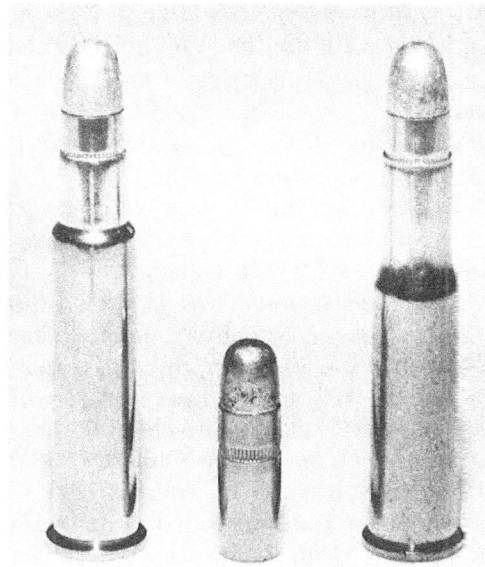

One of the author's favorite close-range loads is the 190-grain Silvertip bullet loaded into the 30-30 Improved (left). This bullet will average about 2,100 fps from the muzzle with a modest powder charge in the 30-30 Improved. The bullet is taken from the 303 Savage factory round (right). Note the round-nose style of the bullet itself (center).

boot. Penetration and all that, you know."

My buddy peered at me from the corner of his eye as if he were looking at a gila monster that had a hold on his big toe. "Yeah," he said. "I guess so." He wasn't real talkative the rest of the afternoon, especially after we set up my bullet box, a test unit, at 200 yards and whacked the box a couple times. My Speer 165-grain boat-tail penetrated round, potent enough and far-reaching in power. And he handloaded the 90-grain Speer bullet with IMR-4350 powder for 3,200 fps MV. That's a muzzle energy of 2,047 foot-pounds, over a long ton at the muzzle. You have to respect that. Still churning along at 2,687 fps at 200 yards, that 243 Winchester 90-grain bullet's remaining energy was 1,443 foot-pounds. My friend has taken several deer and antelope cleanly at 200 yards and more with that 90-grain bullet load.

"By the way," I said with a grin, "this old 30-30 with the 165-grain bullet at 2,400 gets to 200 yards still peddling along at about 2,041 fps. It has more energy at 200 yards than your hotrock 243, which you say is dynamite on deer. And it's a 165-grain 30 caliber bullet to

A superior long-range load in the 30-30 Improved is the 150-grain Speer Mag-Tip bullet. *Never load this bullet in the tubular magazine.* By using only two rounds in the rifle, there is never a bullet touching the primer of the round in front of it, because one round is chambered, the other remaining in the magazine. This tough bullet does well on game when driven from the 30-30 Improved at 2,550 to 2,600 fps muzzle velocity, which is attained from a 24-inch barrel with less-than-maximum loads from a Lyman manual.

about double the depth of his 90-grain bullet.

I said earlier that the Improved 30-30's gain was not necessarily in the ballistic force of the Improved round. So what values are offered by the 30-30 Improved over the standard 30-30? One is reloading ease. Let's look at that 165-grain bullet load for a moment. After you stuff 34.0 grains of IMR-3031 into a standard 30-30 case, there isn't enough room left over for an aphid to make a home. Seating the bullet often brings that unwanted sound . . . *crunch!* The powder charge is being invaded by the base of the bullet.

With the 30-30 Improved version, that fine load is easier to make than a peanut-butter sandwich. The powder should still be settled, which is accomplished by lightly tapping the case as the charge is poured, but there will be room for the bullet because the case has been blown out through fireforming.

A second virtue of the Improved case is less neck stretch. The 30-30, I admit, is an offender here. Case stretch can be a problem for the handloader. But the 30-30 Improved case—because of the sharp shoulder, I surmise—helps in this problem considerably. I still check my case length with a gauge when loading the Improved, but I have found case stretch to be minimal.

Third, case life is improved. This is partly the result of less case stretch, but overall fatigue of the brass is apparently less. I can get several loads per case with the Improved, but with the 30-30, cases sometimes show signs of "getting tired" after four firings or in some instances only three reloadings.

Also, depending upon the rifle in question, there can be *some* increase in muzzle velocity with the Improved round.

For example, I don't like using 39.0 grains of W-748 with the 165-grain bullet in the standard 30-30 cartridge. There is no room for the powder charge with that long bullet. In fact, I do not use 39.0 grains in my Improved, but I could if I wanted to, and if I did, that bullet would sing out at about 2,500 fps MV for a muzzle energy of 2,290 foot-pounds.

Others have found that in their rifles they can use considerably more potent charges in the 30-30 Improved case than in the 30-30 standard case in terms of smooth ejection of the fired hull. One experimenter who worked with the 30-30 Improved was John E. Traister. Like so many of us, Traister wanted to stay with the Model 94 for its lines, carrying style, feel, speed of action and light recoil, but he did want just a bit more authority from the round. He went Improved. In his article in *Handloader's Digest*, 9th Edition, Traister says, "It seems almost impractical to consider any improved cartridge these days, but for a fan of the Winchester Model 94 carbine for hunting the hills of Virginia, there just ain't nothing else beyond the 30-30 and the 375 Winchester. That's all the reason I needed to try the 30-30 Ackley Improved."

This shooter went on to compile a long testing history on the round, including accuracy runs. His usual group, using a scope sight, was two rounds touching one another at 25 yards and one right in there, for a three-shot group of under three-quarters of an inch. I don't believe Traister's Model 94 was tuned, so this is good accuracy and certainly hunting accuracy. Interestingly, Traister and I used very different loads but arrived at almost the same velocities for the rounds we both liked very much.

I find that my 150-grain bullet at 2,550 fps MV is quite effective. Traister ended up using 32.5 grains of H-4198 for 2,557 fps MV. I like the 170-grain bullet at 2,350 fps MV. Traister's 30-30 Improved load for that bullet weight is 32.0 grains of H-4198 for 2,383 fps MV, quite close to the 170-grain velocity I ended up with. Traister also loaded a 180-grain bullet in his 30-30 Improved for a muzzle velocity of 2,217 fps using 31.5 grains of 3031. Traister had used 32.0 grains of 3031, too, the load I ended up with, but in his tests he gained no added velocity for the extra half-grain weight of powder. Incidentally, he shows "Mod. pressure" for this load, in his judgement.

One more thing — all in all, I think I'm getting better accuracy out of the Improved case. I realize that this hypothesis is as scientific as wetting a finger and holding it up in the air to determine wind velocity and direction, but so far my data shows the Improved to be slightly ahead of the 30-30 standard. And remember that in three of the four guns tested, the firearm is one and the same for both tests. It used to be a 30-30, and the rifle was then rechambered to 30-30 Improved. So the tests for 30-30 vs. 30-30 Improved were made with the same rifle with only a chamber change.

Accuracy is *mainly* a function of good bullets out of good barrels. But other factors do enter in, such as bedding and action/barrel fit, chamber and so forth. I doubt very much that the case shape has a thing to do with the slightly better accuracy levels I achieved with the 30-30 Improved. My guess is that the Improved case loads better than the standard case, especially in the area of powder damage. In the standard 30-30 case with safe but strong hunting loads, the powder charge is often crunched by the base of the bullet. This means broken kernels of powder. Even ball-type powders seem to react to being crushed, and the reaction is in the negative.

There is also bolt thrust. I cannot prove that this is a factor here. I only offer the idea because a couple of my colleagues believe it to be pertinent. The cartridge, of course, does swell out to cling to the walls of the chamber during firing. This is why we urge shooters to use clean ammunition, but *never* oily ammo. Oily ammo can cause a problem with case cling. Another problem with case cling is that the thrust upon the face of the bolt is, at least in theory, going to be greater when the walls of the case slope, thereby encouraging the case to push back on the face of that bolt. But with the straight walls of the blown-out improved case, case cling is improved and bolt thrust reduced. There may be nothing to this phenomenon at work here, but it sure sounds good, doesn't it?

Don Roberts penned an article on the 30-30 Improved, and though its thrust was mainly negative toward the round, he did obtain 2,630-feet-per-second muzzle velocity with the 170-grain .307-inch Sierra flat-nose bullet, using 37.0 grains of IMR-4064 and Remington 9½M primers. Don called this his "most accurate load tested." (Page 37, *Handloader* No. 107, January/February 1984.) While I agree with Don that the 30-30 Improved is not going to whip the standard 30-30 in the power department, or not by much, that 170-grain bullet at over 2,300 is a good 300 fps faster than some of the 170-grain factory loads I tested.

Don also obtained a muzzle velocity of 2,518 feet per second with the 150-grain Sierra hollow-point bullet using 37.0

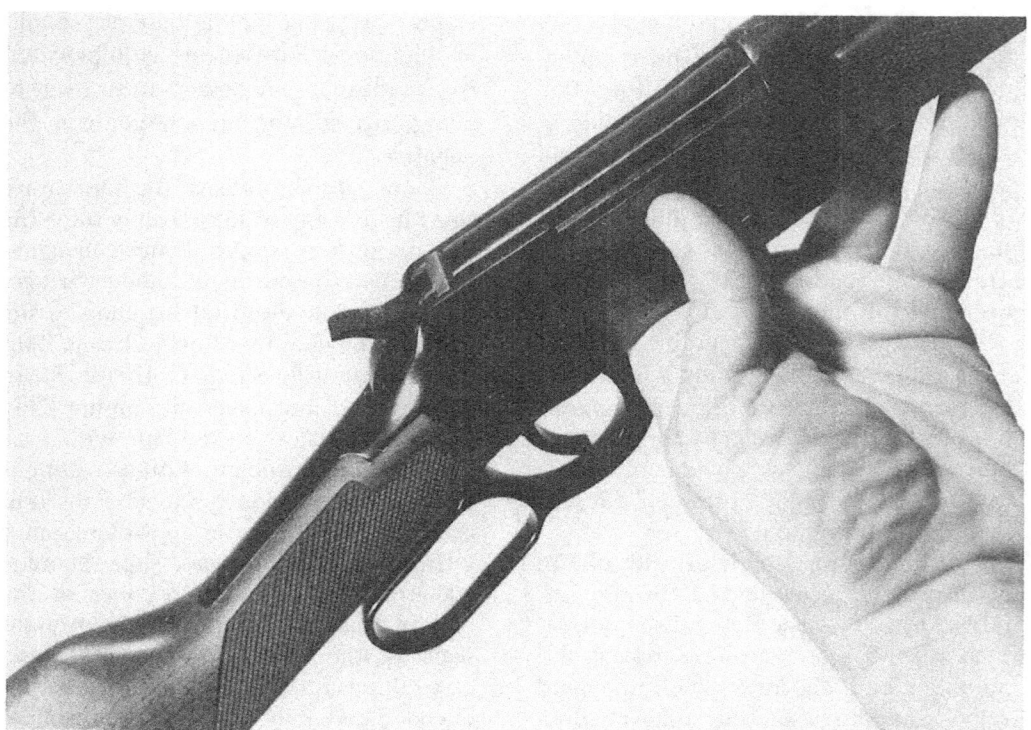

The action of the new Model 94 Angle-Eject is stronger than that of the older 94. Therefore, the Angle-Eject can use rounds such as the 307 Winchester, which turns out to be a 30-30 Improved in ballistics, or even better.

grains of IMR-3031 powder and CCI 200 primers. He called this one "maximum; good groups," on page 37 of the same article. With 40.0 grains of IMR-4320 and the same bullet, muzzle velocity in Don's test was 2,505 average, CCI 200 primers again. He called this load "compressed; good accuracy."

Should a shooter wish to have his standard 30-30 Winchester switched over to 30-30 Improved, I suggest the Ackley configuration. You can get reloading dies in the Ackley style from RCBS — order from your local dealer or write Omark Industries. This, in my opinion, is the improved version which is more of a standard than some of the other modifications. I have used three different sets of Ackley 30-30 RCBS Improved dies owned by two other shooters and me, and reloads fitted all of our arms perfectly.

The 30-30 Improved does seem to offer a better case for the reloader. And it is a very nominally priced switchover, under $50 as this is written. Also, the Improved's suitability for reloading does not alter the fact that one of the prime reasons for owning a 30-30 is the wide availability of ammo — out-of-the-box factory ammunition works just fine in the 30-30 Improved, with no loss in accuracy and only an insignificant and yet-to-be-proved loss in muzzle velocity.

The past few seasons, I have taken part in what is known in my state as the depredation hunt. Antelope have become too populous in a few regions, and the excess animals must be cropped or they'll be lost to the hard winter anyway. In fact, a tough winter is terribly rough on an entire oversized herd because when it gets truly bitter, all the remaining animals are in trouble. So hunters have been allowed to take several antelope per season — only one buck, but several additional non-horned animals.

My family and I like antelope meat and have good recipes to cook it, and of course, I have taken the opportunity to test loads during these hunts. I have found that with my Storey Conversion and the 150-grain bullet beginning its journey to the target at 2,550 fps MV, I can drop an antelope at 200 yards instantly with one shot in the chest area, and with minimal loss of edibles if the shot should stray and hit the shoulder.

My last harvest was a very old doe — and you can tell the older ones from the younger. She had paced her way onto a high plateau some 8,000 feet above sea level. I was on foot, and the hour was growing late. I cut below the rim in hopes that the 'lope's high-power eyes would not detect me, and tried to work in for a closer shot. But when I topped the rim again, the old doe, all by herself, was on the move and the sun was eating into the horizon like a live coal. I sat, wrapped up in the sling and used my walking staff to help steady my aim. The Model 94 cracked on the silent plains, and the antelope dropped immediately at over 300 of my longest paces. a full 200 yards from the muzzle, I estimated.

I dressed my game carefully and attached the antelope to my packframe. Slipping the sling of the Model 94 Winchester 30-30 Improved on the hook provided on my packframe, and with walking staff in hand to help balance the load, I headed off the plateau in the direction of my vehicle, now a tiny speck disappearing in the twilight. The harvest would have been welcomed with any gun, any caliber, but that old doe antelope was a real trophy and a memory-maker for me mainly, I think, because of the rifle I was carrying.

5

Sights, Sighting, and Trajectory

Good loads make the 30-30 perk like strong camp coffee, but ballistic force is not effective unless it's properly directed — in other words, it doesn't mean much if you miss the target or misplace the bullet on game. Putting that projectile on the money is a matter of good sights, proper sighting technique and firearm handling. This chapter is about sights, sighting in and also about the behavior of the bullet from muzzle to target as it follows its parabola — in other words, *trajectory*.

The Model 94 has worn many different types of sights. Study old Winchester catalogues, and you find that dozens of different patterns were used. In the main, however, we need to look at the open iron sight, the tang sight, the "peep" and, of course, the telescopic sight. All four have advantages. All four have disadvantages.

Knowing what to select as a Model 94 sight and how to use it is a big part of the success story of the lever-action 30-30.

The open iron sight is the crudest of the types used on the Model 94. But it works. It has worked for many, many years. In theory, a shooter is not supposed to be able to see well enough with iron open sights to create a four-inch group at 100 yards. I have many witnessed targets with two-inch groups, and a few groups near an inch center to center. Open iron sights work, especially at the closer ranges. Are they the best sight for the Model 94? Possibly not. But for close-in shooting in brush or forest, they're not bad.

The iron sight is strong, and it stays sighted in well, too. It's very light in weight. It does not take away from the balance of the firearm, which is impor-

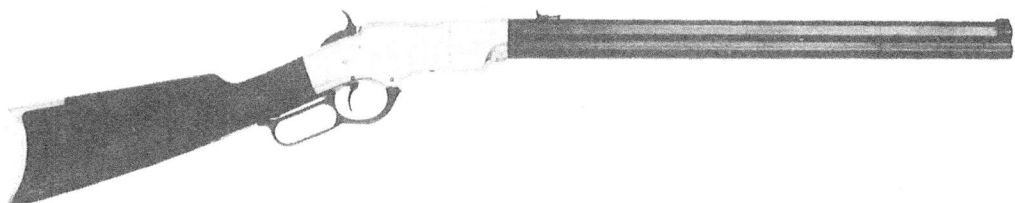

Navy Arms Company's replica of the Henry Carbine in 44-40 caliber displays the open sight pattern which was to continue with the Model 94 and countless other rifles. Though not the most refined of sights, the iron open does work.

tant in the Model 94 Winchester. Also, the iron sight allows the firearm to be carried neatly, in the hand. Mount a scope, and the middle of the rifle gets bulkier than a sumo wrestler.

The tang sight is good, but out of vogue. I have one on an old Model 94 rifle, and it does work well. The tang sight is close to the eye, so it is fast, but a hunter would seldom have the tang in the up position, so that factor is of no account at all, really. Furthermore, the tang sight was probably installed to increase the effectiveness of aim at longer ranges. That's where it shines. On my 94 rifle, I use the tang sight only for faraway shots. I use the open sight the rest of the time.

Although many thousands of receiver or "peep" sights have been sold in this country, this type of sight has never been terribly popular here. That's too bad. It is the best of the iron sights. It still allows the flow of the Model 94 to be maintained. It is not bulky, not heavy, and it works remarkably well. I have achieved many one-inch groups at 100 yards with my Storey Conversion Model 94 custom rifle using the peep sight. The one thing about the receiver sight which bothers some shooters, including this one, is that it is not beautiful. I know the old cliché concerning beauty and the eye of the beholder. I behold the receiver sight as a lump of metal which does not add to the graceful lines of the 94, but this factor is superseded by the superior aiming properties of the peep sight. This is a good sight for the 94.

Of course, the finest rifle aiming instrument in the world to date is the telescopic sight. The scope is wonderful because it magnifies the target, of course, but it also offers the most precise and clear aiming point. And the scope has something else going for it — a "flat" picture. With open iron sights, the eye has to focus back and forth on three points, the rear sight, front sight and target. The peep reduces this number to two points. The scope has one flat optical plane, and that is it.

Speed? In my opinion, the man who learns to use the aperture or peep sight with a large hole in the disc or with the disc removed entirely is going to get off the fastest *well-aimed* shot. I said this in Africa, and thought they were going to get a lynch mob after me. The African hunter insists that an open iron sight is the only one for fast shooting. The open iron sight is fast, but in terms of alignment, the peep is faster. The scope can be very fast, too, if it is mounted correctly so that the shooter can see through it the second he mounts the rifle.

As for sight picture, which is vital to understanding the use of any iron sight, the important thing to remember with the open iron sight is that there must be a *frame of reference*. In other words, the notch should be just large enough so that there is light on both sides of the front bead or blade, optically speaking. We do not want the front sight to fit optically into the rear sight notch so that the shooter has no frame of reference. If the shooter can see some light around that bead, he can align the sights with the same amount of light on both sides of the bead.

A large bead is good for close work. But I like a fine bead on my Model 94s because I feel I can see it well and I like the added precision gained by not covering up the target with the bead. The bead on my Storey Conversion and my old-time 94 is one-sixteenth of an inch in diameter. I have a little Trapper 94, 16-inch barrel, with a larger bead, but I use that little gem only in heavy brush and for close encounters.

The peep sight is so easy to use that it confuses shooters. They want to work at centering the bead in that little hole. The idea is to forget any such notions. Using a peep sight means simply looking *through* the hole, ignoring the hole itself altogether and putting the front sight on the target. The eye will automatically focus in the dead center of the peep sight hole because the highest concentration of light is there—optically speaking more than physically speaking. So you look *through* the peep, put the front sight on target, maintain it there and squeeze off the shot. That's the sight picture for the peep. For hunting, use a larger aperture with a very small disc, and if a small disc is not available, remove the disc altogether and just aim through the threaded hole into which the disc used to fit.

One thing to watch for with the aperture sight is lint or dirt, snow or any debris stuck in that hole. If the foreign object is big enough, it will be seen readily. But sometimes, a little lint gets hung up in the hole of the peep sight and it's terrible. I took aim on a 4 x 4 mule deer buck in the mountains one day and simply could not get a sight picture on him. There seemed to be an eclipse of the sun when I looked through the peep sight. "I knew my eyes would go on me one day," I said to myself, "but I didn't know it'd happen all at once!"

In less than an hour, I had another chance. Same thing. The picture was hazier than a foggy day on the riverbottom. I didn't have the good sense to check the aperture in the receiver sight for lint or dirt. Finally, after the hunting day was a closed book, I found out what was wrong. In wiping down the rifle that night, I decided to take a closer look at the peep hole of the sight. It had a bit of lint in it, the kind which sometimes comes from a soft gun case. There was not enough lint to totally block the view, but just enough to make a lopsided sight picture. Check the peep sight aperture before every hunt.

Sighting in is not difficult with any of the Model 94's sight styles. First, get a good target. A nice black dot or square on a piece of clean, white paper is good, but for sighting with irons, I get a piece of black paper and paste a six-inch-diameter white circle in its center. In order to sight in the open iron, simply move the rear sight in the direction you want the next bullet to hit. If the rifle is putting its bullet to the left, move the rear sight to the right, which will put the next round

Sights, Sighting, and Trajectory

to the right. If the rifle is shooting low, raise the rear sight; if it's high, lower the rear sight. Any 30-30 Model 94 should sight in easily with rear sight adjustment only. But if the front sight has to be drifted, remember to do so in the opposite direction. To hit more to the left, move the front sight to the right, in other words.

Pick a bright day if possible. With the sun on the target and not in the shooter's eye, even iron sights create a decent picture. Use a benchrest setup, too, if possible. Put the rifle's fore-end, not the barrel, over the sandbag. Resting the barrel can change vibrations and point of impact. Make sure that the right elbow is

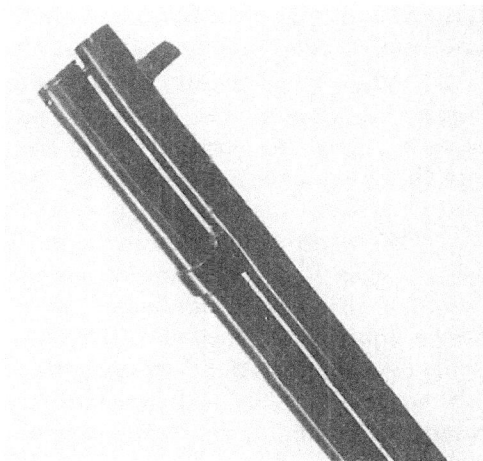

The basic front sight has remained with us for a long time. This is the front sight on the Winchester Model 94 7-30 Waters rifle.

Sighting in is vital to good field shooting with any rifle. The Model 94 is sighted from a rock-solid bench, and with great care and plenty of ammo. Most likely, it will be sighted in but once, with periodic bench checks to ensure that the sights have stayed put.

also rested (for the right-handed shooter). An elbow waving around means an unsteady hold on the firearm. The idea is to remove as many human factors as possible by using the bench. Hold a half-breath during shooting, and *squeeze* that trigger as if you were defusing a bomb.

The micrometer receiver sight is easy to sight in, too. The shooter adjusts by moving it a certain number of "clicks" in the appropriate direction. If the gun is shooting low, move the peep upward. If it's shooting high, move the peep downward. If shooting to the right, move the peep left; if shooting to the left, move the peep to the right. How many clicks? It depends upon the sight. My sight has a "quarter-minute" click.

A quarter minute means one-fourth of an inch at 100 yards. So, to move the impact of the bullet an inch, it takes four clicks. With a half-minute system, two clicks right would get the next bullet one inch to the right. A minute of angle subtends about an inch at 100 yards. Scientifically, it's not truly an inch, but that's close enough for our purposes. Of course, at 200 yards, the value of each click *doubles*. So the quarter-minute click is worth a half inch at 200 yards. One click moves the point of impact a half inch instead of a quarter inch at 200 yards. Remember, a minute of angle, for shooters, is an inch at 100 yards, two inches at 200 yards, three inches at 300 yards and so forth.

Sighting the scope is a cinch. Remove the cover on the turret, and turn the adjustment in the direction of the arrow. How much? Each scope has its own value. Some scopes will have adjustments in clicks, just like the micrometer sight. Others are continuous, but will have some sort of mark to indicate the value of the adjustment. The arrow indicates which way to move the dial for bullet impact. The arrow will be marked for "up" or "left," and so forth.

Which sight should you choose, then, for the Model 94? My custom 94 wears a peep sight. I like the fact that I can shoot both fast and accurately with the peep, and yet the lines of the 94 are not violated by this little lump of metal. I'd like a smaller unit if possible, but can live with the size of the peep as is. My Trapper has its original open sights, but I don't do any shooting past about 100 yards with it. Scope? I love scope sights, but for my own Model 94 purposes, I prefer irons. The new Angle-Eject 94s, however, wear a scope beautifully. If I were using one of these, perhaps in 356 Winchester caliber for brush or timber work, I might mount a low-power scope. Nothing to date offers such an advantage in aiming as the modern scope, and it is tough as whang leather and reliable. A scope sight is a good choice.

The bullet describes a parabola as it flies from the muzzle to the target. This curve means that we have to point the barrel up if we want the bullet to "drop into" the line of sight down the way. Of course, the faster the bullet, the less we have to tilt the bore upward. But all arms today, including the 220 Swift or 22-250 Remington, require this upward angle in order to put a bullet on target out yonder. Trajectory is the path the bullet follows, and in sighting the 30-30, we have to know what the trajectory looks like so that we can aim correctly for various distances.

The data here are helpful. And they are correct, though not precise. Inherent in the very group size is enough error to rule out perfection. In other words, when sighting in at 200 yards, the group you

Sights, Sighting, and Trajectory

This informal target shows what can be done with the Model 94 from modest range, in the 100-yard class. One of the author's special Model 94s, the Storey Conversion, will create groups of one inch center to center at 100 yards from the bench.

get is not a single 30 caliber hole, but measures maybe three inches. If the gun is sighted in perfectly for 200 yards, in theory the bullets would be 1.5 inches high and 1.5 inches low as well as clustered in an area three inches in diameter.

But that's no big problem, because hunters don't shoot at targets only three inches in size at 200 yards. A buck mule deer's chest will go about 18 inches in depth, for example, and a whitetailed buck may be a little bit less on the average. So the sight-in suggested here works very well.

Start all sighting in at 25 yards. There are two important reasons for this. First, at 25 yards, the gun will at least be "on the paper." Or it should be. If a shooter begins his sight-in at 100 yards and the bullet does not even strike paper, it's tough finding out how to adjust the sights so that the next missile will cut the target. Also, if sighted right in at 25 yards, the majority of 30-30 loads will put the bullet near the bull at 100 yards, so a lot is accomplished with this preliminary 25-yard session.

After the load is sighted on the money at 25 yards, use the 100-yard target. Remember that values for those sight adjustments change at 25 yards. One click of a quarter-minute micrometer sight at 100 yards moves the point of impact a fourth of an inch. But at only 25 yards, it will do but one-fourth of this. At 25 yards, it takes 16 such clicks to move the point of impact an inch.

The trajectory figures given here will help the shooter in sighting his firearm. For example, let's say that you are in whitetail country and that your favorite bullet is a 170-grain flat nose. Since you're a handloader, you have that bullet going out at 2,300 feet per second at the muzzle. First, of course, the sight-in takes place at 25 yards to put her on the paper. But what next? If you wanted to sight in for 200 yards, you would have to see that the bullet prints 4.5 inches high at 100 yards. That's because of the arc of the trajectory pattern.

This means that at 100 yards, the sights would have to be held 4.5 inches *low* in order to hit center. Most deer at close range are missed because the hunter shoots *over* them. I don't think sighting in for 200 yards is the way to go. You can sight in 2.0 inches high at 100 yards, and the bullet will be right on at 150 yards and 5.0 inches low at 200 yards. That is more like it, especially if the shooting is going to be up close most of the time.

In my charts, energy figures are also given. Energy figures are interesting.

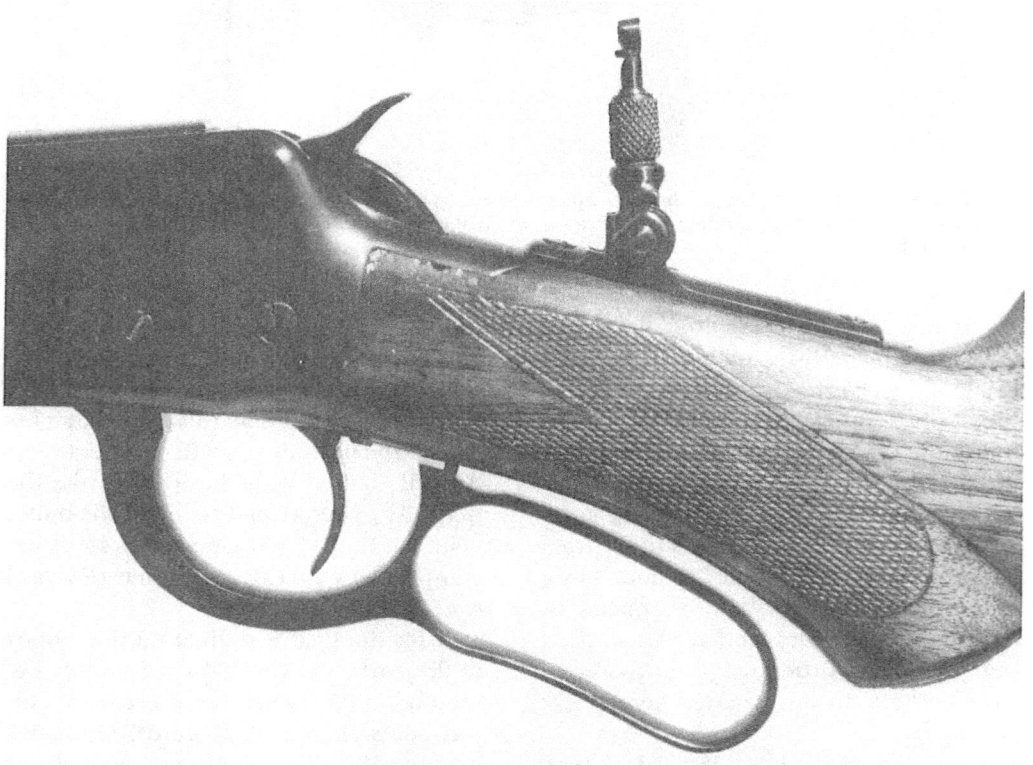

A tang sight was once popular on the Model 94, but has not been a factory offering for some time. This Model 1894 30-30 rifle is shown with the tang peep sight in the raised, ready-to-go position.

Sights, Sighting, and Trajectory

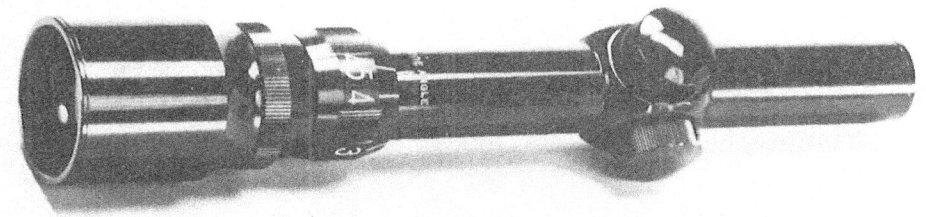

The modern Model 94 takes to a scope like a teenager to hamburgers. This little 1.75X to 4.5X variable from Bushnell would be excellent for both close and modest-range shooting.

They don't tell the whole story, but they are worth something by way of comparison. Bullet diameter, construction and weight . . .these and many other factors dictate what will happen when the bullet strikes, as well as its energy in foot-pounds. The figures are shown here for comparison.

The shooter who can professionally handle his Model 94 rifle and round is the one who knows his sights, how to take a good sight picture with them and where to hold at the approximate ranges at which he's firing. The following information should give that shooter an ace to play the game with, stacking the deck in his favor when it comes to harvesting game in the field.

A superb iron sight for the Model 94 Winchester is the micrometer aperture type. This Lyman model is shown in relation to how low it mounts on the receiver, making it very fast to use.

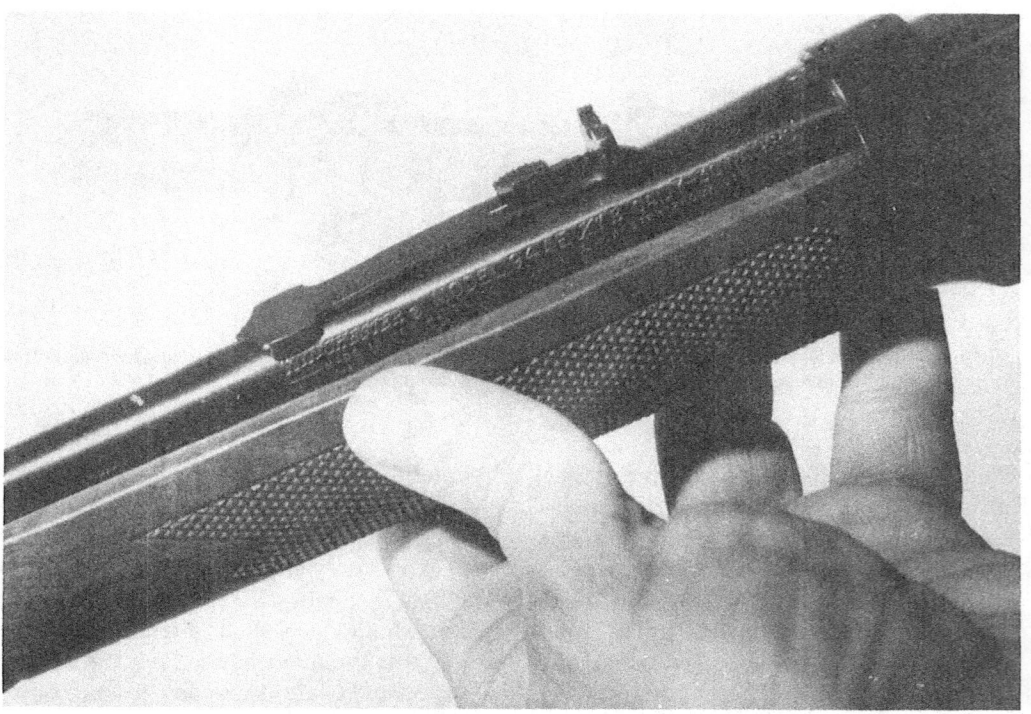

A Modern Angle-Eject 94, the 7-30 Waters rifle, uses a standard iron open sight with elevator bar. But the receiver is drilled and tapped for a scope sight.

100-grain round-nose bullet

Muzzle Velocity	100 Yards	200 Yards	300 Yards
2,878 fps	2,150 fps	1,540 fps	1,250 fps

Muzzle Energy	100 Yards	200 Yards	300 Yards
1,840 f-p	1,027 f-p	527 f-p	347 f-p

Trajectory	100 Yards	200 Yards	300 Yards
	+1″	−4″	−15″

Comments

The effective range of the 100-grain round-nose bullet, sighted an inch high at 100 yards, is about 200 yards on varmints. Energy is still sufficient for most varmints at 300 yards, but you must dope out a hold-over of about 15 inches. Remember, the muzzle energy of a 22 rimfire magnum with a 40-grain bullet at 1,900 fps is 321 foot-pounds, so this load has more energy at 300 yards than the 22 magnum rimfire has at the muzzle.

WARNING! Never load pointed bullets in a tubular magazine.

Sights, Sighting, and Trajectory

130-grain spitzer bullet

Muzzle Velocity	*100 Yards*	*200 Yards*	*300 Yards*
2,680 fps	2,370 fps	2,100 fps	988 fps

Muzzle Energy	*100 Yards*	*200 Yards*	*300 Yards*
2,074 f-p	1,622 f-p	1,273 f-p	988 f-p

Trajectory	*100 Yards*	*200 Yards*	*300 Yards*
	+2.5"	0	−11"

Comments

The shooter must never use a spitzer bullet in the magazine, but in single-loading the 130-grain Speer bullet, I did find a good trajectory pattern out to about 225 yards, or even 250 yards on larger varmints of coyote size. The energy at 200 yards is sufficient for big-game hunting.

WARNING! Never load pointed bullets in a tubular magazine.

150-grain spitzer bullet

Muzzle Velocity	*100 Yards*	*200 Yards*	*300 Yards*
2,550 fps	2,325 fps	2,075 fps	1,800 fps

Muzzle Energy	*100 Yards*	*200 Yards*	*300 Yards*
2,166 f-p	1,801 f-p	1,434 f-p	1,079 f-p

Trajectory	*100 Yards*	*200 Yards*	*300 Yards*
	+3"	0	−11"

Comments

Using iron sights with the 150-grain spitzer single-loaded in the Model 94, a shooter can put the bullet on the money at 200 yards by sighting in three inches high at 100 yards. Though enough energy remains at 300 yards for deer-hunting power, the sights limit bullet placement at this range. About 200 to perhaps 225 yards should be the limit, with the hunter taking the challenge and getting close to his game through stalking.

WARNING! Never load pointed bullets in a tubular magazine.

165-grain spire-point bullet

Muzzle Velocity	100 Yards	200 Yards	300 Yards
2,400 fps	2,190 fps	1,993 fps	1,809 fps

Muzzle Energy	100 Yards	200 Yards	300 Yards
2,111 f-p	1,758 f-p	1,456 f-p	1,199 f-p

Trajectory	100 Yards	200 Yards	300 Yards
	+3"	0	−12"

Comments

The 165-grain bullet describes an arc much like that of the 150-grain bullet when the former takes off at 2,400 fps MV and the latter at around 2,550 fps MV. As far as raw energy is concerned, this load could harvest a deer at 300 yards, but 200 yards or closer is much more practical, especially with iron sights, since bullet placement is always a big factor in a clean harvest. The 165-grain bullet must be single-loaded only.

WARNING! Never load pointed bullets in a tubular magazine.

170-grain flat-nose bullet

Muzzle Velocity	100 Yards	200 Yards	300 Yards
2,350 fps	2,100 fps	1,845 fps	1,600 fps

Muzzle Energy	100 Yards	200 Yards	300 Yards
2,085 f-p	1,665 f-p	1,285 f-p	967 f-p

Trajectory	100 Yards	200 Yards	300 Yards
	+3"	−1.5"	−13.5"

Comments

This is the 170-grain Speer bullet with its .304 ballistic coefficient as fired from the 30-30 Improved. Note that it does extremely well out to 200 yards. This is due to the good ballistic profile of the bullet coupled with modest muzzle velocity. The Speer Flat Nose is designed to be used in a tubular magazine, such as the one on the Model 94.

WARNING! Never load pointed bullets in a tubular magazine.

170-grain flat-nose bullet

Muzzle Velocity	100 Yards	150 Yards	200 Yards
2,300 fps	2,077 fps	1,869 fps	1,678 fps

Muzzle Energy	100 Yards	150 Yards	200 Yards
1,997 f-p	1,628 f-p	1,319 f-p	1,064 f-p

Trajectory	100 Yards	150 Yards	200 Yards
	+2"	0	−5"

Comments

Note that the longest trajectory range shown here is 200 yards. Sighted to strike 4.5 inches high at 100 yards, this bullet is on at 200 yards and about 20 inches low at 300 yards, but such a high sight-in at 100 means a hold-under of too much at close range. The flatter-nose 170-grain bullet load should be sighted at 150 yards instead. The flat nose is exceedingly fine as a hunting bullet and is an excellent choice for brush and timber hunting.

WARNING! Never load pointed bullets in a tubular magazine.

190-grain round-nose bullet

Muzzle Velocity	100 Yards	200 Yards	300 Yards
2,100 fps	1,725 fps	1,450 fps	1,200 fps

Muzzle Energy	100 Yards	200 Yards	300 Yards
1,861 f-p	1,256 f-p	887 f-p	608 f-p

Trajectory	100 Yards	200 Yards	300 Yards
	+3"	−3"	−24"

Comments

Don't let the energy levels cloud the true picture of the 190-grain bullet out of the 30-30. Because energy figures are based on the Newtonian formula which squares velocity, lower velocity produces much lower energy figures. But at close range, this bullet penetrates well. This bullet and load are a good choice for black bear hunting in timber or brush.

6

Small-Game Hunting with the 30-30

One of the mountains in the chain was called the Sawtooth, after its namesake range of rugged peaks in the Rocky Mountains. I knew why it was so called the moment I saw the jagged peaks. A hunter leaves a lot of shoe leather behind in that terrain, but it was negotiable enough, even for a mediocre mountain man like me. It was easy to mark a path through this country by simply making my trail coincide with a stream. The tools of my trade—cameras, notepads and pencils—stayed behind, and though I packed a valid deer tag, I felt no pressure to fill it.

Food? Mostly what I could find along the way, plus what I packed on my back. Rifle? My old handmate usually came along, a Model 94 30-30. Shots at deer would not be that long, and there were small game as well as mountain grouse in season; and it was and still is legal to harvest both rabbit and grouse in those mountains with a rifle. I'd carry the little 30 with empty chamber but with the hammer back, a safe method and still very fast, too. Should a buck show up close, I could flick a round up into the chamber faster than a bullfrog catches a foolish green fly. If I spotted a buck in the distance, which I often did with my binoculars, I could lever a round home and set the rifle on halfcock prior to the stalk.

And if I spied those wonderful small-game edibles along the upcountry trails, I could ease the lever downward just enough to slip a special round directly into the chamber without the carrier picking up a big-game round. This special round would be a small-game handload. You see, the Model 94 30-30, for the handloader, is both a big-game and a

Small-Game Hunting with the 30-30

small-game rifle and round. Out of my shirt pocket comes that special squib load, the underload, the round that turns the rifle into a 32-20 or even a 32 rimfire, depending upon the powder charge.

Earlier I cited a 16.0-grain charge of MP-5744, the Accurate Arms powder which gave the little 110-grain round-nose bullet a mild muzzle velocity of only about 1,500 fps MV. It will work fine on small game. Go for a head shot, of course, for even at this low level of energy, the 30 caliber pill may act too forcefully on a delicate mountain grouse.

But can a hunter depend on hitting such a tiny target with a 30-30 firing that squib load? The answer is a resounding yes, but remember that the shot must be close, real close. Accuracy with the squib load and a small charge of powder is not always fantastic with the 30-30 — in my tests and my rifles anyway — but most of our small game is actually harvested at only 10 or 20 paces, especially in the outback where this game is not hunter-wise.

Sight-in is very simple with the small-game load. Don't bother. Don't worry about it. With the rifle sighted for big

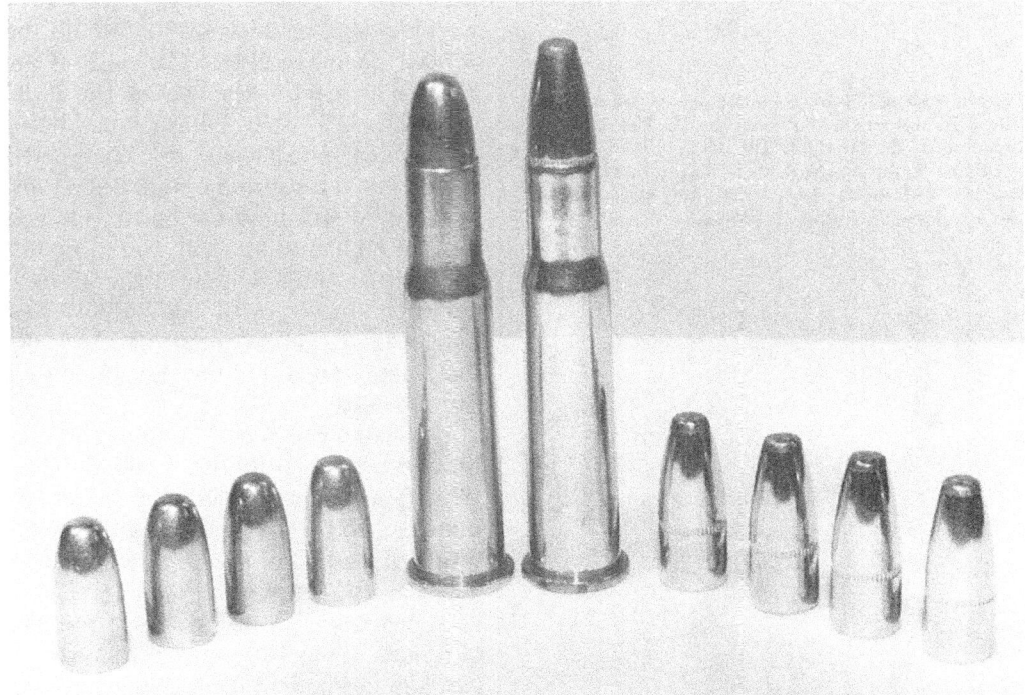

The 30-30 with specific handloads becomes a relatively good small-game rifle. Displayed here on the left is the 110-grain full metal jacket — check local laws for legality of using the full metal jacket bullet. It is loaded down to about 1,500 feet per second in this handload. Four 110-grain round-nose full metal jacket bullets are on the left-hand side of the load. On the right is the 130-grain Speer flat-point bullet, also loaded down, and to the right are four 130-grain bullets. The 110-grain Hornady "full patch" bullets would be useful for wild turkeys and any delicate game, also for pelts. The 130-grain is a tough bullet, too, and when loaded down does not "mushroom" much.

game, at perhaps 150 to 200 yards, the little load seems to drop nicely into the parabola at very close range, putting the rifle on the money at 25 yards or so. Actually, many of the big-game loads do hit right on at 25 yards, too, when sighted for 150 to 200 yards. In other words, the bullet crosses the line of sight first at 25 yards when it is on its upward arc to strike the target at 150 to 200 yards.

So either way you look at it, the little small-game load is on the money up close. Of course, the real secret to success here is to learn exactly where *your* light load hits at 25 yards or less. Then there is no guesswork. As I said above, accuracy is

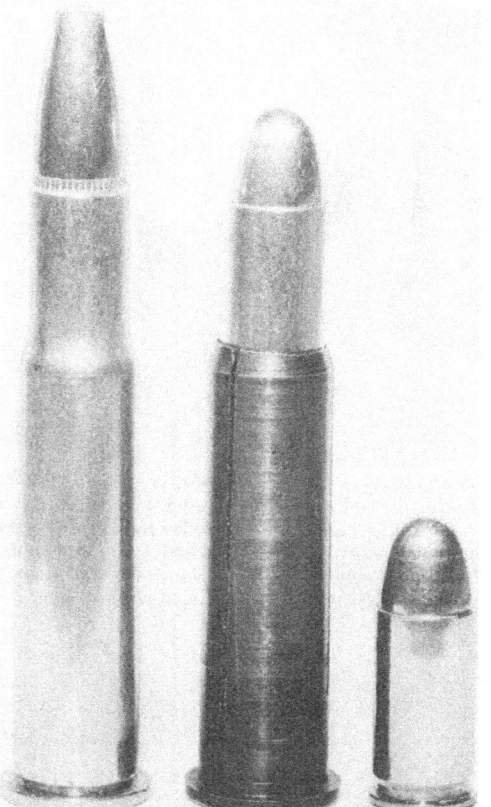

Shown with a 130-grain underload, on the left, is the cartridge insert that uses the 32 ACP round, which is on the far right. The device allows the 32 ACP's use in the standard 30-30. Again, be aware of the law. Full metal jacket bullets may not be legal for any game, including small game.

sufficient for such shooting because of the close range, so a hunter only needs to know where to hold those sights when the squib load is in the chamber. The rest is easy—aim with care, hold your aim and *squeeze* that trigger.

There are four different bullet types which can be successfully employed in the 30-30 for small-game hunting. These are the lead cast projectile, the full metal jacket and the soft-nose bullet in the blunter forms such as the round nose, and the 32 ACP (Automatic Colt Pistol). The last bullet is used in its factory-loaded form by placing the 32 ACP pistol cartridge into a 30-30 insert cartridge— merely a shell of sorts that will hold the 32 ACP round in place. The walls of the 32 ACP case act as the neck of the 30-30 cartridge. My Storey Conversion will not accept this unit, because it is chambered for the 30-30 Improved round, but a standard 30-30 will hold the 32 ACP insert, sold through gunshops. Of course, no full metal jacket bullet, even in the 32 ACP cartridge insert form, should ever be loaded in a tubular magazine. Use any full metal jacket bullet in single-shot fashion only.

If accuracy is your main desire, it's hard to beat a cast bullet. Loaded to low velocity and using a good alloy of the Lyman No. 2 type, the cast bullet causes minimal leading of the bore. A gas check also helps in preventing leading, and if some leading does occur after a number of rounds, it can be removed. A gunsmith can handle the bad cases, but I have yet to see a 30-30 badly leaded from lightly loaded cast bullet rounds.

Generally, those lead bullets with a lot of shank do best, accuracy-wise. But close-range small-game hunting can be handled with a host of cast bullets. Using a Lyman 120-grain cast bullet, No. 2 alloy, and 7.0 grains of PB powder, muzzle velocity will be about 1,300 feet per second. With the same 7.0-grain charge of Red Dot powder, muzzle velocity of the 120-grain cast bullet is about 1,400 feet per second. Gas checks are useful with most of the cast bullets which fit the 30-30 case, but may not be imperative for such low-velocity loads. I use them, even with the low-end charges.

Even a little 22 rimfire can spoil edible meat with the wrong bullet placement; conversely, the much heavier 120-grain lead bullet mentioned here will spoil virtually no good meat, given the proper bullet placement. Everyone knows that the head shot is right for small game. If this is the case, why not simply use a full-power 30-30 load and go for the head shot? I don't care for that much noise when I can employ the little popgun load and get the job done very well.

Another cast bullet which can work for low-power 30-30 loads is the Lyman No. 311242, which turns out to weigh about 125 grains; yet another is the Lyman No. 311410, which goes about 130 grains. There is also a 150-grain cast bullet, the Lyman No. 311466, but it weighs about 151 grains. Ten grains of Red Dot pushes this one at about 1,400 fps MV in the 30-30. I have noticed good accuracy with this bullet. Using 7.0 grains of PB, muzzle velocity is about 1,200 fps with this cast projectile, and 8.0 grains of SR4756 gains about 1,275 fps MV.

Now for the full metal jacket bullet—which must *never be used in a tubular magazine*. You should check the legality of "full patch" bullets for hunting in your area. In my state they are legal for mountain grouse and wild turkey hunting, possibly because it is legal to use the full

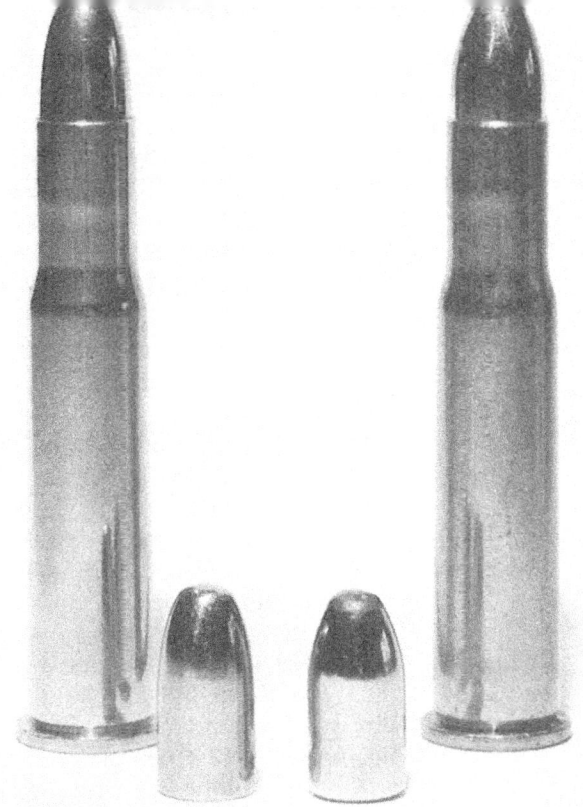

The 30-30 as a small-game load—both of these rounds use a 110-grain bullet, but the one on the left is the full metal jacket; the one on the right is a soft-point, but meant for high velocity, so it does not disrupt too much edible meat at low velocity.

metal jacket bullet in the 22 rimfire magnum. But if I use a full metal jacket bullet for wild turkey hunting, I do so only in single-shot fashion.

In fact, I don't even carry a pocketful of full metal jacket round-nose bullets with me, but rather only one round. The rest of my rounds will be round-nose soft-point type, and at low velocity, these bullets, made for much higher velocity, destroy little valuable meat.

The soft-point round-nose 110-grain bullet is super for small game in the 30-30 when down-loaded. After all, the 110-grain soft-point is often constructed to withstand very high velocity. A good example is in the 300 Weatherby Magnum, where a 110-grain round-nose bullet may be driven at muzzle velocities exceeding 3,900 feet per second. Using a soft-point but strongly built 110-grain bullet in round-nose form at under 1,500 fps MV out of the 30-30 means minimal smashup of tissue.

Burning so little powder in the 30-30 case does not always strain the accuracy potential from the round. I'll say again that at close range, accuracy is sufficient. I repeat the accuracy disclaimer for the benefit of the shooter who might be looking for a really fine target load with a cast bullet. I suggest he at least try something like the RCBS 180-grain lead missile with gas check at a load level designed for about 1,600 or 1,700 fps MV.

Hunting small game with the rifle is a process of moving very slowly and looking a lot. I admit that I'm a binocular-lover from way back, but the glass truly does help, even on small game. Out West, especially in the wilder reaches, a hunter can often sit on a rise and simply glass the medium distances to find sitting rabbits and other game. Then he can stalk in for a good, clean, close shot.

But slow-pacing the terrain works, too. Sometimes you'll jump your quarry at a few feet or yards, and off it goes. I don't worry about these lost opportunities. There are many other times when looking a lot and walking slowly has produced sitting small game at close range.

Another game trophy that is suited to down-loaded 30-30s is the turkey. The wild turkey is often hunted with a rifle, and I say that some of the best rounds ever for it were the old-time 25-20 and 32-20. Both were offered with lead bullet loads, and these were pretty tame. The 25-20 fired an 86-grain lead bullet at about 1,380 fps MV. The 32-20 fired a 100-grain lead bullet at about the same muzzle velocity. As one of my older friends once told me about these two rounds, "Why, you couldn't do no better than them on the turkey!" I think he summed it up quite well, for these loads had enough oomph to down the tough turkey, but were not disruptive of that fine meat.

Many of the 30-30 loads listed here and elsewhere duplicate the 32-20 for all practical purposes. I took a bird on the riverbottoms not long ago with one of my 30-30s, the one I call the Storey Conversion. She was "loaded light" that day. I did not have a big-game round in the magazine, as I would during a big-game hunt where I'd sometimes use the 30-30 on small game. I had only the low-velocity loads along.

I stayed to the high points above the riverbottom, looking into the trees below me, especially with my binoculars. That day I was carrying a pair of Bushnell 10 x 40s around my neck, and the idea was to find a flock of birds as they fed in the bottomlands. I knew the birds were there because they had left plentiful sign. There were a tom's J-shaped droppings by the waterhole and the more amorphous leavings of the hens scattered here and there. And the magnificent tracks of both sexes graced the soft places in the earth, especially along one trail which looked well used. And there was a roost, too — a bare-branched tree that provided a nighttime home for the wildbirds.

I used that roost as my home base, hunting within a half mile of the tree's bony arms. The birds were feeding in that area and drinking from a little pond there. Before long, the glass scanned the

Small-Game Hunting with the 30-30

right hunk of terrain and the flock appeared as black lumps against the dry grasses through which they moved.

I simply "cut 'em off at the pass." I could see which way the birds were heading, so it was no big problem to slip ahead of them and more or less wait for the group to show up. There wasn't a tom in the bunch, however. I watched as the last bird went out of sight. And no sooner had I climbed back on my highland post to glass again than I located another bird—this one alone, and bigger-looking than those in the flock. Down I hiked again. And this time, the 30 barked just once, a mild little report quickly lost in the heavy growth of trees and brush. The lead bullet took the tombird at the pinion, where wing and body join. Not much disruption and hardly a thimbleful of meat lost.

Another good shot with the 30-30 low-power load on a wild turkey is in the lower back as the bird is going away, but a hunter must be aware that these big birds are tough, and though hit hard can get away. Shoot straight, and immediately close in to make sure of the shot. Nobody wants to hit a fine wild turkey twice with a rifle, but it's better to lose some meat than to allow the bird to wander off.

The 30-30 proves its versatility when applied on small game and wild turkeys. Each hunter will enjoy using the 30-30 in his own way, but one of my favorites is on small game and wild turkeys, especially when coupled with big-game hunting. The 30-30 is especially useful when given a feeding of low-velocity ammo as well as the high-power stuff.

One of my best hunts coupled large and small game. I was above the Platte River most of the time. Antelope were up there in good numbers. Below, I could see deer standing along the river's edge. What I did not see from on high were the many cottontail rabbits which also inhabited that little stretch of riverbottom. I found no antelope buck to my liking that first day, so I slipped down from the high country into the rich valley.

I had my little five-pound Coleman Peak 1 tent for shelter, along with a small down-filled sleeping bag and a neat little lantern called the Quiklite. The lamp worked with a flick of a lever. I had my house. I had my bed. I had light, and there were staples in my packsack. A little frypan, the kind with the miracle finish which wipes out clean as a mountain spring even if you burn potatoes in it, was also along. And some cooking margarine along with lemon pepper and a small vial of garlic powder.

I flicked the big-game loads out of my Model 94 and replaced these with my small-game cartridges. I had only an hour of light left, if that, but it was plenty. I saw dozens of cottontails in the brush along the banks of the river. I took but one, sitting no more than 20 paces from the muzzle of my rifle. There was not a shred of edible meat lost.

The rabbit meat, sprinkled with lemon pepper and garlic powder, was fried in the margarine over hot coals. The Quiklite lamp created a halo of light around my campsite. While the rabbit fried, I prepared my home by setting up the Peak 1 and unstuffing my sleeping bag from its home in the packsack. I ate some homemade bread, plus a few mushrooms and dried onions which I had quickly sautéed in margarine.

I own and often carry a fine 22 semi-auto pistol, with which I could easily have harvested that rabbit supper. But often I enjoy making that workhorse 30-30 do it all. Part of that "all" is the small-game aspect of this old round and its equally old lever-action rifle. Having a few rounds for small-game or wild turkey hunting is always a must for me. These tame loads just about duplicate an interesting round of the past, the 32-20. The 30-30 can be that 32-20 for the handloader. And at the same time, it can maintain its famous "deer rifle" image. It's all a matter of how you load her and what you do with the loads after you have them.

7

Varmints and the 30-30

The San Carlos Apache Indian Reservation backcountry seemed to be pushed back at least 100 years in time. I strolled among the Ponderosa pine trees and past a few well-stocked fishing ponds. No one was fishing, or hunting, either, on that day. My partner and I had the place to ourselves. Our major interest was the interesting tassel-eared squirrel, for which the San Carlos Reservation is well known. For this quarry, my 30-30 was loaded with 130-grain Speer bullets at a modest 1,500-feet-per-second muzzle velocity.

A small dab of nail polish on the head of each case told me which rounds were the mild ones, and that was necessary, for the next cartridge in line was no blooper—it was also a Speer 130-grain bullet load, but with enough H-335 powder to propel that accurate bullet at full throttle. Why the hot backup round? Varmints. We had seen coyotes walking around in midday, and we had the proper credentials to hunt them, along with the blessings of one of the Apache game wardens, who suggested we help out by lowering the boom on any of the little "wolves" we might encounter. All I had to do, when the coyote connection was made, was flick the lever rapidly and switch from squib load to varmint round in rapid snick! snick! fashion.

Varmint hunting has brought mixed reactions from hunters and non-hunters alike for many decades, and there has been considerable change in game department recognition and classification of varmint animals. Hawks and owls were once placed on the "wanted list" by game officials, but studies showed that these birds—though they will certainly

This is a varmint rifle? Technically, no. But the old Model 94 30-30 has accounted for a good many varmints because it is handy and because ranchers and outdoorsmen have faith in the little gun.

eat a dove, quail, rabbit or other small game animal—were no great threat to these populations because of their short-lived nature. Population dynamics show that quail, for example, perish at astonishing rates whether hunted or not hunted, and that predation and hunting, within reason, will have no disastrous long-range effect on numbers.

The same intense studies, however, have also shown several species of wildlife which are harmful to both game animals and farmland activities, and therefore game departments still list a special category of open-season wild animals: the varmint class. As an example, a study in Arizona showed that as high as 90% of the antelope fawn crop was killed by coyotes before the kids were able to really get around on their own. Man has always put a premium on certain animals, and in this case, antelope were deemed very important and the recommendation was to remove some of the coyote population. Never fear—eradication was neither desired nor contemplated, nor, by the way, possible. There are still plenty of coyotes among the antelope herds of Arizona, but mortality of the antelope kids has dropped as the coyote population dropped. Non-hunters, incidentally,

place the same values on wild animals. They trap mice, which they see as threatening to the welfare of the home or farm, and they remove gophers from the garden so the tulips can grow.

Varmint hunting has become very specialized in America. And the 30-30 is not a varmint rifle. A varmint rifle is a far-shooting piece with a fine scope sight. Usually, this means a bolt-action rifle, caliber 22, though there are varmint rifles in 17 caliber and in 6mm caliber, as well as other sizes. The idea is to raise the velocity to such a point that these guns "shoot flat" out to 300 yards and more, meaning that the hold-over is minimal at long range.

But we would be ignoring an important function of the old 30-30 if we disassociated it from varmint hunting. Though the 30-30 is definitely not a varmint caliber specifically, it has been used on varmints since its 1895 unveiling. Why? Because it's handy in the flat-sided firearm, a gun which fits into crevices and corners and pickup-truck gun racks without poking into our living space. The working rancher, for example, may have an old 30-30 tucked into his outfit somewhere, for the rifle is rugged and he likely knows how to shoot it straight. This man is not interested in hunting varmints specifically. But when he rounds a bend in the road and sees a prairie wolf loping along there, he can jump out of his vehicle or off his horse, grab a 94, shuck in a round and fire away.

I like a 30-30 as a varmint round and rifle for several reasons. First, I enjoy the practice. On a Wyoming ranch I was invited to help thin the prairie-dog population. Unfortunately, keeping the prairie dogs in check by shooting is not generally effective enough, and then poisoning programs are instituted. But in many places, hunting the dogs can help hold numbers down. Prairie dogs undermine grazing lands and can leave huge holes in the earth, precluding the raising of fodder and also serving to break the legs of livestock. In my own prairie-dog hunting, I'll use mostly those firearms I want to stay in tune with, especially my handy sidemate, the 30-30. So my first reason for hunting varmints is the practice factor, which helps me become a good shot and stay that way.

Second, varmint hunting is *hunting*. We can get a lot of hunting know-how and fine-tuning in the varmint field. I have tested hunting gear and accessories in the varmint field, too, especially new binoculars. For example, I found out just how good my 8 x 42 Bausch & Lomb glasses were on a varmint hunt. I was finding animals at great distances with these high-resolution glasses. So varmint hunting can be a proving ground for gear, as well as a good way for a hunter to keep his senses in high tune.

Third, I like the challenge. A 30-30 user has to stalk his quarry, and a small target, even at 50 yards or so — especially with iron sights — is indeed a challenge.

A fourth reason for varminting with

When rodents have become a menace, their numbers must be reduced. Gene Thompson, a superior rifleman, hones his skills with the 30-30 on ground squirrels, very small targets.

the 30-30 is the enjoyment factor. I enjoy carrying and shooting the 94 and its 30-30 round, and I like to test my handloads in the varmint field.

A fifth factor in favor of the 94 is its handy nature. Sometimes varminting is really incidental to other types of hunting, especially for me, since I am not usually engaged in "formal" varmint hunting. The light, easy-to-pack 94 30-30 is no millstone about the neck.

Varmints include many different types of animals. Mainly, the varmint class is those wild animals which do damage to something precious to man. Again, this is a value judgement, to be sure. A coyote

The jackrabbit has caused great destruction to farm and pasture in the West. John Fadala dropped this one with an original Model 1894 30-30.

has his own nature to live by, and he's not "evil" because he likes sheep meat. But sheep raising in some parts of the West has been brought to a halt because of the coyote. In such situations the varmint aspect of this animal comes down hard on a rancher. One ranch in Arvada, Wyoming, ceased the herding of sheep because the coyote problem was just too great to overcome.

Sometimes a varmint's status changes. Today the mountain lion is accorded big-game status in most places. And yet it was once on the varmint list. I recall the days when the lion hunter went forth from a ranch to locate a cat which was dealing out destruction to cattle. Mountain lion permits were unheard of then, and I'm not talking about very long ago. Today the lion is often hunted during a specific season, and a tag must be purchased. The jaguar is another animal which falls into the varmint/big game class. Down in Mexico, the jaguar is certainly hunted as big game. But to most of the people who live in his territory, the jaguar is more menace than trophy. It all depends upon viewpoint!

The 30-30 has long been used on both mountain lions and jaguars. My friend John Kane, professional hunter, considers his 30-30 totally adequate for all mountain lion hunting. He prefers the 170-grain bullet to any other, and I recently provided John with a couple of boxes of 170-grain Hornady Flat Point loads for his lion chasing.

Great True Hunts, a book edited by Peter Barrett, Prentice-Hall, 1967, contains a story entitled "The Last Stand of a Wily Jaguar," in which Dale Lee, a noted lion hunter, pursues a very special jaguar. Frank C. Hibben tells the story of this amazing cat, an ancient fellow named "Old Bruno." This jaguar lived in Nyarit, Mexico, and at the end of the tale he's finally dropped with one shot from a 30-30. Choice of firearm did not surprise me. I met a hunter in Mexico who had used his 30-30 for years in jaguar country.

So there are some pretty big animals which wear, or have worn, the title of varmint. But there are also some animals which are both varmint and furbearer. Two examples are the fox and coyote. Where I live, both fox and coyote are listed as varmints and can be hunted fairly much at will, but both are also furbearing animals whose prime pelts have brought good market prices from time to time. At the same time, there are furbearers which cannot be hunted strictly as varmints. Two examples from my area are the mink and badger. Only the holder of a trapper's license can harvest these

Surely, the fur-hunter who is seriously pursuing coyote and fox pelts should go with a rifle tailored for the job. One of my associates, Jim Osborne, uses a 17 Remington for his fur-hunting. This tiny caliber, with its 25-grain bullet at a muzzle velocity of over 4,000 feet per second, enters but does not exit a coyote. Fur loss is minimal.

But there are others who take fur incidentally in their outdoor travels, and they may well prefer a strong bullet from a 30-30, which will not destroy a pelt. The exit hole can be sewn closed. Furthermore, there are quite a few trappers who carry the 30-30 on the trapline. Once upon a time, light squib loads could be purchased for the 30-30. I wish this were still true, but it isn't. However, with cast bullets or with a solid (full metal jacket) bullet, either one loaded way down, a furbearer can be cleanly dispatched without loss of the pelt.

And there is another big point to consider—varmint hunting is not a long-range game all the time, not by a long shot! Many varmints are taken at very close range. In fact, in calling—one of the most popular means of hunting coyotes, foxes and similar animals—the shot is going to be at very close range much of the time. That fast-handling 30-30 is not just so-so for this type of work. It is downright perfect for it.

I'm not the only one to feel this way. A professional hunter by the name of Wyman Meinzer wrote an article entitled "Try The .30-30 On Coyotes." This work appeared in *The American Hunter* magazine for August of 1984. Meinzer says, "It seems that in this era of high-velocity mini-bullets and hot .22 center-fires, everyone has forgotten about those thousands of hunters who have stashed away an old, dust-covered .30-30—whose life as a dependable varmint buster seems to have screeched to a halt half a century ago—in a closet or behind a kitchen door. Well, search the attics and basements and clean the cobwebs from the actions because there is life after death, and the .30-30 will prove my point."

The author is right. Many hunters have forgotten that the middle-of-the-road 30-30 is a varmint number under certain circumstances, and even better than a 220 hotrock at close range. Meinzer continues, "You must first realize that I am not a casual hunter who occasionally fires a shot at a target, much less an animal in the wild. For years I hunted for a living, so if anyone can appreciate fast bullets and accurate rifles, it is definitely me. I will say, however, that I'm always looking for a new challenge. So a couple of years ago when I spotted a Winchester Model 94 Classic hanging above a cabin doorway, the cogs began to turn."

The cogs turned in the direction of using the 30-30 in varmint-calling circumstances. This hunter finally went to a cast bullet at even less velocity than is possible from the 30-30. He found that his coyote-calling was rewarded with a totally reliable harvest, without pelt loss. Telling of one such encounter with the 30-30 152-grain cast bullet underload, Meinzer says, "My hunting companion and I went to the spot where the coyote had been, then followed the fleeing animal's tracks. Perhaps 20 yards behind where the predator had stood, my partner scooped up something. Closer inspection showed it to be the 152-grain bullet, almost completely undamaged after its flight of 50 yards. After another 60 yards, we found the coyote punched through from stem to stern. The bullet entered the coyote's chest and exited its rear."

Many of us have had similar experiences. The 30-30, especially because of its chambering in that reliable and fast-handling flat-sided rifle, is just right for hunkering in the brush and dispatching a predator lured in by a varmint call. So indeed, not all varmint shooting is accomplished across the field at 300 yards. A lot of it is at much closer range.

There are at least four different types of varmint/predator/furbearer loads for the 30-30. First, there is the factory ammunition seen on the shelves of gunstores. The Remington Accellerator load, as discussed in the chapter on factory ammo, will serve for varmint hunting. Here we have a 55-grain 22 caliber bullet at high velocity, with consequent explosiveness. If a pelt is sought, this load is probably a wrong one. But if the varmint hunt is for jackrabbits, the Accellerator might be just the ticket.

There is also the fine Federal load with

The coyote has made things tough for some sheepmen, hence it is ranked a varmint. The custom 30-30 is posed here with a "prairie wolf."

Varmints and the 30-30

a 125-grain hollow-point bullet. I have used this factory offering on prairie dogs and jackrabbits, and again, explosiveness is the byword. One afternoon I was plodding along a meandering stream in an out-of-the-way spot, mostly scouting the territory, but also keeping an eye sharp for varmints. I was packing a Model 94 30-30 loaded with the Federal 125-grain pill. A jack took off from underfoot like a furred cannonball, and I pulled up and took a shot from about 25 yards. The result was an instantaneous kill, which is part of the varmint hunter's code. The 125-grain hollow-point from Federal will offer rocket-like disruption.

The second type is the hot handload. There is already plenty of explosiveness in the factory hollow-point load, but it can be increased with a full-throttle handload. A perfect example is the Speer 110-grain Varminter bullet, which approaches 2,700 fps MV from a 20-inch barrel using RE7 powder, 34.0 grains (Speer load). Lyman (page 282 of its 46th edition) lists the 110-grain bullet at a more scintillating velocity—2,842 fps MV—with 43.0 grains of H-335 powder, again from a 20-inch barrel.

A third type shows a very different approach. This is the mild handload. Some of our so-called varmint shooting takes the form of dispatching furbearers, often on the trapline. And there is no point in destroying the pelt of a coyote or other predator called in close. So the light load is also a value.

Where allowed by law, the full metal jacket bullet can be used for furbearers. Hornady offers a fine 110-grain round-nose bullet in full metal jacket. Their own recommendation for the bullet (page 37 of the Third Edition) is "Velocity: 1,800-3,100 f.p.s., Varminting/Hide Hunting." This bullet can actually be driven at 1,500-1,800 fps with good accuracy—certainly good enough for close-range shooting, and the load is meant for close-range shooting only. However, as I have noted many times, no full metal jacket bullet should ever be loaded in the tubular magazine of the rifle. The trapper may carry the full metal jacket load, but he must single-load it only. Or, as Hornady suggests, put one load in the magazine only and one in the chamber. But never load these full metal jacket bullets one behind the other in the tubular magazine.

The fourth class of varmint load for the 30-30 is the cast bullet. Since a cast bullet at modest velocity, even in the 1,800-2,000 fps area, will not "blow up," the hunter can use this bullet type for predators which may have valuable hides. At the same time, muzzle velocity need not be held way down here. Some trajectory flatness is certainly desirable, even for calling 'em up close, and the properly loaded lead pill will serve admirably to the century mark and even beyond. I have taken a few varmints of the fox/coyote size out to 125 yards with the 180-grain cast bullet at a beginning velocity of close to 2,000 fps. It's not destructive, but it is effective. However, since there is no bullet blowup, the hunter must be extra careful to check after each shot, making certain whether his shot was a hit or a miss. The varmint may wheel and dash off, but drop in the brush 50 or 60 yards from where it was hit.

Nothing will turn a 30-30 into a 220 Swift. Various calibers accomplish various things. For long-range work on varmints, choose the varmint rifle, but for day-in, day-out rifle-toting in the outback, the old slabside does all right for

Some fur hunters like to carry a full-power rifle on the trapline, and a 30-30 is often selected. A 30-30 with subloads will take furbearing animals cleanly and without undue destruction of the pelt. Where legal, a 110-grain round-nose full metal jacket bullet is a good choice.

itself. It's a rugged little devil, and it has all the ballistic authority necessary for varminting, even at 200 yards and better. The iron sights limit the 30-30 in terms of shooting at smaller targets much past 100 to 125 yards, naturally.

One of my favorite 30-30 articles is a story by H.V. Allen, Jr., back in the February, 1948 *American Rifleman*. On page 26, Allen sums up a five-year hunting record for his 30-30 carbine, "Little Eva."

He says, "Looking back at Little Eva's record for that five-year period, I find it goes as follows: Three deer, one bear, eight turkeys, one elk, the Lord only knows how many coyotes, and some broomies. Every animal shot at was killed, and no cripples escaped." He got those predators not because the 30-30 is a crackerjack varmint round, but because the 30-30 was handy. It was in hand or nearby when opportunity presented itself. That's the way I look at the 30-30 in terms of varminting.

Varmint rifles have big barrels with little bitty holes in them. And out of these tiny bores, little projectiles come shrieking forth at triple to quadruple the speed of sound. These rifles usually wear bolts and beautiful glass sights that magnify the target and offer precise aiming points, and they shoot flatter than a desk top. But some of the time, a varmint rifle is the rifle you're carrying, and I'm likely to be toting a 94 30-30 when I encounter that predator or tunnel-building rodent. Over the years, the 30-30 has dropped quite a number of these animals, and it is probably going to account for quite a few more for the users of handloads, especially those who skillfully operate a varmint call.

8

Best Deer Rifle in the Woods

The buck moved like smoke out into the meadow. He stood in the thin early light for a moment before melting back into the dimness of the trees. I never saw the buck again. Maybe I should have tried a shot. It was legal shooting light, and I was not that far away. But it wasn't surefire, so I held off. For a moment, my faith waned in the little slim-sided rifle I cradled in both hands. "With my scoped 6.5mm," I said to myself, "I could have downed that old boy easily."

We have to make choices. If we accept the challenge of the bow and arrow, or the muzzleloader — or, for that matter, the 30-30 as opposed to a scoped, high-intensity-cartridge rifle — then we have to live with the challenge, enjoy it, savor it, find pride in the special achievement gained by successfully using the less-than-modern tools of the harvest. I left my self-assigned post at the edge of the meadow that morning and went on to take a better buck at the close of day. It won't always happen that way. Sometimes an opportunity is lost forever.

My lost opportunity above had nothing to do, really, with the 30-30 I was carrying. But it had something to do with iron sights. Had I a scope on that 30-30, I could have managed a clear sight picture and placed a bullet just right. To gain a true aiming point on that buck, I would have needed a bit more light. Later in that same day, however, that slick little Model 94 flowed cleanly to my shoulder and I put a bullet on target so fast that I surprised myself.

All in all, then, my rifle was adequate. As for the round, that old 30-30, let me assure you that with a good soft-point bullet, factory or handload, no deer that ever scraped antlers on a bush will stand up to one well-placed shot. I know this is true. I've seen it happen a lot of times.

The 1895 round raises the very hairs on the backs of many gunwriters' necks, of course, because it is so ho-hum when compared with many other cartridges of the hour. After all, the 30-30 isn't a magnum! And it was never our military round, either. Its only claim to fame is that it was our first commercial sporting cartridge to burn smokeless powder, and even that truth is a shared one, for the 25-35 came on the scene at the same time.

A flock of similar rounds flushed out of the grass like quail soon after the 30-30 hit the scene. Know why? Because the 30-30 *worked*. There was the 303 Savage, a 30-30 with a 190-grain bullet. There was the 32 Winchester Special and the 32 Remington, both the same, ballistically, as a 30-30. None of these, of course, would exchange with the 30-30, as the brass dimensions differ. But they were and still are ballistically no more or no less than the old 30 WCF.

Today factory sales show the 30-06 to be number one among rifle cartridge ammo. But the old 30-30 is number two, and that's pretty significant. That popularity results because the 30-30 is a premier deer round, especially for brush and woods, and for *anywhere* the hunter is willing and able to stalk within modest range of his quarry. I won't go through all the reasons the 30-30 is right for deer. That was done earlier. But it is very important, I think, for the 30-30 fan to employ his round and rifle in a special way in order to gain the most from both in terms of deer harvesting. That's what this chapter is all about, harvesting deer with the 30-30, and I'll talk power and range, sight-in and hold, as well as the most im-

Bill Hirsch, son of outdoor writer Bob Hirsch, poses with his first deer. Many hunters use a 30-30 as their first big-game rifle. If the neophyte is trained to use the 30-30 well, that's fine, but the 30-30 is mainly a veteran's tool.

portant aspect of 30-30 deer hunting, *method*.

You shoot a deer rifle very little. I hunt deer regularly in several states each year, and yet I certainly don't fire my deer rifles many times in the field. Even if I were to hunt five states, that would be only five or six deer to harvest (I get two deer tags where I live). At that rate, I would harvest only 60 deer in 10 years, maximum. No, you don't shoot your deer rifle at deer much, unless your aim is pretty wild and you burn up a couple of boxes of fodder every time you hit the field. But you darned well *carry* a deer

A long-time resident of Gates of the Mountains area north of Helena, Montana, took these nice deer back in the good old days. She used a Model 94 Winchester, and a closer look will show the tang sight up in position for shooting. The Model 94 30-30 has a rich history. It truly has been America's Rifle. *Montana Department of Fish, Wildlife and Parks*

rifle a lot, even in areas where drives are better than stillhunting.

I think this is a major reason for the continued success of the 94 rifle, or carbine if you will. It's easy to pack. It's not that long, and it's slim. Even my special 94, the Storey Conversion with its 24-inch barrel, is not that long or heavy. But even so, I'm glad it wears a sling. Generally, a sling adds to the beauty of a rifle about as much as a dried chicken bone through the septum of the nose adds to the loveliness of a woman. But since we must carry a rifle a lot more than shoot it, I'm going to say that a sling is a good thing to have on a deer-hunting Model 94 30-30 rifle.

There are exceptions. If toting does not bother you, forget the sling. And by the way, even if the 94 does wear a sling, don't carry it slung over the shoulder like a seabag as you hunt deer in the thick stuff. Carry the rifle safely, of course, but *ready for action.* The 94's beauty in close cover is the fact that it's very nice to carry at the ready, due to features already enumerated, such as the flat receiver.

As for sights, the new Angle-Eject wears a scope as naturally as a debutante takes to furs. The scope sight does detract from the 94's carrying ease, to be sure, but it gives the shooter extra hunting time. That's the truth. At those prime moments of deer hunting, very early and very late in the day, the scope shows the target better than iron sights do. I love scopes; however, my favorite 94 is fitted with a peep sight instead because I think of this rifle as my easy-to-carry deer piece, and I accept the added challenge of the iron sight.

Now what about power for deer hunting? I think the owners of the 30-30 should understand the potency of his round as a deer-taker, not only to give himself confidence in his firearm, but also to help him understand the limitations of his caliber. The 30-30 is no 300 Magnum. Everybody knows that. If it were one, it would be wrong as a premier deer round. You don't need a 300 Magnum to harvest a deer. But the 30-30 is limited in range. With my own handloads, I feel I could cleanly take a deer out to 250 yards. But with my iron sights, in spite of the fine handloads I use for deer hunting, I am largely confined to the 200-yard range.

I like the words of Francis E. Sell pertaining to 30-30 power. Sell has hunted deer for a lot longer than most of us have occupied space on this planet, and this is what he had to say in *Gun Digest* for 1985 (page 178).

Nancy Fadala poses with a buck taken in the high sagebrush country just 100 yards from the beginning of timber. Stalking is the key to success in this terrain. Find that buck before it finds you.

> The so-called wounding potential of the 30-30 and its 170-grain round nose soft point raises several questions in my mind. Prowling the wilderness for the past 65 years, seeing hundreds of deer killed cleanly with the 30-30 and similar calibers, I am of the opinion that the 30-30 is a clean killing deer caliber at all average ranges. It seems obvious to me that if the 30-30 was a wounder, it wouldn't have survived and kept growing in popularity.

No hunter of deer can consistently do well without faith in his round and rifle. Taking a deer down means good bullet placement, of course, as well as bullet authority. A hit in the tail with a 458 Winchester is still a hit in the tail, and I contend that faith in the firearm and caliber aid in good shooting on game. So this part of the chapter is geared in that direction.

Warren Page, in an October, 1962 article in *Field & Stream*, said that:

> The sixty-eight-year-old .30-30 [over 90 years old now], by the way, cussed by devout riflemen as inaccurate, is actually a balanced round capable in the right

rifle of very close shooting. Most lever guns chambering this handy perennial may be three-inchers, true, with an alarming tendency as the barrel heats to walk shots downward, but this isn't always the case. I recently gave a straight-gripped Marlin 336 carbine a serious workout under a 4X Marlin scope. With forty rounds of over-the-counter ammunition, the little piece shot five-round groups running from three inches at worst down to one inch at best. The average was a hair better than two inches. Such clusters we might expect from a bolt-action. No hot-barrel walking either.

I want to add to those words by saying that the chapter on tuning deals with hot-barrel walking, and I believe that with the proper fiddling, the 94 can be made to shoot into a two-inch cluster at 100 yards from the bench.

So power and accuracy are there for deer hunting, fellow 30-30 shooters. Have confidence. From modest range, your 94 30-30 is capable of hitting the deer when you do your part, and the bullet is capable of cleanly harvesting the game. Go for it! But go for it with a plan. Hunt 30-30 style. Don't beat around the deer country as if you were carrying a ray gun with cross-canyon trajectory capability.

Sight-in was given its place earlier in this book, and the only reason I bring it up again is to remind the shooter to sight in for the best possible use of the trajectory potential of the particular 30-30 load. Second, and just as important, the good deer hunter using a 30-30 or any other round knows approximately *how to hold* at ranges from very close to the outer limits of his round. How to hold! If you reckon your deer to be 200 yards away, how do you hold for a perfect strike? With my 170-grain handload at 2,300 fps plus, I would hold the bead full on the chest, maybe fudging it just a bit toward the topmost part of the chest area—but not holding over, for a hold-over here would mean a high shot. Know where she shoots. Apply that knowledge in the field.

There are two broad categories to consider in 30-30 deer hunting. We'll call one the brush/woods method and the other the open-country method. I use the round in both types of terrain with total success, but these areas dictate a very different approach to taking venison with the 30 WCF. Mostly, the 30-30 is a brush/woods number—the very title of this chapter suggests that fact. Best round for the woods, it says. However, I like the challenge of the 30-30 in open country, too, in spite of the fact that many other cartridges shoot much flatter.

Brush/Woods Hunting

Stillhunting is the number one method used for deer in close cover. Stillhunting —and I have looked the term up in many books—does not mean "staying still," although I read just this definition in an outdoor magazine, where the writer said that stillhunting meant sitting on a stump and staying still until a deer showed up. Stillhunting is walking quietly, in a still fashion, through the terrain in order to encounter a deer. But you have to still-hunt partly in accord with the abilities of your firearm. If you're walking along the edge of a big meadow, for example, and your rifle is really flat-shooting, then you can tromp out on the edge of that meadow, knowing that if you see something on the other side, even 300 yards across, you can nail it. Forget that with the 30-30. You are out of "field position" when you tromp openly with this rifle at the meadow's edge, and field position is a big part of stillhunting.

Stillhunt with the wind in your face, obviously, since the deer's nose can be its first line of defense in close cover. I realize this is difficult to do at times, but a hunter works at it the best he can. And maintain field position as much as possible. I maintain my field position by playing a little game in my head. As I carefully walk along, trying to be quiet, I set a scene in my mind, a little motion picture show.

"If a buck broke from that cover in front of me," I say to myself, "could I get a shot?" That, fellow 30-30 fans, is field position in a nutshell. Could a good shot be made? If the answer is yes, then field position has been satisfied. If the answer is no, field position has not been met. Example — you're walking along a dense riverbottom where some little trails cut in and out of the thickets. Follow one of them? I doubt it. Rather, I would see if there were any higher points in the area, and I'd occupy those higher chunks of land in order to see anything that might take off in front of me.

I have gotten less than careful and failed to observe field position. It has cost me more than one shot. On one low-country hunt, I approached a hill in the very center of a big brushy area. The hill was also dense and tangled. I had a choice. I could maintain my field position by climbing up on that hill as quietly as possible, or I could skirt the hill, which would be a lot easier. It's usually very simple to convince ourselves that we probably won't gain much by going the hard way, so I skirted the hill. Smack on the other side, a buck broke cover, took a nose dive into a thicket and was gone. From ground level, I could not get a shot.

Had I climbed that hill, I would have come out darned near on top of that buck. Field position. Maintain it.

In hunting with the 30-30 or any shorter-range firearm, stillhunting with field position carefully in mind can mean a close shot. The example of the meadow, cited earlier, comes to bear here. The 30-30 man simply has to work the edge of that meadow for the close shot, and forget about shooting across the meadow. This may mean looking at the other side of the meadow, but through binoculars. If game is spotted, a stalk is made for that close shot.

No human hunter is totally noiseless as he walks through the woods. We just do the best we can. I have hunted along streams where the rushing water masked my approach, and I have hunted when lusty wind gusts covered the sounds made by my clumsy feet. But a deer has radar ears. On a still day, away from a stream, he's going to hear you coming. Bet on it. So you try to maintain as much silence of foot as possible, and you hope the deer won't bolt until you can get a shot at him. Ever wonder how many deer we spook unseen, as compared with how many we do see? I have no figure to offer, but I have seen plenty of deer sneaking out ahead of hunters.

Being quiet means mainly two things. First, wear quiet clothing. Big old boots make noise. Soft-soled outdoor footwear is much quieter. Pants should be of material which does not shriek out a warning. I have owned pants that scrape together like giant cricket legs. I try to avoid such clothing. Second, move slowly. The slower you move through the woods, the easier it is to be quiet. Keep the feet close to the ground when possible; raising the feet high tires a walker and makes more noise through extra contact with ground cover. And walk with the toes pointed straight ahead if you can. Splayed-out feet tend to kick into debris along the trial. Walk slowly on soft-soled shoes or boots in soft-finished clothing.

Now let's look at stand hunting. A stand can be a formal, manmade hideout in which the hunter takes refuge for as long as a full day. It can be on the ground or in a tree. The hunter can be camouflaged naturally by foliage or by camouflage cloth or netting. The success of a stand is based on several things. It must be located in an area known to be frequented by deer, of course, and preferably near a path used by deer. It is also smart to set up the stand so that the shot will be at 30-30 distance. A hunter in a stand on the side of a hill looking at another hill 375 yards away may see deer, but if he must use this stand, I suggest a long-range rifle. The 30-30 user should set up his stand 50 or 100 yards from a likely runway for deer.

Get comfortable on stand. Wear the best possible clothing in terms of insulation. I know this advice is important because I have failed to observe it in the past. One wintry morning I sat on a stand for a couple of hours until I became as stiff as a cigar-store Indian. It seemed to take 20 seconds for messages from my brain to get my fingers to move. No fun, that. And besides, it's counterproductive. A hunter on stand should be well-dressed and comfortable. And, by the way, he should be able to see clearly all around him, and be able to get a shot off when a chance shows up.

A third manner of brush/woods deer hunting is the drive, and in some areas it's by far the best way to encounter a deer, especially in thick country. But drives must be organized, and that is best done by a hunter or hunters who really know the area and the movement of the deer. Sure, some drives—I call them minidrives—are simple. You see a big patch of heavy growth and know deer are in there, so one hunter takes a high point while a couple of others beat the brush. Out comes a deer, perhaps heading toward the stationary hunter.

Here, too, use the wind in your favor. Sometimes it's not possible to take a post downwind of the drivers, but generally this is the best way. On some minidrives, it's just as well to post a person with the wind at his back, but generally it's better to let the deer scent the drivers instead. They move away from the drivers and often toward the waiting hunters. I have used this plan in small canyons out west; one of us takes a point on the ridge, while the other meanders about in the bottom of the draw, hoping a deer will scent the walking hunter and slip away from him right to the stationary hunter.

I want to add here that heavy brush does not rule out the use of optics. I have found deer in thick terrain by using binoculars. This usually means studying brushy areas across open meadows, but it can also mean looking into thickets right in front of you. For heavy brush, I like the tiny binocs which are popular today. I have a pair of 7x20 glasses of good optical quality, and they work well for me in dense cover.

One little trick which helps the 30-30 deer hunter is to constantly check the wind's direction by using a "smoke bag." This is simply a cloth bag, such as those in which bulk cigarette tobacco is sold. The cloth pouch is filled with the fine white soot from a campfire or fireplace. To keep the user's clothing clean, the bag is placed in a plastic sandwich container. From time to time, the hunter takes the bag out and "pops" it into the air. A little puff of white "smoke" comes forth, and it tells the way of the wind far better than wetting your finger or kicking dust up with the toe of a boot.

Open Country Methods

Field position is important here as well as in brushy areas. Stillhunting is the basic method of covering open deer country. That little smoke bag is useful, and so is being quiet if possible, though I sometimes think it's better to sound like a herd of cows coming through the country instead of like a sneaking hunter who snaps twigs and rustles leaves.

Mostly I like to 30-30 hunt the open deerlands by stillhunting along, maintaining field position so I can get a shot if something bursts out, watching the wind so the game won't sneak out of a draw ahead of me unseen, and taking to good lookout points where I can use the binocular. The glass has been my number one means of finding deer in the West. Most of those deer were spotted while they were feeding in early morning or late afternoon, but I have located a good number of bucks which were bedded down in midday.

Most hunters use the glass to look at something they have already seen with unaided eyes. I use the glass to locate deer which I would not otherwise know existed. There are a few rules to glassing which can help the hunter. First, get steady. I often use a walking staff to steady the binoculars, or I will sit with back against a boulder, elbows on knees, to steady the glass. A shaky glass is a curse. Deer are hard enough to locate because they wear that wonderful gray camouflage suit that blends in well with most of their terrain.

Focus the glass constantly. Pick out a hunk of terrain and study it completely, focusing the glass soft and hard, back and forth. This helps to sort out the bucks from the brush. Look for the little stuff. Don't look for a whole deer. In mule deer hunting, look for that white rump patch, but also watch for the glint of an eye in the grass or the shine of an antler. It's amazing how far away these things can be seen by a careful observer using high-quality binoculars.

I believe in quality optics. Give me a used 94 30-30 right off the wall, and I will sight it in and go get a deer. But please don't give me a cheap glass. I'll use the glass all day long—the rifle will likely fire but once. Sure, the "moment of truth," the actual shooting, is important, but if you can't find a deer, you can't harvest a deer. So give me binoculars with fine optics, meaning superior *definition*—the optical ability to help my eyes distinguish between a gray boulder and a buck off in the distance. Uninitiated binocular users often don't believe what can be done with a good glass.

Not long ago, I was studying the side of a rock cliff. It was steep, but it had deer trails running along it like lines on the weathered face of an old outdoorsman. I mustered up my patience, which I have in small quantity, and forced myself to study the rock face intently with the binoculars. There, looking out of the cliff as if he were in the mouth of a mine shaft, was a buck, only his head showing. A stalk produced a close shot and a harvest.

And that's the way it's done in open terrain with binoculars. The glass does part of the walking for you. And when

Reliable, that's the 94 and the 30-30. Even in the snow, the deer hunter can rely on the 94 to feed the rounds in and fire them, with good ejection.

the deer is located, you make a careful stalk, putting to use all of the precepts of stillhunting. But the beauty of finding the game before the game locates you is the fact that the deck is now stacked in your favor. You can stalk with the wind in your face because you know where the deer is in relation to the wind. You can take the quietest route and the one that offers cover for the stalk. Suddenly, the 30-30 is more than adequate in the open country, for you can stalk in for a close shot—you need not shoot from hill to hill.

One last note on the 30-30 for deer: I love to backpack into the quiet places. A hunter can live off the land as he goes, for there are small game animals and birds in season, available to the handloader who has down-loaded ammo for his 30-30 or who is carrying a 22 pistol. Getting the deer out means boning it, where legal, and leaving hide and offal for the wild creatures to clean up. I am hardly the only hunter who enjoys the outback in this manner. Read the words of Charles J. Farmer, a friend of mine, who often heads into lonely places for deer. He says in *The American Hunter*, November, 1984, on page 34:

> I walked slowly along an old logging road that meandered along a series of ridges. My pack creaked slightly with each step, and I had the .30-30 ready just in case of a chance meeting with a buck. Every time I don a pack, carry a rifle, and hike through a remote land, I identify with mountain men, trailblazers, and trappers who depended on their wits, hunting skills, and stamina to survive. My hunt was no survival mission, yet it offered challenges beyond those encountered on conventional deer hunts. Eating, drinking, sleeping, creating shelter, staying warm, and fine tuning hunting alertness blend together on such a trip to keep the senses at high frequency.

I know what Charlie means about the high-frequency senses, and I attribute a part of the excitement to the tool of the harvest that we carry. I truly admire the modern firearm, and everybody knows it. But on such a backwoods hunt, that 30-30, nearing a full century of existence, seems to fit in—not only my original Model 1894 rifle manufactured about 1899, but also the well-balanced custom 30-30 I like to carry.

More venison has been taken with the 30-30 than with any other cartridge ever developed. When I hear that it is no good for deer, and that its bullets simply bounce off a deer's hide like spent BBs. I sit back and chuckle, and visions of cleanly harvested bucks dance through my head. All that hooting and hollering about the ineffectiveness of the 30-30 on deer amounts to what you find on the ground in a corral occupied by a big Hereford bull.

9

The 30-30 on the Plains

Always I return to the wide open plains. I can view a vast panorama in all directions and somehow regain the belief that man will not build edifices over every square foot of the original earth. There is a sense of freedom on the flatlands. Therefore I am a lover of the plains and plains hunting. In America, that means the pronghorn antelope, as far as big game goes. This chapter is devoted to hunting that fine trophy in the open reaches of western America, but not with the usual tool of the harvest . . . no, sir. This chapter is about another challenge, the old 30-30 on the flats.

My first encounter with the 30-30 on the plains was through that noted Arizona game warden, Levi Packard. He used a standard Model 94 30-30 carbine for his pronghorn hunting, and he expressed the idea that its less-than-super-flat trajectory and iron sights gave him a sense of accomplishment when he harvested antelope, a trophy sought generally with scope-sighted rifles firing flat-shooting rounds. On the one hand, the 30-30 seems about as modern as spats and knickers when compared with the sizzling hotshot calibers used today for antelope. But history reminds us that at one time the 30-30 was a prime flat-country round. I sometimes like to turn the pages backward in the shooting history book for reward and enjoyment.

Our famous shooting president, Teddy Roosevelt, expressed his joy in shooting the then-new 30-30 on an antelope hunt, and his words are a reminder that not so very long ago, an antelope hunter—no, any hunter of open spaces—had to stalk close for a shot if he wanted to consistently bag his quarry. In *Outdoor Pas-*

Taking game with an original Model 94 rifle is a real thrill. This rifle, a 94 30-30 manufactured about 1899, is much like the one Teddy Roosevelt used to hunt antelope.

times of an American Hunter, the Charles Scribner & Sons text of 1923, Roosevelt described using the smokeless powder 30-30 in the year 1896. He said, on pages 196–201:

> In the fall of 1896 I spent a fortnight on the range with the ranch wagon. I was using for the first time one of the new small-calibre, smokeless-powder rifles, with the usual soft-nosed bullet. While travelling to and fro across the range we usually moved camp each day, not putting up the tent at all during the trip; but at one spot we spent three nights . . .
>
> The last shot I got was when I was out with Joe Ferris, in whose company I had killed my first buffalo, just thirteen years before, and not very far from this same spot. We had seen two bands [of antelope] that morning, and in each case, after a couple of hours of useless effort, I failed to get near enough. At last, toward midday, after riding and tramping over a vast extent of broken sun-scorched country, we got within range of a small band lying down in a little cup-shaped hollow in the middle of a great flat. I did not have a close shot, for they were running about 180 yards off. The buck was rear-most, and at him I aimed; the bullet struck him in the flank, coming out of the opposite shoulder, and he fell in the next bound. As we stood over him, Joe

The 44-40 on the left was used often for plains game in the "good old days." The 45 Colt on the right was a common big-bore pistol of those days. The 25-35 Winchester, in the rear, represented a new school when it came along, and so did the 30-30 smokeless.

shook his head, and said, 'I guess that little rifle is the ace;' and I told him I guessed so too.

A short time ago, I enjoyed a similar experience. I was hunting with my son John, and we had located a good antelope buck with his harem, the group feeding at the mouth of a cut which went up into a long draw of rocks and stunted trees. I was carrying my original Model 1894 rifle. John and I used the rock cover to hide our stalk, and yet the pronghorns got some kind of message concerning our proximity to them, or perhaps there was another hunter nearby whom we could not see. At any rate, the herd bolted. John and I made a mad dash for a little coulee which seemed a possible avenue of escape for the herd, for we figured they would head out into the plains, not up into the rocky hill behind them.

We were lucky. They did use the long draw as a road to the flatlands, and we were able to cut 'em off before they broke into the open. Crack! The buck was down and cleanly harvested. The range? Maybe 150 yards. Had I taken the nice buck with a flat-shooting rifle, it would still have been a trophy head, but because I dropped it with the old 30-30, the event was very special for me. I recalled Roosevelt's long-ago hunt, looked down at the rifle in my hands and muttered under my breath, "I guess you are an ace."

I truly enjoy cruising the flatlands on foot with the 30-30, packed in the hand or, if I'm using my Storey conversion, slung over the special strut on my packframe. A muzzleloader has been an important tool for my antelope hunts, too, and I've taken bucks in the 15-inch to 15½-inch class with a smokepole. But that 30-30, well-fed with handloads, makes a fine middle-ground pronghorn piece. While I consider 125 yards about far enough for the muzzleloader, I feel that 200 yards, maybe 225, is no big trick for a properly loaded, well-sighted 30-30.

My favorite antelope load for the 30-30 comes out of a Lyman reloading manual, Number 46. I cut the charge by two grains and gain a very respectable muzzle velocity with it. On page 283, Lyman's 46th shows a 150-grain bullet with 39.0 grains of H-335 powder. My own load is 37.0 to 37.5 grains of the same powder with a 150-grain pill, and out of my 24-inch barrel 30-30, using standard 30-30 cases, the muzzle velocity averages about 2,550 fps.

On the plains, I turn my own 30-30 into a two-shot rifle—one in the magazine, one in the chamber. Or I carry two in the chamber and *none* in the magazine; then I can flick the lever and enter a round into the chamber, but the magazine will still have but one round in it. In this way, as previously reported, it is safe to use a bullet with a profile a bit racier than a round nose. Remember, it is forbidden to load pointed bullets into a magazine in such a way that the nose of one rests against the primer of another. But with the two-load measure, there is no chance of a problem because there is only *one round* in that magazine.

Now the 150-grain Speer Mag-Tip goes to work, or the 150-grain Hornady Interlock, both fine bullets at 30-30 muzzle velocities. Neither is terribly destructive at these 2,500–2,600 fps starting speeds. Yet both will drive totally through an antelope or a deer and harvest either quickly and cleanly without undue loss of meat.

About the Mag-Tip: fear not that the profile is truncated—no nice pointed tip of lead shows there. That pretty little tip of lead on the front of a bullet, be it spitzer or spire-point design, is smashed fairly flat when the bullet crashes into the atmosphere at its high muzzle velocity. Speer knows this. There are actual photos to prove the fact. That is why Speer offers a bullet which has no lead tip, such as the Mag-Tip style. I like this bullet for *two shots only*—never with more than one in the magazine. It feeds great into the 30-30 because the bullet is short, thanks to its lack of a tip.

The big factor in hunting the pronghorn with the 30-30—or any firearm which does not have that taut-wire trajectory pattern we are used to obtaining from the 243 Winchester, 6mm Remington, 270 Winchester and other hot numbers—is to *know thy game.* Understand the antelope as best you can. Learn his ways. Try to discover the patterns he follows in a given day. And remember this—the harvest of antelope is important to the herd. When a herd is too large going into winter, the entire group may suffer badly from competition for food supplies. Antelope herds have suffered huge winterkills. It's right to harvest the pronghorn, and it's downright exciting to hunt him using a modest firearm.

The pronghorn is unrelated to any other big-game animal in the United States. He has no living relatives in the Old World, either. His large eyes are so situated on his face that he can almost see behind. He can see extremely well. In fact, his eyesight is incredible. Some people believe that the antelope has a sort of binocular ability I don't know. I do know that through binoculars I have spotted a herd which was totally invisible to the naked eye, and yet that herd was watching me. I would wave a hand, and the herd would react to the movement. The 'lopes could see me, and yet I didn't notice a single one of them wearing Bushnell binocs!

Another thing antelope can do very well is run. Boy, can they run. I have definitely clocked an antelope at 55 miles per hour for a short stretch. The antelope has very strong bones in its forelegs. In a test, a cow's foreleg bone broke under a stress of 41,300 pounds while an antelope's foreleg bone withstood a pressure of 45,300 pounds per square inch—even though the antelope weighed about one-seventh as much as the cow. The pronghorn's feet have special protective cartilage, too, to pad them for fast running.

The heart of an antelope is twice the size of a sheep's heart, though both animals weigh about the same. The trachea (windpipe) of a man will be about .76 of an inch in diameter. The trachea of an antelope will be more like 1.6 inches in diameter, though the man will weigh about 180 pounds and the antelope maybe 125. The pronghorn is well-suited to life on the plains, and the 30-30 hunter has to understand the abilities of this quarry so he can work around them.

The antelope takes in about four pounds of food a day, mostly forbs and grasses as well as brushy materials. He feeds a lot, and he feeds much of the day. So the hunter knows he must look for pronghorns all day. Take your lunch. Stay out there. The antelope may be found up and moving about at midday, while his deer friends may well be loafing in the shade of a bush.

Antelope usually take water on a daily basis. Look for watering spots. When I see a windmill in the distance, I often make my way to it so I can study the water situation. I have many times found little water troughs which were being used by pronghorns in these areas. When a waterhole is located, the idea is to hunt in the vicinity for herds of antelope. Antelope will come to a waterhole to drink during daylight hours, whereas most deer will use the watering location at dusk or in the night.

I have bowhunting friends who wait by waterholes for antelope to come in. I don't hunt that way with my 30-30, because I don't care to stay still that long. I much prefer being up and about. But a hunter may notice that a specific spot, either a waterhole or a crossing, is used a lot by antelope, and if he wishes to park himself in the brush and wait for Mr. Pronghorn to show up, that's fine with me. I sometimes think that the fellow who does this has as good a chance as the hunter who moves around.

Make no mistake—an antelope can jump a fence. But he prefers not to. I have seen antelope glide over fences like a jackrabbit clears sagebrush. Also, during the terrible winterkill of 1984 in Wyoming, I found many antelope caught on fences, proving that they had tried to jump them. All in all, however, the pronghorn will go under a fence or along it if he can avoid jumping it. And the 30-30 hunter can use this information to his advantage.

One season I watched a big herd of antelope moving in the distance. It was heading right toward a long fence line. I figured that the herd was not going to jump that fence. So I paced as fast as I could to a corner in the fence where I felt the herd would tarry. The group stopped right where I figured it would. It turned out that the bucks in the bunch were not large, so I passed 'em up, but had I wanted to harvest one, it would have been a 50-yard shot.

Another thing—stick with it. Don't drop out before the end of the day. Antelope often lose caution in the late afternoon for some reason. I have seen it many times. A buck impossible to approach at noon might be less wary in the latter part of the day, allowing a 30-30 hunter to close in for a killing shot. One day I kept on the trail of a nice buck from first light through the noon hour. I felt like giving up. That buck seemed to know where I was even when I was behind a hill. I would walk 500 yards and then take a look over a bump in the earth I had used for cover, only to find that the pronghorn had also moved 500 yards. But late in the afternoon, I found it much easier to approach him and ended up with a shot at less than 100 yards.

Antelope are creatures of the open, to be sure, but do not neglect what I call "the fringe." Big bucks often seem to prefer areas where the brushlands and the prairie join. I have seen loners on the fringe many times—big bucks, all by themselves, feeding and bedding in rolling country, even among small trees. So look hard into all those rolling, grassy pockets in your area. A big boy could be lingering there.

Antelope are quiet, most of the time. But I have discovered more than one herd by using my ears. An antelope may be looking right at a hunter, but he simply won't see that pronghorn at all until the animal gives forth with his little yelp—*Ow*! It's a bark, I suppose, more than a yelp. That warning cry can help a hunter locate an antelope which otherwise might never be seen.

Of course, antelope hunting is a game of optics. I have had a few chances for antelope which I located simply by pacing the countryside on foot and spotting them as I came up over a rise. But most of the time, hunters use binoculars or a spotting scope to find antelope. If it seems incongruous to use modern optics while carrying a more challenging firearm like the 30-30, worry not about this. Jim Bridger, the mountain man, used a telescope to find game and foe in the 19th century as he fur-trapped the Far West. There is no need to feel that the use of optics is a too-modern approach.

I use both binoculars and spotting scope in my own antelope hunting. Once again, the idea is to locate a fine buck,

This nice antelope buck was taken with the Storey Conversion, the author's custom Model 94 Winchester 30-30. The shot was from more than 200 yards.

then stalk in close for a sure shot. It can be done. The flatlands are not entirely flat. There are hills and many little depressions and waterways—normally dry stream beds, actually—which can hide the hunter on the way to his pronghorn buck. And there is brush. I've picked some cactus out of my body due to belly-crawls through the sagebrush, but I always felt the few needles were worth the reward of getting close to a fine antelope buck.

Sometimes I'll carry my spotting scope with me in the field. It's perfectly honorable to drive backroads, stopping and searching from time to time, as long as no shooting takes place from a vehicle in chase, which is illegal and immoral. So the hunter can mount a spotting scope on a vehicle's window. When he finds and judges his quarry, then he dismounts his trusty iron pony and proceeds to stalk his game on foot. But the spotting scope can

John Fadala poses with a buck taken by the author. Such harvests are always memory-makers, but when the rifle is an old-timer, the memories are even sweeter.

also be carried into the field by the walking hunter. Bushnell offers a neat little tripod which is useful in steadying the spotting scope for good viewing.

My favorite antelope hunt is via the backpack method. This puts the hunter into the land with his game. I like to choose an area which lets me leave the roads behind. Striking off from a backroad, I'll walk into the roadless area, camp on my back. Today's backpack gear is so advanced that it is simple to enjoy overnighters in comfort.

I use a good frame, such as the L.L. Bean model with its shelf unit, coupled with a daypack of good size. The daypack has all my incidental gear in it—first-aid supplies, emergency firestarter, matches, compass, cutlery gear, flashlight, and many other outdoor necessities. The sleeping bag, a smaller mummy type for easy carrying, is strapped onto the frame after it has been tucked into a stout plastic garbage sack to keep it dry. A tarp can serve as a covering. The new plastic tarps are strong and lightweight. Or you may choose a little tent. Mine is from the Coleman Company and weighs only five pounds complete, yet it houses two hunters nicely. Food staples are carried in a separate container. I have a feed bag which is waterproof and strong.

All of this sounds like a lot of gear, but even with my lantern aboard—I like light in camp—there's nothing to carrying this load. When dusk arrives, I unlimber my gear and start the lantern, either a Peak 1 or the newer Quicklite, which lights instantly with the flick of a lever. A stove may be necessary in places where there is little wood supply. A backpack stove need not weigh much, even with liquid fuel or a gas cartridge.

Sometimes I carry a little bundle of charcoal briquettes and a steak. The added weight is not too bad because on the first night in camp, the steak will be eaten and the coals used up. A tiny backpack grill turns a steak and a few mushrooms into a delight. I also have a small Silverstone frypan for no-stick cooking and easy cleanup.

Food can also come in the form of wild fare. Sage-hen and antelope seasons often coincide, and I own a tiny double-barrel blackpowder shotgun with 11-inch barrels, which is perfectly legal. This little jewel easily puts sage grouse in the pot, not to mention cottontail rabbits.

And the 30-30 tops it all off. I don't know—it fits in. In the light of the campfire, that old lever-action rifle seems a correct part of the scene. And it does get the job done. With a handload such as mentioned earlier, the 30-30 delivers an antelope or deer punch well past 200 yards, even 250 yards for the hunter who can hit the chest from that far. Remember, this load requires a sight-in of three inches high at 100 yards and it's right on again at 200 yards, so there is no guesswork about hold-over out to 225 yards or so—you don't need any hold-over.

Some parts of the plains have deer, too. And watch for varmints such as the coyote. A little 22 rimfire pistol can bag small-game edibles. An easy-to-pack shotgun, such as my little blackpowder model, will put upland birds in the pot. And, of course, there are the squib loads for the 30-30, as mentioned in the small-game chapter.

At first, it may seem inappropriate to carry the little 30-30 in open country. After all, I called this round a premier woods caliber, not a long-range shooter. And it isn't a long-range shooter, certainly. On the plains it does not begin to compare with a well-loaded 30-06 or any of the fast cartridges chambered up in fine bolt-action, scope-sighted rifles. The 30-30 puts the *hunt* back in hunting, though, and it's plenty strong enough for all plains game when loaded properly for this sort of challenge.

10

Larger-than-Deer Game

Colonel Townsend Whelen said in *The Hunting Rifle*, his 1940 text, "Most of the deer I shot with the .30-30 cartridge did not go 10 feet from where they were hit." Whelen dropped 43 deer with the 30-30, his records showing 50 shots fired. He missed two bucks. This sort of accomplishment for the old 30 is commonplace enough, but what about larger-than-deer game? Is the 30-30 adequate? Al Miller, on page 43 of his often-quoted Rifle Magazine No. 37 article, said, "At one time or another, every species of North American game has been taken by a .30-30."

So does that make the 30 WCF correct for larger-than-deer animals? Let's look a bit closer. "In the Canadian North the .30/30 cartridge is by far the most popular, and ammunition in this caliber can be obtained at any one of the hundreds of trading posts," Jack O'Connor said in his *The Rifle Book*. But is popular always good? Is popular always right? Let's go back to the argument concerning the availability of 30-30 ammo. I know of hunters who like the 30-30 because ammo for it is found just about everywhere. They intimate that the 30-30 is popular because you can buy fodder for it at a crossroads gas station. This is in fact just backwards. You can buy ammo for the 30-30 everywhere because the round proved itself and became that popular.

I asked my friend John Kane, a professional hunter working out of the West Slope in Colorado, why he packed a 30-30 on so many of his big-game hunts, and he came back with a bunch of reasons which seemed to repeat what so many have said before—reliable, easy to pack, can be carried empty and yet a round can

The big-game hunter on the left collected this warthog in Africa with the 30-30 He also got a nice kudu bull and other game, and said, "Contrary to what everyone thought, the 30-30 knocked 'em dead over there."

be quickly flicked into the chamber, fits into tight spaces, handy in transport and for storage, rugged—the 94 takes a licking and keeps on ticking—and powerful enough. John felt the round had enough power for most game, but he added, "in the hands of a cool shot." I'd agree, adding, "in the hands of a professional."

This chapter will give some background data on the 30-30 in use against larger-than-deer game, exclusive of bears. The 30 WCF on blackies and even grizzlies is covered in the next chapter. Here the main aim is to give the 30-30 fan some history on his round. It is not my intention to promote the 30-30 on game bigger than the deer. But, like it or not, the 30 has been used extensively on elk, moose and other big boys of the backwoods. "Despite his years," said Al Miller from the same article mentioned above, "he [The Colonel, a friend of Miller's] managed a deer hunt every season, and whenever he drew a license, tried for elk as well. Despite the availability of several first-class hunting rifles, he invariably chose a well-worn 30-30 when he headed for the mountains. He carried it on his last hunt and dropped an Imperial elk with it."

Much information exists on the famous 30-30 for animals much larger than deer.

I think one of the most interesting accounts is in the book *We Live in the Arctic*, by Connie and Bud Helmericks. This couple ventured on their own into the Arctic regions, living off the land. Their 30-30 was a tool which spelled out life or death to these two adventurers. On pages 26 and 27 of their book, here's what they had to say about the old round:

> So we picked up a couple of Winchester .30-30 carbines, the old cowboy's favorite, attached buckskin thongs for backpacking them, and let it go at that. This little carbine, the saddle gun of the West, is also the favorite of the Eskimos. The sportsman in Alaska uses guns of high caliber, such as the .30-'06, but 35,000 natives don't know what one is. The common little .30-30 carbine, which has journeyed around the world because it is cheap and does the job where jobs are being done, kills more animals in Alaska today than all other guns together. Hundreds of tons of moose, caribou, walrus, polar bears, seals, big grizzly bears, and so on are shot yearly by the brown man with this little gun, in the northern part of the world.

I don't know what the native sportsman uses in the northlands these days (the Helmericks' book dates back to 1947), and I don't think it matters here. The historical approach in this and the next chapter dictates that we must tell it the way it was. The 30-30 did it all for the native up north, and for Bud and Connie as well.

Another person who used the 30-30 in a meat-getting situation was Olive Frederickson. Recently, a motion picture was made depicting the adventures of this plucky lady who lived in the wilds of western Canada. In her book, *The Silence of the North*, she says, "The Reamer family was out of food." Olive, then Olive Reamer, found that "The moose season wouldn't open until fall, but at the time, British Columbia game regulations allowed a prospector to get a permit and kill a moose any time he needed one for food."

Olive had children to feed. "I got little Olive and Louis and Vala ready, loaded them into the big clumsy canoe, poked four shells, all I had, into my old .30-30 Winchester Model 94, and started upstream against the quiet current of the Stuart River." Then she met her moose.

"The moose was feeding," she said, "pulling up weeds from the bottom and putting his head completely under each time he went down for a mouthful. I paddled as close as I dared and warned the two little girls to put their hands over their ears and keep down as low as they could, for I had to shoot over their heads! I put the front bead of the Winchester just behind the bull's shoulder, at the top of the water, and when he raised his head I let him have it. He went down with a great splash, and I told the kids they could rise up and look."

There were so many others who relied on the 94 for the big stuff that the modern-day 30-30 devotee may be surprised by the facts. Frank Golata, widely known a couple of decades ago as a north-country sheep guide, used the 30-30 to hunt big game, including grizzlies. I have an article from a November, 1951 *American Rifleman* in which a record of moose harvests is given, and though the author is not a 30-30 fan, his tabulation shows quite a few moose popped with the old 30, most of them knocked out pretty handily.

Of course, each harvest is unique. For example, one of those moose was taken with a 32 Remington, which is just a 30-

Good bullets are a must no matter the caliber, but a proper bullet is even more important when a smaller round, such as the 30-30, goes up against big game. The fine 170-grain Remington Hollow Point Core-Lokt bullet on the left hangs together quite well and has proved effective for lung shots. The 190-grain Silvertip on the right, taken from a factory 303 Savage round, is another bullet known for deep penetration.

30 ballistically, and had to be whacked four times from 225 yards, three in the head region and one in the neck. But with the same round the author dropped a moose with one shot from the same distance, striking the hump. It seems that when a bull was hit right with the 30, it was moose meat in a hurry.

In C. E. Hagie's book, *The American Rifle*, the author lists the results of elk harvesting with the 30-30. His bullet collection includes 170-grain Core-Lokt and a 170-grain Western Boat Tail. From pages 83 and 84 of the book, here are the author's remarks

1. 170 gr Core-Lokt — bull elk, ribs, less than 50 yds, ranged through lungs and liver and lodged in opposite flank.
2. 170 Western B.T., bull elk, broadside, 75 yards, travelled directly across lung cavity to lodge under the skin on opp. side, breaking 2 ribs.
3. 170 Western B.T., hit elk, *big* bull, neck, abt. 250 yards, hit vertebrae, little mushrooming.

Does all of this make the 30-30 a marvel against the mighty bull elk? Of course not. But there's no denying that the 30-30 has been used successfully on much game larger than deer.

But is the 30-30 *right* for game larger than deer? This time, I'll answer the question: only in the hands of the practiced shot and expert hunter. The 30-30 is not right for the hunter who sets forth into the outback a time or two each year. He should carry a lot more gun. I'd suggest at least a 30-06, scope-sighted and well sighted in. He should also practice as much as possible before his hunt for game larger than deer, because even with big medicine, you still have to hit 'em right.

He might be embarrassed, so his name will not be stated here, but one fine hunter I know happens to use the 30-30 for a lot of his hunting. He guides other hunters, and has more than once put a big bull elk down instantly after that elk had been hit not so perfectly with much larger calibers. The professional—the hunter who gets out plenty, who stalks for close shots, who works hard at his activity, who is a good, cool shot—that fellow may use the little 30 on game larger than deer. Even for this pro, I can offer a few comments.

Your hunting style probably has to change if you want to successfully drop the big boys with the 30-30. First, it is my recommendation that shots be placed in the shoulder area—the scapula, in other words. The bone-breaking ability of the stronger-jacketed bullet in this area can be a knockout. Also, there are quite a few nerves where the shoulder blade and shoulder bone come together.

The American hunter is often trained to shoot *behind* the shoulder, not into the shoulder itself. This is, of course, good advice because a hit behind the shoulder means the "boiler room" is invaded by the bullet, which knocks out the lungs and sometimes, if it hits lower, the heart. No normally edible meat is lost, either. So, sure, go for that behind-the-shoulder chest hit. But this placement with a very powerful projectile means plenty of tissue disruption. Hit a deer behind the shoulder with a 270 Winchester and he'll drop as if struck by a bolt from above, because the bullet is explosive. But with a bullet that does not have that type of shock going for it, like the 30, the strike into the shoulder is often a better one.

When hunting in Africa, I was handed a 264 Winchester Magnum with handloads. One was a 140-grain bullet at between 3,100 and 3,200 fps muzzle velocity. The other was a 156-grain bullet in the 3,000-fps niche. I was warned by the owner of the rifle that these loads were not all that wonderful on greater kudu, waterbuck and similar African big game, but that it was the only rifle and round available to me.

I thought things over and decided that I would go for bone. I ended up taking three nice animals—a record-class kudu bull, another good kudu bull and a fine waterbuck—with three shots. I went for hits in the shoulder area on the kudu and into the spine on the waterbuck. "Where are you hitting those animals?" the owner of the rifle wanted to know, and I explained that the "boiler room" was not my aim.

So with the 30-30 on bigger game. Give me a good 150- to 170-grain soft-nosed bullet on a deer or antelope, and I'll go for a lung/behind-the-shoulder, boiler-room shot. But for game larger than deer, I'll try to put those bullets into the shoulder region, if not into the neck/

spine area or the brain. Also, the hunter who uses the 30-30 on bigger animals should recognize that his 94 is a repeater. Use that second or third shot. It's no disgrace to have to hit game with more than one bullet. But it is a real shame to lose a big-game animal. Follow-up shots with the lever-action 30-30 are very possible indeed. But they should all be *aimed*. Supposing a strike in the shoulder brings that big animal down. Shoot again. Put another into the shoulder region, or drop this one in behind the shoulder, since you already have one bullet into bone.

In my opinion, a bullet of 165 grains weight should be about minimum on game larger than deer if the 30-30 is to be used. I have to quickly add, however, that if given a choice between a strongly constructed 150-grain bullet, such as the Hornady Interlock or Speer Mag-Tip, and a softer 170-grain bullet, I'll opt for the stronger bullet every time on any big game requiring real force to bring down.

The stronger bullet will stay intact, driving deep into the vitals, leaving a blood trail if it exits, and also will be much more likely to break bone. The softer bullet may itself break up on bone instead of breaking it. The handloader has the edge here, of course, because he can select bullets which match the game. The factory ammo made for the 30-30 is mostly aimed toward deer hunting, as it should be. As a handloader, I have the option of using bullets of strong construction. Also, the 170-grain Silvertip bullet and 170-grain Core-Lokt, as well as Frontier's Interlock 170-grain bullet, are all fine designs which usually retain core and jacket in one unit.

On the other hand, a 180-grain bullet extracted from the 307 Winchester is built quite strongly; another stout bullet is a 190-grain Silvertip, which must be stolen from the 303 Savage load and handloaded into the 30-30 case. Another bullet which could be quite useful for larger game with the 30-30 is offered by a factory. Federal now has a Premium brand of ammo using a 170-grain Nosler partition bullet. This is the familiar Nosler bullet with its H-style jacket which separates the lead core of the base from the lead core of the forward portion of the bullet. While the nose of this bullet is fairly soft, with a tapered jacket, the bullet can't strip its jacket from the core due to the design. So, the shank section of the bullet remains intact on penetration, offering a longer wound channel and greater bone-breaking possibilities.

In my 30-30 Improved with 24-inch barrel, but using standard 30-30 loads, I find a 180-grain Winchester bullet moving out at over 2,200 fps MV and a 190-grain bullet taking off at about 2,100 fps MV. That is not magnum force by any means. On the other hand, such ballistics are not exactly in the same league as chucking a spear A strongly constructed 180-grain bullet, for example, at *close* range, even with a modest 2,200-fps starting velocity, will break bones and penetrate well.

Bullet weight and bullet construction are the key here. I have found fine results on big game using a bullets in the 30-30 designed for the 30-06 class of cartridge. So the hunter who feels he wants the easy carrying and fast pointing of the 30-30 Model 94 or similar lever-action firearm should select handloads with strong bullets at approved upper-end muzzle velocities. In factory form, I think the 170-grain is the choice. Handloaders may want the 180-grain or the 190-grain bullet.

Using terrain wisely can help the hunter get that "30-30 shot." In this country, it is important to watch the wind and to keep field position in your favor.

As discussed in the deer chapter, hunting style must be matched to the lower-key punch of the 30-30. The 30-30 man is going to have to get closer than the 300 Magnum shooter. And he's going to have to place those slower-moving pills on the money. If he does get within the working range of the 30-30, maybe under 100 yards for the larger-than-deer varieties of big game, he will find that a flat-nose or round-nose bullet in the 170- to 190-grain weight class will do good work, producing long, straight wound channels.

In Mexico, a rancher friend of mine was having trouble with some feral bulls. These were truly feral — mixed-breed animals with temperaments to match their ill-begotten looks. Though it may sound melodramatic, one of those bulls could easily break a good horse down and ruin him, and if the rider happened to get in the way, the bull would try to smash him flatter than a tortilla. I always had the feeling that the Mexican ranchers were truly proud of those dangerous misfits which they had on the ranch. Instead of the typical docile corral-raised beef cattle, those bulls were truly formidable opponents with which the ranchers could match courage. And matches were indeed made.

The only big-game rifle on that ranch was the Model 94 30-30. So it was bull vs. 30-30 all the way. I was interested in obtaining as many facts as possible concerning encounters between the vaqueros and their ferocious, free-roaming bulls. What I learned was this: the cowboys soon found that the only way to bring a bull down quickly was a hit in the brain or a broken bone followed up by a well-placed shot in the spine or other vital area. The range was usually quite close, too close for me. But at such close range, bullet placement was not too difficult, and the bulls lost each bout with the cowboys. Most amazing to me was bullet penetration. Only factory fodder was used, but often a bullet broke a shoulder and lodged up against the opposite shoulder.

Finally, it's only fair to state that the Model 94 lover of today should think about other calibers if he wants the light-packing lever-action as a firearm for game larger than deer. Let's face it, today's Angle-Eject and Big Bore 94s are offered in some pretty potent rounds. I have tested the 356 Winchester at length, and it's a powerful round. So is the 375 Winchester. Both shoot a 250-grain bullet. I have handloaded 270-grain bullets in the 375 Winchester. In my opinion, either of these rounds will serve admirably on elk, moose and similar game at close range. Of course, we are still talking about close range. These are not flat-shooting numbers. They are larger of bore than our old 30-30, firing heavier bullets at modest velocities.

Therefore, I'd have to suggest that a potential customer who wants to employ a Model 94 on big stuff take a long look at the 356 and the 375 Winchester. The 307 Winchester isn't at all anemic, either. It shoots a 180-grain bullet in factory-loaded form. Besides, the Angle-Eject allows normal scope mounting, so the hunter has a chance to place that bullet correctly even if he's not quite an expert with iron sights.

If I were to hunt elk in the black timber or moose in the high forests of my state, where the big boys generally hang out, I'd be not the least bit afraid to pack my 30-30 and my handloads, provided I was in physical tune and had the time to truly *hunt* 30-30 style. But if time were short and if I felt that cross-canyon shots were possible, I'd go for bigger ballistics.

The old 30-30 has accounted for every type of big game this country has to offer: elk, moose, grizzly, caribou, bighorn sheep, wolf, mountain goat, wild boar and so forth. But times have changed, and so have hunters. The man who wants to stroll along one hillside popping off big game on the other hill 300 yards off has to leave the old 30-30 behind. It's not the right caliber for that type of work. But the hunter who is willing and content to stalk game close, learning the habits of his quarry so he can keep the odds in his favor when he crosses paths with it, this man may indeed enjoy the challenge of the modest, no-frills 30 WCF, even when the quarry is larger than a deer.

11

The 30-30 and the Bear

Bears! Blacks and even the fearsome grizzly have been hunted with the standard 30-30 since that round saw the light of day. The 30-30 was, still is and always will be a good black bear cartridge. As for Old Ephraim, the grizzly, my personal opinion is that something larger than a 30 caliber bullet at twice the speed of sound should be employed. I've lived in grizzly country, and though I don't know all that much about this fellow, I have learned enough of his size, stamina and general nature to respect him greatly. In my mind, a basic bottom-of-the-line grizzly round is something in the 33 caliber plus domain, with bullets weighing at least 250 grains pushed out of the muzzle at over 2,500 feet per second.

All the same, the history of bear hunting is replete with documented stories of the mighty grizzly falling to the little 30-30. This chapter has two distinct "flavors." One deals with the history of hunting the ferocious grizzly with the 30-30. This part of the story is important and interesting to 30-30 fans in spite of the fact that we do not intend to use that round on the grizzly today. And let's face facts—there's very little grizzly hunting going on these days, so our interest in the 30-30 on these big bears is academic.

On the other side of the ledger, the second "flavor" in this chapter smacks of roast meat, meat from the black bear, an animal which has done very well in the face of civilization's encroachment. Lots of black bears are running around in the forests of America, and there are plenty of good hunts for the blackie. Furthermore, the 30-30, with the right loads, has proved to be quite useful in harvesting the black bear. I have no qualms over hunting this animal with the little 30, especially with strongly constructed factory bullets or good handloads.

Thirty-thirty Jack was a documented figure who earned his name by hunting bears with the old 30-30 cartridge in a Model 94 Winchester. Frank C. Hibben, admired researcher and bear hunter, spent some time with Jack, who apparently saved the lives of both Hibben and his wife. Hibben tells the story in *Hunting American Bears*, a book from the University of New Mexico Press:

> We had progressed only a few yards when there was a splash ahead of us. I stopped in the middle of a stride and put one hand back to signal Eleanor behind me. But she had heard it too. There were shallow pools of water in the path where we walked and we could hear the little sounds of the dripping forest around us. But this had been a splash like a heavy stone thrown into a puddle. There it was again just in front of us on the trail. I straightened and looked ahead. The screening salmon-berry bushes hid everything with only a shaded glimpse here and there of the larger trees. As I strained to see through the thick foliage, a hemlock limb pulled to one side, then snapped back in place. The top of a clump of bushes shook visibly as the stems were agitated from beneath. Some huge form was coming down the path!
>
> The torpedo is more terrible as it approaches unseen beneath the water. Death by night is a hundred times more awful than the same danger by daylight. This ominous animal that splashed toward us was neither under the water nor in the dark, but it might as well have been both. That cursed Alaska vegetation had been the death of people along this coast before ourselves.

Unless a person has been in the thick vegetation along the Alaskan coast, where the big grizzlies roam, it's difficult

John Kane with a black bear taken by the author. The 30-30 has long been used successfully on blackies.

to appreciate what it's like to sense one of those big brutes close by. As it turned out, it was no blackie in the bush in front of the Hibbens. The author goes on:

> Even as I spoke a wet thing of matted hair pushed out from the agitated bushes before us. It was a pointed head with ears and a black nose that swung among the wet leaves like the head of a cobra. It was no wonder that the animal used its nostrils in that way. Where one eye should have been was only a fleshy hole, and there was an inflamed scratch across the empty socket.
>
> In that instant the other eye of the grizzly fixed upon us. The camera hit the mud of the trial with a wet 'thump' as it dropped from my hand. The inexorable

wheels of time stood still. We were so close to the awful beast that we thought we could read decision in that one staring eye. The grizzly growled menacingly and lunged at the same time. The gray body came out of the screening bushes and raised half erect with forepaws swinging clear. The long hooked claws spread wide for the charge. It would be easy there in the narrow trail.

The blast of the shot was deafening in the confined space. A spurt of fur flew from the grizzly's throat at the instant of the clap of noise. But the bear hesitated only a second. With a powerful thrust of his hind quarters he surged toward us, goaded by the pain in his neck. Again the rifle roared just in front of us and the leaves at one side of the trail blanched before the muzzle blast. The grizzly also suddenly saw his real antagonist and seemed to turn in mid-air, although whether from indecision or the impact of the bullet it was not clear. An empty cartridge case gleamed momentarily as it arched out of the leaves and plopped in the mud. Whang! The gun blasted again as the bear twisted and dropped forward into the bushes . . .

This lengthy quote gives the reader an idea of grizzly bear encounters, and there is plenty of evidence to show that stories of grizzly attacks are more fact than fiction, in spite of modern talk to the contrary in some circles. The 30-30 student must recognize that though we don't consider the old workhorse caliber right for the big grizzly today, it was better than plenty of other rounds in use at the turn of the century. And the 30-30's use on Old Ephraim is a part of the overall grizzly bear story today.

The reader interested in the history of the 30-30 will find much merit in the accounts of grizzly hunting with the old favorite round. *Notorious Grizzly Bears* by W.P. Hubbard, a 1960 Sage Books printing, has a good story in which a hunter packed into northern British Columbia, transporting explosives to a mine. The mules were charged by a grizzly bear. The 30-30 was used to finish this bear. Hubbard himself used the 30-30 on grizzly. On page 42 of his book, he says, "I favor the 30-06, but have used a 30-30 Winchester on one occasion, at close range, and found it most effective."

The naturalist William T. Hornaday went for grizzly with a smaller caliber, a 303 Savage. He describes in his book *Camp-Fires in the Canadian Rockies*, Scribners, 1906, how that 30-30-like round took out the mighty bear.

Harold McCracken, in *The Beast That Walks Like a Man*, a 1955 publication from Hanover House, hunted the big bears with a 30-30 under the tutorage of a Cree Indian. And in *The Grizzly Bear*, a 1966 book from the University of Oklahoma Press, B. D. Haynes and E. Haynes relate the interesting story of Old Ephraim of Utah. I made it a point to study materials on this monarch grizzly when I was in Utah, and if the figures are correct, that bear was truly a giant.

Old Ephraim was a renegade, a killer bear. He cultivated a taste for livestock and then did his best to see that his stomach was always full of his favorite fare. This preference did not please the ranchers of Utah, and the bear was on the "wanted list." Frank Clark trapped for the bear from 1914 until he got him in 1923. Although the huge bear was not taken with a 30-30, I include his story here because he was dropped with the 30-30's little sister, the 25-35 Winchester, a companion smokeless-powder round.

Clark's account of catching up with Old Ephraim is an interesting one. He says, "Finally, more out of fear than any other passion, I opened up with my small

25-35 caliber rifle and pumped six shots into him. He fell at my feet dead..." The editors of the book state that the statistics on the big bear read:

OLD EPHRAIM'S GRAVE
(Grizzly Bear)
KILLED BY FRANK CLARK,
MALAD, IDAHO
AUGUST 22, 1923 — Weight Approx.
1,100 pounds — Height 9 ft. 11 in.
SMITHSONIAN INSTITUTE HAS
EPHRAIM'S SKULL

This information is from the Utah Department of Fish and Game, and if the bear did weigh 1,100 pounds, he was indeed one of a kind. Whatever his weight, I am sure the renegade was a big boy and as formidable an animal as any hunter would want to meet up with.

When I was in the Yukon, I had a chance to study some documented information on grizzly bear assaults upon humans, and will leave the reader with one case which has always struck me as indicative of what a mad old boar grizzly can do. The aftermath of the attack found three victims lying dead. One was the bear. The other two corpses were those of a couple of miners. Both of the men had 30-06 rifles. Both had fired. And both had apparently made hits because the bear had absorbed seven 30 caliber bullets in the chest area. However, before expiring, the grizzly managed to wipe out the two riflemen. Mighty is the grizzly bear.

But the black bear is no circus clown. I have read stories which suggest that the blackie is really a cute little overstuffed cutup in a black suit, and the suggestion is that this shy little fellow is no threat to man. Normally, he's not. And yes, the black bear is very shy and generally non-aggressive to man. However, the exceptions are somewhat remarkable. Black bears have attacked men. In fact, black bears have attacked *and eaten* humans.

The 30-30 has gone up against blackie with great success. The black bear is most often hunted in dense cover, though there are several exceptions to this rule. I have seen bears in Alaska feeding on one hillside as I glassed from another hillside 300 or 400 yards or more away. Even with a stalk to the narrowest distance between the hills, the shot would have been a very long one. Also, blackies have been hunted on waterways, where they sometimes feed out in the open. All in all, however, the black bear is usually a creature of dense cover, forests of one sort or another.

The 30-30 is at home in this type of habitat, and is effective on this game, even though some blackies weigh 600 pounds. Most of these bears weigh far less than that. Also, though there is no such thing as a round which can truly break through the brush, the 30-30 with a 170-grain flat-point bullet does about as well as any, and so is right for the task of hunting black bear in thick vegetation.

Ben Lilly was a professional bear hunter. He lived when the ranchlands were being cleared of the grizzly, and his task — somewhat self-assigned — was to hunt down the worst of these killer bears. That time has slid into the recesses of the past, never to return; however, professional bear hunting for renegades is still going on to this day, although the bear doing the livestock damage is most often a blackie.

Such a black bear was making waste of sheep and cattle in Colorado. My friend and hunting partner, John Kane, a professional bear, lion and predator hunter,

No clown, the black bear — this tree-climbing bruin may look like a teddy bear, but it is a wild animal and has given many hunters a memorable chase.

was assigned to locate this particular bruin and put an end to his career. Interestingly enough, I noticed no animosity whatsoever in the tone of the rancher who was having trouble with the bear. In fact, the man admired the animal, but he also had a problem. It's easy to be magnanimous when someone else's living and dollars are at stake. In this case, a lot of the ranchers dollars in the form of prize livestock had been chewed up by the bruin, so the hunt was on.

In my own imagination, I always see these stock killers as tough giants of their race, and the tough part is certainly true, but some of the most aggressive sheep- or cattle-killing bears have turned out to be very ordinary in stature. One such was this particular black bear. Kane's rifle was of special interest to me, an older Model 94 30-30 with a bent tubular magazine.

"How'd you bend the magazine?" I asked, and John told me he had to use it in an emergency when his horse somehow got a foot caught between two rocks. John felt that the horse was about to break a leg, and there was no time to run and look for a pry bar. So the little 30-30 ended up being the pry bar. Though the tube has remained bent, rounds still feed perfectly from the magazine into the chamber.

John will do what he must in order to locate and dispatch a specific stock killer. One time he spent 32 days in the Arizona mountains before he got a lion which had killed thousands of dollars of prize livestock. He had only a pup tent as a home, and it rained for several days in a row, but John ended up with the cat, taking it with his 30-30. "It's just about the only rifle I've tried that really holds up in the saddle scabbard and in real rough use," John told me.

A lot of people think that bear hunting with dogs is a lark. They figure you sit in camp by the fire roasting marshmallows until the dogs bark treed; then you glide into the saddle and jog on over to the tree, where you find the bear sitting up on a limb, snoozing, while the dogs patrol the base of the tree to give you enough time to ride leisurely to the site and make the kill. I'm afraid not. If you want to get your face torn off by a tree limb, ride with Kane or any other professional bear hunter in pursuit of a pack of dogs. Hang on, friend, because there are forests of trees to dodge, and in some terrain you find yourself inching along cliffside trails with a dropoff which will end things in favor of the bruin if your horse slips.

John used his pack of hounds and his horse to capture the bear that had become so fond of lamb chops and prime ribsteak. The chase lasted a few days. Sign was cut the first morning, but rain washed it out. In fact, the chase might have been over right there, but the bear killed again, giving the hunter a new starting point. The spoor led up into huge wooded canyons and across many mountain streams 9,000 feet above sea level and higher.

Another overnighter was inevitable as the bear continued to wind up into the mountains. With a tarp to keep Kane and his gear comparatively dry, the pursuit continued. Food ran out, but leaving the trail then would have given the bear a chance to lose himself in the wilderness area. At last the reward came in the form of a throaty howl from a lead dog and a fast-paced gallop through a maze of obstacles.

The shooting in such a situation is anticlimactic, and few deny that. At the end of the line, the little carbine is slipped from the scabbard and a round is fed into the chamber. Then the hunter takes careful aim and drops the bear, usually with one shot. For pure memory-making material, the first phase of the chase is best, but this part is often business, the business of professional hunting.

So one means of hunting the black bear is with dogs, which usually translates as dogs and horses. I do not rank this method as my favorite, and though I have but a few black bears to my credit, I have hunted and seen quite a lot of black bears, passing up the bulk of them. I wanted a "trophy" and had no use for a smaller, or even an average, blackie. Having eaten a couple of bears, I've altered my opinion of hunting them for food. They are food. Their meat is excellent when handled and cooked properly.

Another means of harvesting the black bear is with a bait. This method is not legal in some areas. Is it sporting? I have

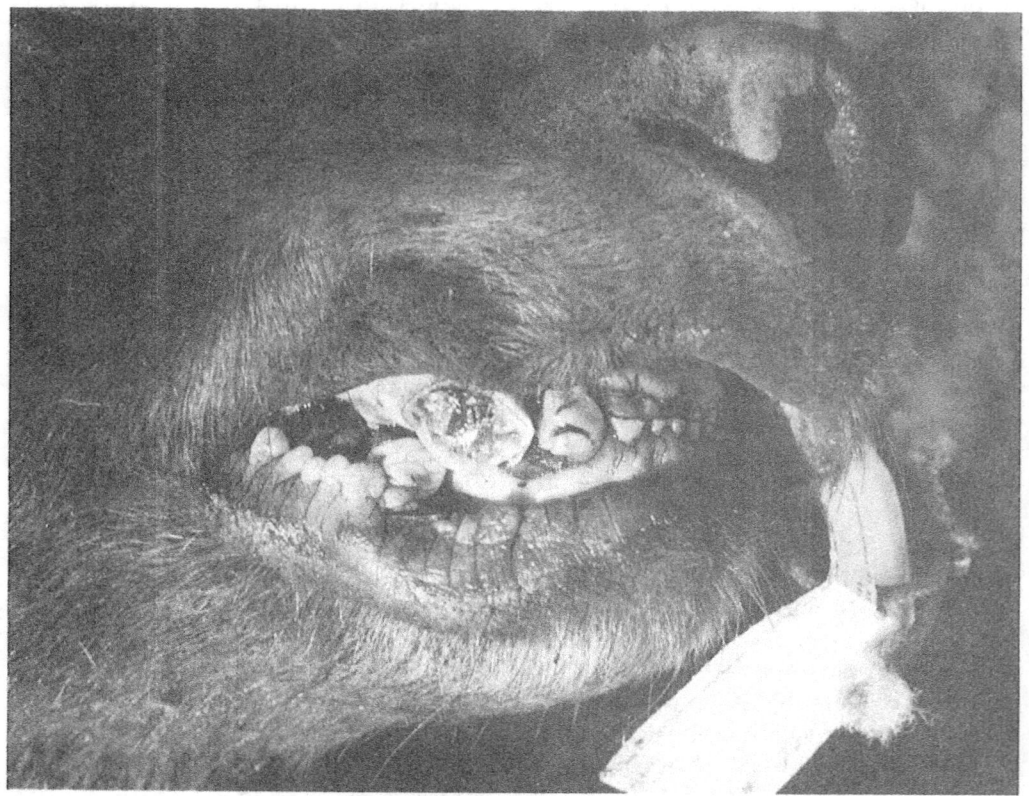

This bruin had a severe tooth problem, and its disposition was probably anything but mild. The bear was jumped off a deer carcass, and there was ample evidence to show that the bear itself killed the deer.

no solid opinion on the matter. I sat over a bait one time, and at dusk a big black form came in, picked up the odoriferous sheep carcass like a dog biscuit and carried it off. It was past good shooting light, so I could not fire. The hair on my neck raised up, and my spine did a tap-dance. Darkness closing in, a strong-smelling bait 20 yards away from me and a bear in the vicinity—it all added up to a pretty exciting moment.

Baits are generally set out in such a manner that the hunter has a pretty good chance of making an easy shot if a bear does come in. From that standpoint, the deck is stacked in favor of the outdoorsman. Is bear baiting different from duck hunting over decoys? The bait is a decoy very much as the little lure on the water is a decoy to ducks. It's all a matter of how you look at it, I guess.

Another way to get a bear is to go hunting for a deer or an elk. In fact, more bears are gotten in this manner than by hunting for bruins specifically. Usually, the hunter is working the deer or elk ranges when a bruin simply shows up. Where I live, the elk tag I buy comes with an attached bear tag. The reasoning is sensible. Bear harvest is very low, and having an "automatic" bear tag while hunting elk makes you a candidate for taking a legal bear.

Then there's the out and out bear hunt—the outdoorsman on foot or horse, trying to locate a bear as he would try to locate a deer. I have gotten bears in this fashion. One way is to hunt in the springtime, in areas which have plenty of good bear food, such as berry bushes, using your eyes to locate the bear as he feeds on springtime goodies. This is a rewarding way to hunt in terms of enjoyment and challenge, but in no way will it bring the results obtained through the use of a good pack of dogs.

Another way to find the black bear is to look for him in the fall of the year in much the same manner as in springtime hunting, except that bears will not generally be found on the more open hillsides at this time. I have hunted right after elk season, searching an area for bears that are feeding on elk offal, the gut piles from hunter kills. All in all, this is pretty tough hunting, and the odds are poor for the hunter, but the outing can be very rewarding.

As with hunts for other game animals, I enjoy backpacking for black bears. But honesty forces me to admit that though my bears have come by no-dog, no-bait methods, I have yet to harvest a bruin on a backpack hunt, though I have seen a couple of small ones during these treks.

He's a fine game animal, the black bear, and the 30-30 is one heck of a good caliber for hunting him in a close-range setting. From a horse, it's hard to beat the scabbard-ready Model 94 or similar flat-sided firearm. And as far as power goes, a good 30-30 load, preferably with the 170-grain bullet, is adequate for black bears. In fact, it can be just about right. Again,

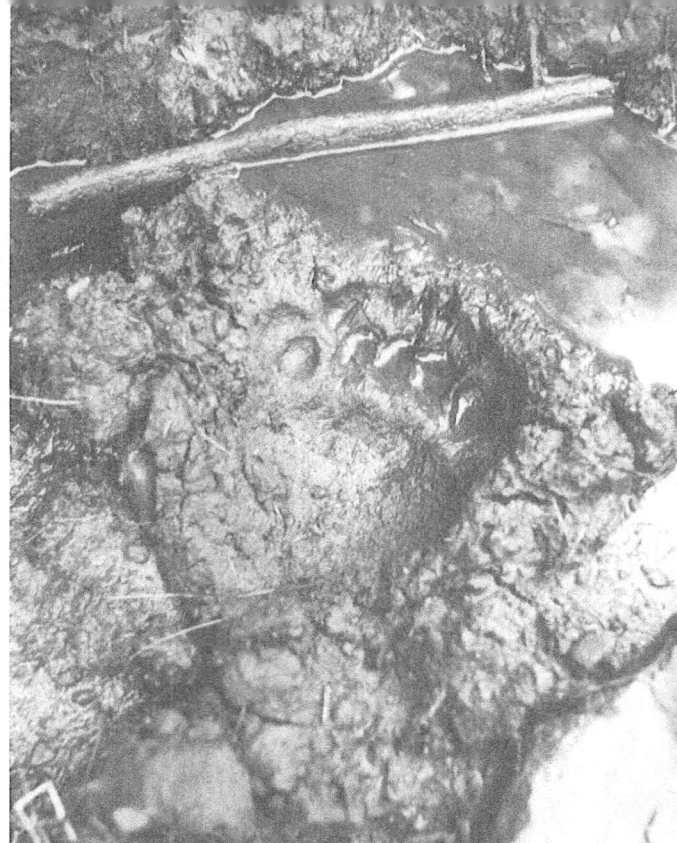

This large bear track was located along a stream at an altitude of about 10,000 feet.

I'd select a tough bullet. Federal's Premium brand, with 170-grain Nosler Partition bullet, would be excellent. So would those handloads often mentioned, the 180-grain and 190-grain bullets. Penetration is important here, just as it is for wild boar, another rugged customer with a hide that resembles a flak jacket.

I once had a chance to watch a treed bear. The bear decided it did not like its perch anymore, so down it started. We began to shout, and the big bruin seemed confused for a moment, and then seemed to get angry, for with one smashing blow of the forearm it cracked in two a live limb on a Ponderosa pine tree. I can't imagine how many pounds of force it takes to break a limb like that, but re-

The rugged little 30-30 has been a bear gun for many decades. Though the author does not consider the 30-30 a grizzly caliber, many of these bears have been taken with that round. A snowstorm does not hamper this 94's ability to shuck out the shells.

spect for this animal's power welled up in me.

Black bear hunting is a rewarding and very interesting sport. Hunter success rates are not high, but there is real thrill here, as well as challenge.

I believe that the purpose of hunting is to take a quarry, not to smell the roses — you can do that in your backyard. None- theless, you can have a wonderful hunt without bringing home any meat. I recall a superb bear hunt on which no bear was taken or even seen. It began with the sighting of a fresh, very large track in the mud in the bed of a glass-clear stream.

My partner and I struck out along that track and lost it quickly in the brush, but got lucky and cut it, or another big bear print, far up the mountain at over 9,000 feet above sea level in a forest of amazing beauty. We were able to stay with the track, thanks to the dampness of the earth at the time. But darkness set in. There was plenty of firewood, and we made dinner from a mountain grouse and a few foodstuffs from the pack.

The firelight played fingerlike over the stock of my favorite Model 94. Our lightweight tarp was extended between tree limps like a lean-to, and the heat of our small blaze banked off a wall of logs my partner had stacked up as a reflector. Here in the country of the evasive and powerful black bear, we spent the night and the next day, and took home with us a memory well worth carrying.

12

Tuning Your Model 94

Reliable as rain in Ketchikan, Alaska, that's the Model 94. In all of my years of shooting the 94, I have never had one jam, not once—not on the range, not in the field, not at all. You might think this fine record of service hinges on simplicity. After all, simple things work well, generally. But that's not the case here. The Model 94's lever-action design is not simple. The mechanical composition of the lever-action is, in fact, complicated for a firearm design. The Model 94 is a rather sophisticated structure, but one that *works*. It's practically infallible, given reasonable care.

As good as the 94 is, however, it can be improved upon in the accuracy department, and this improvement comes through tuning. The first step on this journey involves understanding the function of the Model 94, in rudimentary terms. After looking at how the 94 works, we can move on to actually tuning her up to give better grouping.

Many things happen when the shooter flicks the lever on the Model 94 Winchester. There is extraction of the spent cartridge case, with the ejector tossing that case out of the action. Meanwhile, the bolt has travelled rearward, cocking the hammer back so that the rifle is ready for the next shot. During the same interval, about as long as it takes a butterfly to flit its wing, the carrier has lifted upward, readying a fresh round for the chamber. The bolt is then slammed forward on the new round as the carrier drops back down to pick up the next cartridge coming along from the tubular magazine. The upward thrust of the lever has also moved the locking bolt into place, which locks up the action for the shot, and the

Tuning Your Model 94

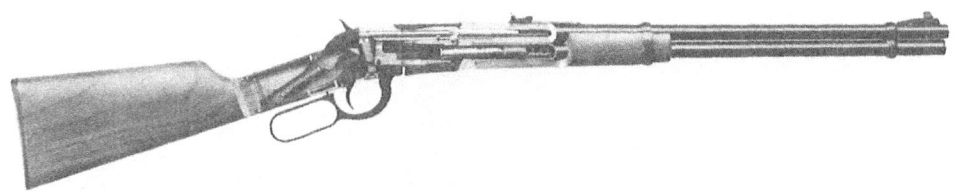

The Model 94 Winchester's lever-action design is foolproof, but it is not simple. This cutaway view shows the workings of the 94.

trigger stop is deactivated as the lever is fully pressed against the lower tang of the rifle.

That all this happens with a simple down-up motion on the finger lever is impressive enough, but that it happens with such uncanny reliability is amazing. The action was designed to handle blackpowder rounds to begin with, and though it is certainly adequate for the 30-30 and similar cartridges, the design had to be boosted in order for the 94 to handle the hotter numbers of the day, such as the 307 Winchester and 356 Winchester. So the "new" 94 is stronger than the old, which is just a side point that seemed appropriate to fit in here. Since there are about five million of the "old" design 94s around, this tuning session has widespread implications. My remarks are geared to the old 94, but they also apply to the new Angle-Eject and Big Bore 94s as well.

The Trigger

Before any good shooting can be done to improve accuracy on the 94, the trigger has to be refined. I do not do my own triggers, and I don't recommend that anyone else, other than a qualified gunsmith, hone his own trigger down to refine it. The best plan is to take the old 94 to a real "gun doctor" and have him do the trigger job. A professional gunsmith put my own 94 triggers in fine order. There is one big point the shooter must impress upon the gunsmith—lightness of trigger pull is secondary to crispness of trigger pull. In other words, it is possible to have a three-pound letoff from a trigger which has creep and backlash.

Tell your gunsmith that you want as *crisp* a trigger pull as possible. An old cliché says that when a crisp trigger is pulled, it feels like a tiny glass rod breaking. I think this is a good description—that is exactly what the trigger pull feels like on my own Model 94 30-30 favorite. A friend has a 94 which has a three-pound pull, meaning it takes three pounds of pressure before the trigger "breaks." But my own Model 94 trigger lets off at 5.25 pounds, which is a lot, but is a pull that can be lived with if the trigger is crisp.

I love light, *safe* triggers. My favorite trigger system is the multiple-lever design found often on muzzleloaders. There are two triggers, a set trigger and a hair trigger. I say this because I want to establish the fact that many of my better black-

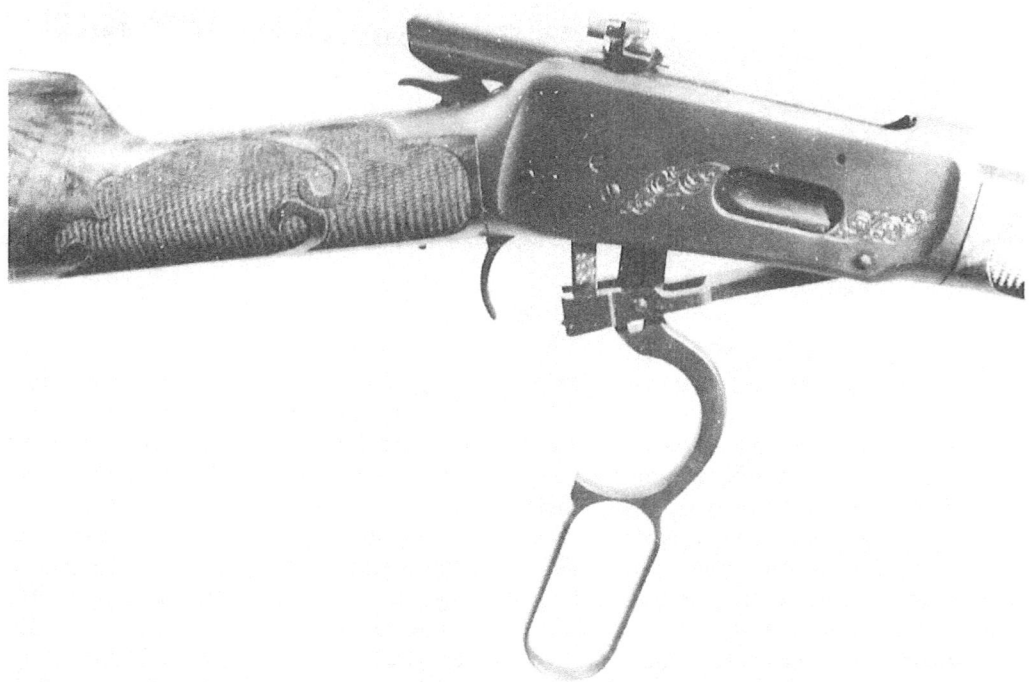

The finger lever on the 94 provides the shooter's entire involvement with the action. The simple down-up movement performs several important functions, as described in the text.

powder rifles have had trigger pulls measured in *ounces*, not pounds. And yet I can live with the 94's 5.25-pound pull because it is crisp. Again, insist that your gunsmith try for crispness first, with light letoff a secondary consideration.

Sights

Sights are a part of tuning. Want the best possible group? Then go with a scope. But it's not that simple for those of us who love the old 94 and its wonderful carrying facility. We like that slim receiver. And though I am a big fan of the scope sight on many rifles, I personally use the Model 94 30-30 as my "middle-of-the-road" round, between my muzzleloaders and my hot, flat-shooting, modern rifles. So I want the challenge of open or peep sights on that 94.

On my original 1894 rifle, the factory sights are intact. I don't want to tamper with the historical correctness of that rifle. But my custom 30-30 wears a micrometer receiver sight — a "peep sight" in other words. It has made a tremendous difference in my shooting. On one recent trip I hunted the wonderful Abert squirrel in Arizona. These squirrels dash up into the tops of the big Ponderosa pine trees which abound in their homeland.

Tuning Your Model 94

They are so hard to see up there that I got all of my squirrels by finding them with binoculars first.

It seems almost funny standing at the base of one of those big trees looking up with binoculars in a search for a squirrel which is usually plastered flat against a limb or against the trunk, only a blob of darkness as seen with the naked eye. So I located each squirrel with binoculars, but what about making the shot without a scope? Using my underloads, as mentioned previously, and with the aperture sight, I managed to make a hit on every shot I tried on those targets in the branches. I think this little story speaks well for the peep sight, and I contend that the serious 94 fan should consider a peep as part of the tuning process.

Handloads

The handload is another incidental part of the tuning process. I find factory ammo totally reliable and very accurate in 30-30 caliber. However, the beauty of the handload is that the components can be juggled until that combination which best suits your Model 94 turns up. There is usually a combination of bullet, powder type and powder weight which creates the best accuracy in a given individual 94. Handloads let you find that combo.

Magazine Plug Screw

On the carbine, you will find a small screw which fits through the end of the magazine plug and up into a tapped hole

The trigger on the new Model 94 Angle-Eject is somewhat crisper than that of the older 94. The shooter interested in tuning his Model 94 should have a gunsmith do the trigger work.

in the end of the barrel. This little screw is often pulled down tightly, and it can cause the shot group to walk vertically. That is, the rounds will tend to string up and down the paper instead of clustering. The way to correct a too-tight magazine plug screw is to loosen it — a brilliant deduction, eh Watson? But this means that the screw may drop away and be lost. So once it's loosened, apply a dab of Loctite or nail polish to the threads of the screw and insert it just enough to help hold the magazine plug in place and no more. A little risk of loss may remain, but not much. The end result is often a modest improvement in accuracy.

Other, similar tuning measures will be discussed here, and though none is a cure-all in itself, together they improve accuracy — except in a particular hard-to-live-with individual 94 that does not respond. But I have seen this one little measure, loosening of the magazine plug screw, help accuracy a lot. As the barrel heats up, the relationship between the muzzle and the magazine tube is altered when the screw is too tight.

Magazine Band (Front Band)

The whole idea of our tuneup is to remove pressures in various locations on the Model 94 Winchester. The first relief mentioned was the magazine plug screw, and here is a second, the magazine band. This band is the smaller one which connects barrel and magazine tube. I wrap emery cloth around a wooden dowel and work the *inside* of the band — only the upper portion which goes around the barrel — until it is relieved. This does not mean a sloppy fit, necessarily, but rather simple relief of tension. When the barrel heats up, the metal band receives more pressure at the point where it touches that heated barrel, and this probably changes the manner in which the barrel is allowed to vibrate.

It's possible to use a fine round file for this job. But any haste will probably produce a bad cut, a sloppy fit and an unhappy Model 94 owner. The goal here is removing a little bit of metal so that the barrel is no longer bound up by the magazine band. By the way, if the shooter has any problem in disassembly of his 94, he should seek help, since these steps do demand that the 94 be taken down before the work can commence.

The magazine band has a screw running through it at that point between the barrel and the magazine tube. This screw fits into a small slot in the barrel (on my 1955 Model 94). Therefore, slight metal removal from this band, only on that inner portion through which the barrel fits, is not a difficult task. Even though tension is relieved at this point, the band will still line up properly. As with the loosening of the magazine plug screw, sensible, slow work is required. Don't ream out the band until you can stick a dime through the opening.

The Fore-End Band

In some instances, the work described above will improve accuracy enough so that the fore-end band can be left alone. However, a shooter may want to remove just a little bit of metal around that portion of the fore-end band through which the barrel fits. It is another point which can restrain the expansion of the barrel as it heats up, causing a change in how that barrel responds to subsequent shots. Take care! Remove only a trace of metal. Polish more than file.

Tuning Your Model 94

The barrel bands on the 94 often need to be relieved, as related in the text. Tight barrel bands may cause shots to "walk" on the paper.

The aim in all of this, actually, is to free-float the magazine tube and minimize tension between that tube and the barrel. Imagine that you are seeking a free-floated barrel. Remember that a bolt-action rifle has a one-piece stock, while the 94 has a two-piece stock, making a big difference in barrel support. The one-piece stock is best in terms of accuracy, generally speaking, but the 94, when tuned, comes quite close to the bolt-action when it comes to clustering the rounds in a group.

Ultimate Accuracy

When Dale Storey and I were working together on the design of the Storey Conversion, a Model 94 Winchester deluxe custom rifle, Dale came up with several ideas on accuracy potential of the would-be rifle. His ideas were well-founded, and the finished product has created many one-inch center-to-center groups at 100 yards from the benchrest with handloads. This was done with the Lyman receiver sight in place, not a scope, but I do feel we are shooting well with the rifle (we wait for windless days and shoot at well-lighted targets).

How does this special 94 gain its accuracy? I think the 94 enthusiast should know because he might want to turn his own 94 into a special personal rifle, too. If you do, here are some points which Dale feels should be observed. First, he made sure that the creep in the trigger was eliminated right away. No creep. While the trigger is on the heavy side, 5.25-pound pull, it is quite crisp and safe.

Part of the workings of the Model 94, in both old and new styles, is the trigger stop, the small protrusion in the lower tang. The finger lever must be fully closed before the trigger stop will disengage and allow the trigger to be pulled.

Remember, there will be some wear, and the 94 trigger is much more basic in design than, for example, a Model 700 Remington trigger. In order to allow for wear, Dale kept his mating surfaces flush and sufficient.

A peep sight was installed as another means of gaining the most from the Model 94. And all those barrel-band problems were whipped by simply eliminating the band altogether. Dale did this by going with the button magazine, a design found on certain older Model 94 rifles. The button magazine meant that the tube was short and fully within the fore-end of the rifle, not protruding. That design cut the number of shots in the magazine in half. It used to hold six rounds, but after customizing, it holds only three. With one in the chamber, this makes my Storey Conversion a four-shot rifle. That is good enough for hunting big game, I feel, and I've always had enough ammo for any task.

Dale next wanted a stiffer barrel, so he went to the octagon design, the barrel being made by the Bauska Rifle Barrel Company of Kalispell, Montana. The octagon is a rigid design, and Dale did not go totally for barrel lightness. We wanted steadiness more than featherweight properties in the custom 30-30. The barrel, 24 inches in length, is modest in weight, but not whippy, not all that light.

When Dale did the rebarrel job, he ensured that the new barrel was fitted with minimum tolerances. His specs were observed to the letter, and his headspacing was minimum. All specs, in fact, were kept within the closest possible tolerances. The thread extension was fitted as tightly as possible. "What I'd really like," Dale said, "is to have the barrel and receiver milled out as one piece, but since that's not possible, the next best thing is as tight and perfect a fit in the thread extension as we can get." And he got it.

The extra accuracy potential of the tuned 94, or the custom 94 built with improved accuracy in mind, can come in handy. Previously, I mentioned having to nip squirrels out of the high branches of pine trees with squib loads out of a 94, and the fine accuracy and sights of my Conversion model helped in that chore. Also, I have enjoyed the extra confidence which better-than-average accuracy brings. I know that my handloads are plenty strong enough for deer at 200-plus yards and antelope out as far as 250 yards, and my own record of clean harvests on such game at such distances is a good one. Get as close as possible, of course—that is the 30-30 challenge. But when a little bit longer shot is desired, it's nice to have both the power and accuracy to get the job done.

What do I mean when I say that accuracy is improved through tuning? Al Miller, now assistant editor of the fine *Rifle/Handloader* magazines, has owned five 94s. He says that his worst groups measured three inches at 100 yards, and they were from a take-down model from the old days. My own take-down 94 rifle groups into two inches at 100 yards, which shows how rifles vary. But Al's rifles, when tuned up, produce two-inch groups as a rule. That's an improvement worth looking for. It means an increase in accuracy of 33 percent at 100 yards. And some fine-tuned 94 rifles have done better than two inches center to center for three- to five-shot clusters.

I had one 94 which started out very unimpressively from the bench. Good ammo produced four-inch 100-yard groups. After tuning it, I could count on a two-inch group any day that the sun shone and the wind did not blow. That is a very significant upgrading in the accuracy of any rifle. By the way, a two-inch group will suffice for big-game hunting, even when you insist that bullet placement be very precise. From the standing position, putting five shots into a six-inch circle at 100 yards is darned good shooting, and my 94s will do it when they group two inches from the bench.

On page 198 of the 1965 *Gun Digest*, edited by John T. Amber, a compilation of data shows the accuracy improvement of the Model 94 Winchester. Based on the work of C.H. Helbig and P.B. Cain, the article is entitled "Lever Action Rifles." Here are their findings:

You can enhance the Model 94's accuracy with an overall tune-up, from trigger work to relief of barrel bands to slicking up the action by polishing.

A. *Unworked Rifle*
Factory ammunition = 3.35-inch groups (100 yards)
Handloads = 3.10-inch groups (100 yards)

B. *Reworked Rifle*
Factory ammunition = not tested
Handloads = 2.21-inch groups (100 yards)
Best Group = 1.55-inch groups (100 yards

I am hardly the only person to make 94s shoot a lot better, as evidenced by the data above. If a hunter uses his 94 in tight spots only—say, boar hunting in thick places where a 30-yard shot is a long one, or whitetail hunting along riverbottoms where bucks jump up right under your nose—then accurizing the Model 94 is probably not necessary at all. But if you want to employ your 94 in an all-around manner, taking a little time to make it shoot straighter is worth it.

It was worth it for me one mule deer season. My heart was set on a range of hills nestled back in a big, rugged valley. This was one of my "quiet" trips, the kind of outdoor adventure meant for relaxing, heading into out-of-the-way places. I had rarely been near the place, and had never made it back into the valley, which for me was only a set of topographic lines on a map.

I set up a base camp which had everything but the kitchen sink, and I almost took one of those along. For shelter, there was a five-pound mountain tent and a light but warm sleeping bag. Light was provided by a backpack lantern. Though I had to pack my supplies and gear in, the distance was not great, for the valley was secluded only because of a mean little mountain-like hill that had to be crossed to reach it. Actually, the road was probably a couple miles away from the beginning of my valley.

A little carbine 94 30-30 was my sidekick on the trip. I had some squib loads as well as my deer-hunting handloads along. Everything was smooth as a greased ball bearing, except one thing.

The map gave an impression of tight terrain, and the rugged hill leading into the valley appeared to be thick, so I assumed close shooting would be the rule.

The valley turned out to be much more open than I had figured, and the shooting was going to be at longer range. The deer seemed to be posted on high points, using their eyes more than their noses to detect the presence of guys like me. My binoculars saved me, helping me locate a couple of bedded bucks, and I did get what for that region was a close shot. But there was a hitch.

The shot I ended up taking was at about 150 yards. However, the bedded buck was mostly hidden by foliage. With my binoculars, I detected an open spot through which a bullet would find a chest strike for a clean harvest of the buck. I had a fine shooting position, prone on a soft bench slightly above the bedded buck. But I would have to drive a bullet through a hole that seemed no larger than a pie plate.

Whack! The little carbine barked out, and its echo seemed to last for a very long time. The buck never even got up. He was instantly mine, at least partly because of the added accuracy gained from the 30's tuneup. I wondered whether the bullet would have found the mark before the tuneup, when the rifle was grouping over 3.5 inches at 100 yards instead of two inches.

Tune her up if you think you need the extra accuracy, or if you simply want your own 30-30 Model 94 to do its best in grouping bullets. Don't mess with the trigger if you are not a trained gunsmith. But try the tuning touches I've outlined. Do them carefully, slowly and patiently. You will thereby relieve the tension on that barrel and allow it the freedom of movement to heat and cool properly.

13

Mastering the 94

The Winchester 94 is an expert's firearm. Though it may be true that hundreds of thousands of shooters have begun their big-game rifle careers with the 94, the fact remains that, especially with the shorter carbine, it takes know-how to truly master the 94. Many times, I've reached back in memory to those days when I wandered over the mountains and flatlands of Arizona toting a 30-30 with me. I was a young fellow with a lot of desire and enthusiasm, and was willing to work very hard for my game, but I never compiled a good record with the 94 in those days.

I had not mastered the 94. And it took me a long time to realize that the only reason my game record was poor with the carbine was my own lack of ability in handling the piece. As the years rolled by, I bumped into several shooters who could handle the little jewel, and fortunately the haze evaporated and the picture cleared. I could see what had been wrong with my 30-30 technique.

The 94 is a personal, handmate rifle. It's a rifle shooters pick up when they mean business. There are no frills. The 94 does not work by itself — you have to make it work for you.

First, the 94 is light in weight. That is very good. It means easy carrying, and you carry a firearm a lot more than you shoot it. But a light firearm must be very carefully managed. If you hold onto it too tightly, especially on the fore-end, the shot is not likely to be well directed. You cannot strangle the fore-end and expect excellent control.

In an old movie, a master swordsman compared handling a sword to holding a bird in the hand. If you don't hold tightly

It pays to attain the most solid stance possible. Too many shooters try to treat the 94 like a shotgun, pointing instead of aiming the piece.

enough, the bird will fly away. But if you hold too tightly, the bird will be killed. With the rifle, the idea is to control it with the butt up snug into the shoulder, but the hand on the fore-end caresses the wood—it does not strangle it.

Second, the 94 carbine is short. There is little barrel weight to steady the piece. The master shooter knows this and is especially careful to get those sights aligned and to keep them on target as the trigger is squeezed. It is very easy to *cant* the rifle—that is, twist it right or left—which can throw the sight picture off badly and cause a miss. Since the 94 is short, it takes extra care to keep it aligned.

Third, because the 94 is flat-sided and neat to pack, and because it is so fast in the hand, the tendency for many shooters is to snapshoot with it. There is nothing wrong with snapshooting if by that term you mean "fast aim," but there is plenty wrong with snapshooting if you mean "pointing the rifle." I used to snapshoot my 94 all the time, and seldom did I hit a thing. Snapshooting is for shotguns, and even then you must carefully align and control the gun. Snapshooting is not for rifles. Aiming is. You aim the 94. You do not snapshoot it.

Fourth, the 94 is still used most often without a scope sight. Many shooters have all but forgotten how to master the open sight. They have grown so used to the superb scope sight that they have for-

The 94 is so fast-handling and easy to pack, as shown here by Dale Storey, that some hunters forget it is a rifle. But it does have sights, and it has to be carefully aimed for good results.

gotten how to use iron sights. Mainly, I think, they fail to gain a truly good sight picture. This entails carefully aligning the sights, as stated in the chapter on sighting. Instead, they pick up a picture of the bead in the notch somewhere and let fly. That is speculation on my part. I can't prove it. But I've seen the targets and watched the bullets miss the tin cans. Furthermore, once a sight picture is attained, it has to be *held* until the gun goes off. Mastering the iron sight, then, is vital to mastering the 94.

A fifth factor is gun fit. A 94 does not fit the shooter the same as a bolt-action rifle does. In the first place, the length of pull is generally shorter than that found on many bolt-action rifles. I love it. It took me a long time to realize that although I can handle a long length of pull—14 to 14.5 inches from the buttplate to the trigger—a shorter length of pull would be faster to handle. So the shooter of the 94 should recognize that he may have to mount, hold and fire that little gun in a different manner, with a slightly different stance.

I like about a 45° angle when firing offhand with a rifle. That is, my feet point out to the right of my target by roughly 45°. I don't change this angle much when firing the 94, but I think I lessen it just a bit. Shooters might try the same when offhand-shooting the 94. Also, a shooter may find that he cannot get used to the shorter length of pull on his 94. Though a recoil pad does nothing for the graceful lines of a rifle, it can be used to extend the length of pull. Some shooters may need this. I thought I did, but practice with the shorter length of pull solved my handling problems.

Here is how I think the 94 should be handled:

1. Hold the buttplate tightly into the shoulder, but do so by pulling in with the right hand. And by "tightly" I don't mean a deathgrip. Maybe "snugly" would be better. The left hand, for a right-handed shooter, does *not* force the rifle back into the shoulder. That hand controls only the fore-end of the rifle. And it does so with gentle pressure.

2. Align the sights with extra care. Make certain that the open sight picture is clear, with equal light showing on both sides of the bead

3. The trigger finger is almost independent of the hand. You "sneak" it into the trigger guard and squeeze that trigger, while steadily maintaining the sight picture. The whole hand does not grip down in order for the trigger to be pulled.

4. Depending upon the individual shooter, the thumb of the right hand either is wrapped around the wrist of the rifle or lies along the wrist, pointing toward the muzzle. In my own 94 shooting, I do better by allowing my right thumb to lie along the wrist rather than wrapping it around the wrist of the gun. My little finger is at the back of the finger lever, and it pulls back enough to help maintain the buttplate into the shoulder.

5. With a shotgun-style 94 (flat buttplate), use the "pad" of the shoulder for the buttplate. But with a rifle-style, curved buttplate, the shooter may have to insert the rifle more into the arm area than the shoulder. Try both stances to see which is best for you.

6. Hold that aim. Instead of thinking about that fast second shot, hold the sight

The lines of the Model 94 are smooth, and there is just enough drop at comb to allow for a good offhand hold. Master the 94 through practice, including dry-firing with snap-caps.

picture and squeeze the trigger. Make that first shot count. Sure, it's great to have a fast follow-up shot, but always make that first shot well-aimed.

7. Left-handed shooters need to reverse the procedures a little bit here, of course, but all in all, the 94 suits the left-handed shooter just fine. Top ejection does not favor the right or left stance, and the new Angle-Eject type tosses its empty cases fairly straight out from the receiver, so there is no problem for the southpaw.

8. In working the lever, do not remove the rifle from the shoulder unless that is the more comfortable way for you, personally, to shoot. One old-time hunter disagreed with this advice, and it is only fair to present his side. This man did drop the rifle from his shoulder in order to lever in another round. He contended that shooting the lever-action was a smooth act with several parts, and he preferred dropping the rifle after the shot, working the lever and then bringing the piece back up to his face for the next shot.

9. I like to leave my hand within the finger lever when firing, but some shooters use the finger lever as a pistol grip. This is a matter of choice, but I find that if I am going to leave my thumb wrapped around the wrist, I'm better off using the lever as a pistol grip. I prefer, however, to leave my thumb straight out along the wrist with my fingers in the lever the whole time.

I consider those nine steps useful in mastering the Model 94. But there's a lot more. One point to consider is that some shooters use the 30-30 as they would a

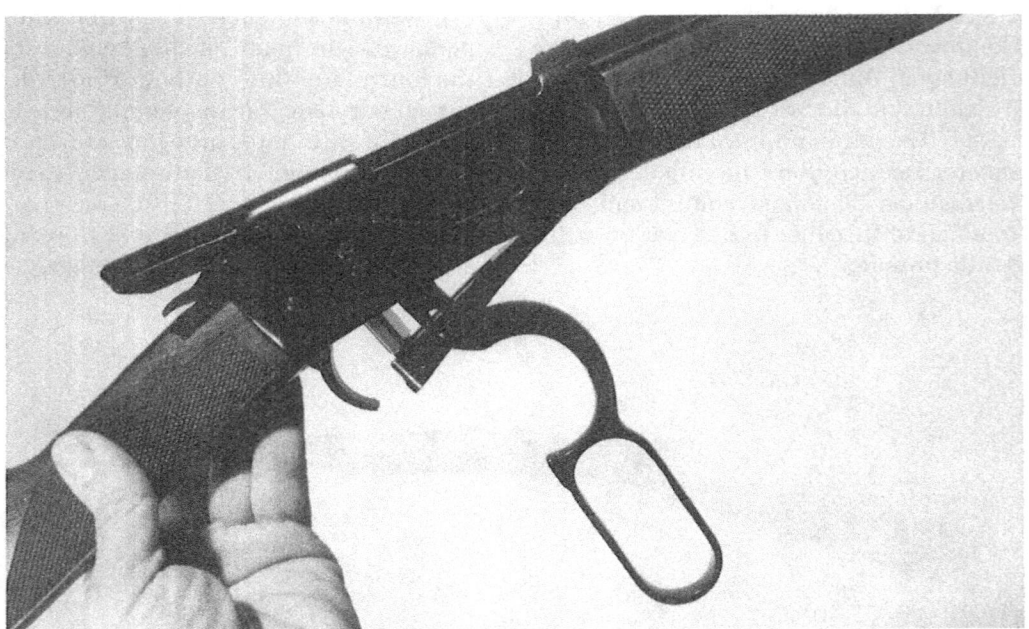

The slick lever-action design on the Model 94 sometimes encourages rapid fire. The Model 94 shooter must remember that *aim* is the goal.

modern long-range rifle. The 30-30, I repeat, is an expert's round, and the 94 is an expert's rifle. I don't mean that only professional hunters can use the 94 30-30. Not at all. I mean that any dedicated shooter can learn to master the 94, but he must treat the firearm in a certain way in order to coax the most from it.

The 30-30 is a round of modest power. Therefore, to use it properly, you have to hunt 30-30 style. Instead of hoping to fire from one hill a couple of hundred yards over to the next, you should attempt to improve your field position to get a closer shot. And you use binoculars where you can in order to locate game before the game locates you. Recently I got hold of a superior pair of binoculars, Bausch & Lomb 8 x 42s. There is no way for me to convey the feeling of being able to *discover* a bedded deer at several hundred yards with these glasses, thanks to their amazing definition — the ability they give the user to optically define the difference between a game animal and its surroundings.

Once that game is located, feeding or bedded, then a hunter can plan a stalk, and he can hunt 30-30 style if he is carrying that caliber. I urge the hunter to hunt 30-30 style because this is the successful way to go. After you have mastered the 30-30, or have upgraded the 94 into a fine custom rifle with high accuracy potential, longer shots are quite possible, especially with strong, safe handloads. But all in all, the joy of the little 94 is its handiness and ever-ready swiftness in use. Both the 94 and its round will do the job within their limits. Just don't stretch the limits.

Never use loads which are too hot for the 94 action. It may seem strange to say that here in a chapter devoted to mastering the 30-30, but it fits in because hot loads tend to slow up the action badly. The older 94 is a very good action, but it's not intended for high-pressure rounds. High-pressure rounds seem to offer too much bolt thrust. Though I went to the straighter-walled 30-30 Improved, which should improve case cling in the chamber, I still found that bolt thrust prevented my using heavy loads, even though the case showed no signs of too much pressure. For good extraction and ejection, stick with milder pressures. There is still plenty of ballistic force in those fine handloads which do not cause the action to bind up.

Safety

There are many handling procedures that can help the Model 94 user faithfully observe safety measures. First, of course, you load with the muzzle pointed in a safe direction. But I've seen some shooters put a round in the magazine through the loading gate, allowing the gate to slam shut each time. This is inconvenient. Instead, the round should be inserted up to the rim, and then the following round pushes the previous one home. Each round is left with the rim to hold the gate open until the last round is shoved home.

Also, though I have never had any problem with the half-cock safety on the older 94 (the new ones have a rebounding hammer and no half-cock), some gunsmiths believe that such a half-cock device is not a true safety. It does not contain any device which actually blocks the firing pin, or the trigger for that matter, although the trigger stop does this on the 94. So some shooters think that the 94 should be carried with an empty chamber. If this is done, I suggest that the hammer be in full-cock when the hunter is in a situation where a fast shot may present itself.

Remember, the chamber is totally empty here. There is no round in the chamber at all. With the hammer at full-cock and the chamber empty, it is easier to flick a new round up from the magazine because the bolt does not have to come back and force the hammer into full-cock position. This makes the levering a little smoother and faster. I work the lever as the rifle is on its way to my shoulder and find that an empty 94 is still a very fast shooter.

I know it must be boring to read by now, but when talking safety, it has to be said again — never use pointed bullets in the tubular magazine of the 94 Winchester or any other similar design, for fear that the pointed bullet may set off the primer of the round in front of it when the gun recoils. Also, never use a full metal jacket bullet in the tubular magazine, for the very same reason.

In unloading the 94, most of us simply flick the lever down and up several times, with the rounds flying out. This is fine, but since the 94 does not have a "hinged floorplate," as is found on some bolt-action rifles, the ammo must enter the chamber in order for it to be expelled, *usually*. The only things to remember here are to point that muzzle in a safe direction while working the rounds through the action, and to ensure that the cartridges fall in a soft place. There's no sense in denting them up. I can also unload a 94 by pushing the gate open, allowing the head of the round to protrude and continuing to work the rounds out back through the loading port, but this method can be slow.

Another safety aspect of handling the 30-30 is to remember that it is a big-game round. It does shoot far. A factory 30-30 bullet will go more than two miles if the muzzle is held at about a 45° angle. With a handload and some of the better-profile bullets, this range can extend as far as three miles and more. Be sure of a backstop. The 30-30 is no toy.

Practice

Mastering the Model 94 also means practice. I believe the major difference between shooting the 94 well and being a real pro with it is the practice aspect. However, I don't want to overstate the issue. I have known quite a number of shooters who did not practice much but who were crack shots with the 30-30. I can think of two right off the bat. Both were miners living near Patagonia, Arizona. I suspect that both ate venison steaks whenever they needed the meat, so they certainly shot at deer more often than sportsmen do.

One day I was near their camp and decided to drop in. The men had not yet hit the bonanza gold strike, but they were their usual jolly selves. In fact, I have often thought since that if they had found much gold, it probably would have ruined their happiness. Anyway, they had gotten some of the yellow stuff and had celebrated by putting in an extra supply of vittles and hardware. Part of the hardware was in the form of some extra 30-30 ammo, and the fellows agreed to show me some fancy shooting.

They were pretty darned good with their little carbines, both of them. A tomato can was in big trouble out to 100 yards. They made it "right hot" for a couple of soup cans at 50 yards, too, keeping the cans rolling at a steady clip

Loading the Model 94 through the port is best accomplished by inserting a round only part of the way into the magazine. The next round pushes the first one into the magazine and so forth.

with shots in rapid fire from the 94s. Those two gents had mastered the 94 and stayed in pretty good form without a lot of practice. But I still contend that most of us will get better and better, up to that point where our ultimate ability has been reached, through a lot of shooting.

The handloader can get in plenty of cheap 30-30 shooting, too, especially if he also makes his own bullets. He simply finds, trades for or buys at a good price all the lead he can afford. Then he makes up his alloy and casts a batch of bullets, and he has very reasonably priced projectiles. By using faster-burning powders, such as 4198 or the newer MR2460 or MP5744 numbers from Accurate Arms (now called Accurate Powders), a shooter can use small amounts; thereby a can of powder goes a very long way. For example, 20 grains of MR2460 with a 160-grain cast bullet produces about 1,600 fps MV, which is plenty for practice.

Practice should have a definite plan. I

am all in favor of common plinking, but even then I like to know my ranges and I like to select targets which give a challenge. Also, it's nice to practice in such a way that there is *transfer* from practice range to hunting field, for the Model 94 30-30 is certainly a hunting rifle. In other words, shooting at 20 yards all the time is not as good as shooting at 100 yards, since even in thick terrain a 100-yard shot on game is not unusual for the 30-30.

Also, it's wise to practice on some practical targets. I like to set up a simple cardboard cutout, a circle of one foot in diameter, prop it up at 100 yards with a safe backstop and shoot at it offhand. A deer's chest is about that size, and this form of practice gives me a practical indication of what I can do on a deer-sized target offhand.

Of course, many other targets are equally valuable. A bunch of tin cans can teach you plenty about mastering the 30-30. But shoot sometimes as if you were hunting. Carry the rifle with an empty chamber. Flick a round into the chamber and take a shot, just as if a deer had jumped up in front of you. But also take longer shots where you dope out the wind and consider drop. I think it all pays off.

Another excellent practice session can be conducted without any ammunition at all. This is dry-fire practice, and it is accomplished with an empty firearm. Dry fire works so well because at the very second the gun goes "click," you can tell if you were on target. That's the whole idea of dry-fire practice. You aim, hold steady and squeeze off your shot, and instantly you can tell if you "hit" or "missed." Calling the shot, that's the ticket. And there is no recoil to confuse you. You *know* how well you did because either your sights are on target when the gun's hammer drops or the sights are not on the target any longer, meaning you have pulled off the mark. Dry-fire practice is almost as valuable as the real thing because a shooter can learn so much about follow-through and trigger squeeze, whereas in actual firing some of this is lost in recoil.

What about the firing pin—won't dry firing damage it in the 94? In fact, it can. A good way to avoid this problem is to resize some cases, full-length, and then fill them with epoxy. Gunsmith Dale Storey uses a special epoxy for his "snap-caps," and they work just fine. This gives the firing pin something to land on, and prevents damage. You can use spent rounds, too, but the primer will eventually dent in so that the blow of the firing pin is not well retarded.

Another practice session can take place right in the hunting field, only this time the 30-30 goes forth as a small-game or varmint rifle. Since the book has chapters on both aspects of this Model 94 function, I won't go into more of the same here. Let it suffice to say that any hunter who can consistently bag a jackrabbit at 100 yards with his 94 is going to be big medicine on the big-game trail with that same rifle.

The Winchester Model 9422 is a counterpart to the big-game 94, but in 22 rimfire or 22 rimfire magnum caliber. Practice with the 9422 can certainly transfer over to the larger Model 94. Incidentally, the little Model 9422s I have shot seem to be very well made and quite reliable, so the Model 94 fan may wish to consider one as his 22 rimfire rifle.

I consider the Model 94 to be a firearm which needs to be mastered with even more care and involvement than a more modern firearm. For one thing, a bolt-action big-game rifle probably wears a scope sight. You don't align a scope—you

Plenty of good practice is possible with the Model 94's little brother, the Model 9422 in 22 rimfire.

just put the crosswires on the target and make sure they stay there. There are still plenty of ways to miss, of course, but the scope makes things a whole lot easier. Also, the good bolt-action rifle has, or can have, a very fine trigger pull — crisp, light and safe. The Model 94's trigger is capable of crispness, but generally speaking, a four- or five-pound pull is the rule.

I go along with the words of Teddy Roosevelt: "But the truth is that all good modern rifles are efficient . . . it is the man behind the gun that makes the difference." (From page 131 of *Ranch Life and the Hunting Trail*, The Century Company of New York, 1966 reprint.) A dedicated shooter can master the Model 94 Winchester. He begins by recognizing that the 94 is much more basic than most of the modern rifles, in sights and trigger at least, and he goes on from there, studying and practicing until the Model 94 is as familiar to him as his favorite quail covert.

14

Accoutrements for the Model 94

The True Model 94 enthusiast has to have a number of accoutrements for his 30-30. Oh, he can do without most of them, I suppose, but it's something like a lady buying a hat; she just has to have some shoes to go with it. Well, the 30-30 man simply has to have something in which to encase his favorite 94, as well as an ammo holder or two, and maybe he'll want to fit a sling to his rifle. If he's a horseman, or hunts on horseback from time to time, he might even need a scabbard.

Here are some ideas concerning accoutrements for the 94.

Slings

I don't believe that a sling adds much to the grace of most rifles, and the Model 94 is no exception. But the practicality of the sling is such that when I had my own special 94 custom made up, it carried with it an integral sling eye in the lower flat of the barrel. This little addition meant that I could mount the sling farther up-barrel so that when the rifle is slung, it hangs lower in terms of the height of the barrel's muzzle. The higher you mount the sling, the lower the barrel will rest in comparison with the hunter's own height.

The rear sling mount, on my rifle as well as most others, is the usual sling eye mounted into the belly of the stock's butt, somewhere near the toe of the stock—about 2.5 to 3.5 inches forward of the toe, for example. The sling swivel itself can be detachable or non-detachable. My sling swivels are the locking type from Michaels of Oregon (Uncle Mike's), and they are detachable. I like detachables on my own 30-30 for their versatility. I have

Accoutrements for the Model 94

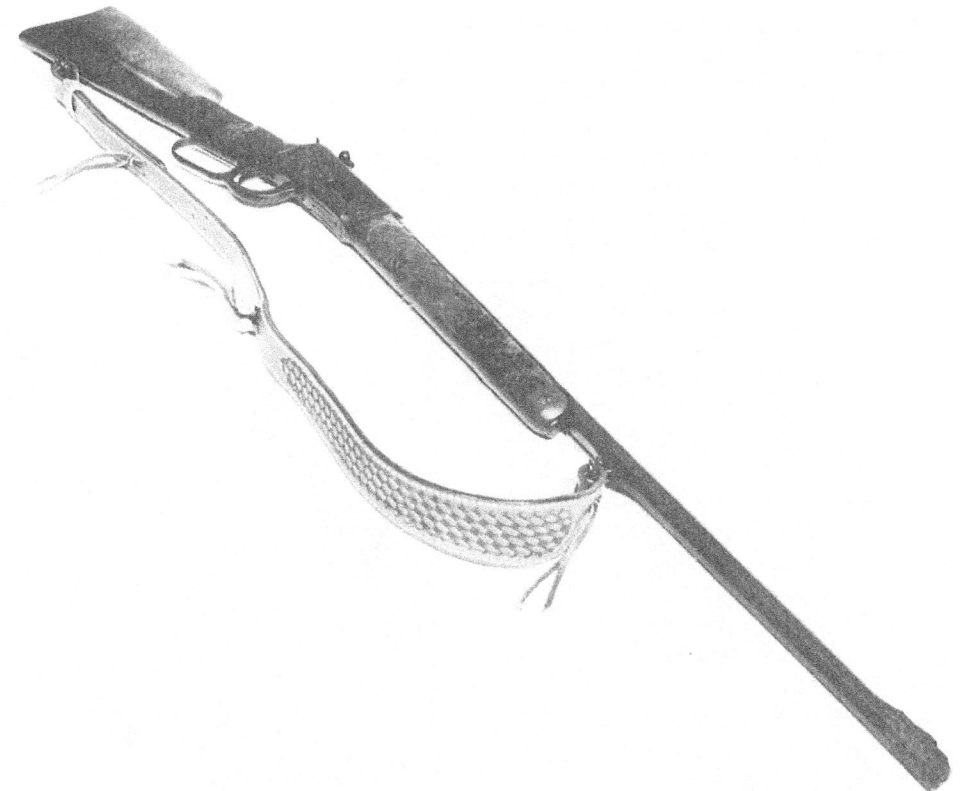

The sling is very much at home on the Storey Conversion because the rifle has an integral sling eye on the lower barrel flat. This is the Uncle Mike's Cobra model.

two slings which I use on the rifle. One is an Uncle Mike's cobra style, with the cartridge holder a part of the sling. It's a very handsome sling, and quite practical.

This cobra-type sling offers a wide area for contact of sling to shoulder, making carrying a bit nicer. But I think it was the extra cartridge holder which sold me on this sling. It's a strong pouch, and it contains two rounds. I'm particularly interested in having two strong handloads ready in the pouch so that I can *single-load* these into the chamber, not necessarily because I have shot up my ammo,

but because I may want to take a special shot on a big-game animal. I can slip the usual load out and slide the long-range load in. Since it will *never* go into the magazine, this round can carry a bullet of better ballistic properties.

My second sling is a simple carrying strap. Actually, the cobra-style Uncle Mike's sling is also a carrying strap, since it offers no loops through which to stick arms. But this other sling is a simple strap and no more—a thin, tanned length of very soft leather, an inch wide. Since it's also on a detachable Uncle Mike's locking swivel, I can exchange it with my cobra sling whenever I want to.

And I want to when I go backpack hunting. The simple sling fits better on the strut which I have provided for my packframe. This strut is merely a loop of metal on the upper part of the frame, but it's handy because the rifle sling goes through that metal strut and then I do not have to pack the firearm on my shoulder. The supple sling slips out just as easily so I can dismount the rifle for use.

I also shoot with the aid of my slings, every chance I get. By slipping an arm through the sling (the left arm for a right-handed shooter), tension is placed on the rifle and the rifle is held much steadier. Often I sit when I spot game, slipping into the sling immediately. Any shooter can head for the range and prove to himself that the use of a sling will benefit his grouping of bullets.

The standard Model 94 will not have a sling eye up front, though one can be mounted nicely in front of the toe of the buttstock. This problem has been neatly taken care of by several companies. The best method, I think, is to use a split-band swivel. This band is easily attached to the tubular magazine of the 94, and it's permanent. In mounting, a bit of Loctite on the threads of the bolt makes the fit more permanent. The split-band amounts to a sling eye, and a detachable swivel fits perfectly through this eye. It's a neat, cheap and strong way of adding a sling to the 94 Winchester rifle.

There is also the auxiliary sling, a unit which simply slips over the butt of the stock and the barrel for temporary carrying. However, it offers no shooting advantage. On a special Model 94, such as an original 1894 rifle, I would not mind this

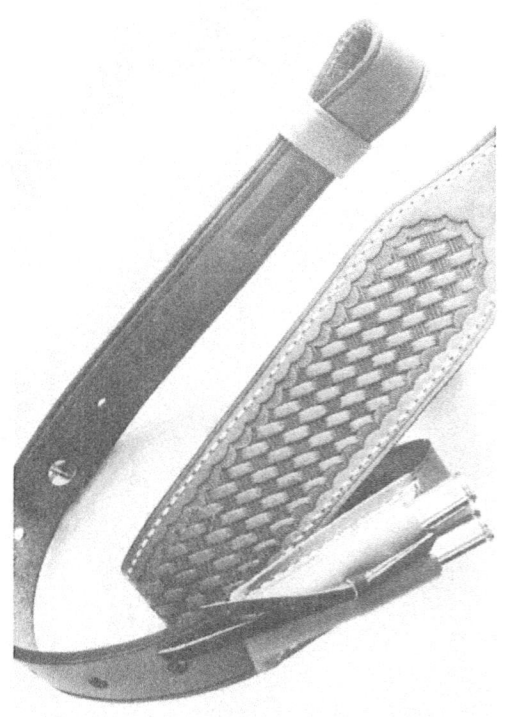

A close-up of the Uncle Mike's Deluxe Basket Weave Cobra sling shows the cartridge holder for two rounds. Author uses this type of sling on his custom 94 rifle.

type of sling, but most of the time, I think a more permanent strap is better.

Scabbards

The scabbard is simply a gun case that fits on a horse. Usually it's leather, but the Kolpin 007 case is made of super-tough plastic. It gives the rifle a lot more protection than the standard scabbard.

Accoutrements for the Model 94

Of course, if the shooter is looking for historical flavor, the old-time leather scabbard is the one to go with. I've seen this scabbard placed on the right-hand side of the horse with the butt of the stock aiming forward. It's not my place to say this is wrong, because some pretty good cowboys have used this method, but I don't care for it. The open end of the scabbard tends to pick up twigs and dirt more easily when it faces forward.

I like the scabbard under my left leg, facing forward with the muzzle downward and the buttstock pointing upward. Since a rider dismounts on the left side of a horse, a hunter hits the ground and slides the rifle free with his right hand grasping the buttstock until it can get hold of the wrist of the stock.

The scabbard should be of good, heavy leather for protection, and it should cover at least the action of the rifle plus the wrist of the stock. Of course, it's a trade-off: if the rifle fits too deeply into the scabbard, withdrawing it is difficult; if the rifle does not fit well into the scabbard, the stock will look like a hunk of old barn wall in no time. It will be scraped, gouged, clawed and chewed into a mass of unfinished wood in a couple of seasons, especially if the user does any bear or lion hunting.

Many people have asked about the old saddle ring found on many Model 94s of the past, and found again on the current Angle-Eject Model 94 Trapper model. In my opinion, the saddle ring was used to accept a piece of thong, and the thong

The Split-Band swivel eye is made for the Model 94 and similar firearms by Michaels of Oregon.

was used to secure the carbine on the saddle or to the saddle scabbard. This ring is so famous with Model 94 collectors that an abbreviation is used today, and you will find it in any listing of older Model 94 Winchesters. The abbreviation is SRC, standing for Saddle Ring Carbine. Those carbines wore the saddle ring on the left-hand side of the receiver. I believe the ring was used in conjunction with a saddle scabbard.

The carbine could be inserted upside down or right side up. I was hunting in Mexico one year, and the ranch foreman and I departed at first light, planning to be in nearby mountains for an all-day deer hunt. I noticed that his Model 94 — which he called his *treinta y treinta*, literally "30 and 30" — was carried upside down in the scabbard and under his left leg. He proved later in the day that he could whip that little 30 out of its boot faster than I could disengage my carcass from the saddle and drop to the earth. Of course, when your posterior feels like it's loaded with Novacaine, movement is retarded.

Gun Cases

Then comes the gun case. I'm sorry to report that too many of my acquaintances over the years have battered their 94s just because they knew the tough 94s could take it. The little carbines, even some of the finer old rifles, were slid into the corner of a closet to collect dust when not in use, and then flopped onto a car's floor or the bed of a pickup truck when transported into the field. I see no reason to abuse any firearm, even a rugged one, so my choice for the Model 94 is a good, strong gun case or a soft case which won't be tossed into the back of a truck.

The choice lies right there. If the 94 is going to be transported in a non-abusive way, then a soft gun case is just fine. Leather and vinyl, as well as other materials, make handsome gun cases, and there are several smaller cases into which a 94 will fit nicely. If the old 30-30 is going to be carried on the floorboards of the old hunting vehicle, go for the hard gun case. Good ones are from Treadlok, Outers and Kolpin, the latter offering that nice Gun Boot 007 mentioned earlier.

The Gun Rack

These days, especially "out West," rifles carried in a vehicle often rest in some kind of rack. The usual rack goes across the rear window of a pickup truck, and the rifle rests in it without bouncing out. Some wear is bound to occur here. A rifle riding and jumping within its gun rack will get marred up a bit.

My favorite gun rack for those hunting vehicles which have bucket seats is the San Antonio Jeep gun rack. This unit mounts on the floor between the two bucket seats and holds the buttstock firmly on the floor with the muzzle pointing up and back. I have hit bumps that would jar a man's false teeth loose, and yet the guns — the unit holds two rifles — did not budge an inch. One caution — the barrel will eventually lose its blue where it touches the upper part of this gun rack. I have wrapped sheepskin around the plastic-coated portion of the rack, and that helps prevent some of this bluing loss.

Ammo Holders

Thirty-thirty lovers are no different from the rest of the hunters in the field:

they have to carry some extra ammo, too. When I was a younger hunter, I prided myself deeply on the fact that I loaded my rifle, by golly, and headed out. Heck, I was a good shot. I did not need extra ammo jammed into my pockets like hard candies. Not me. I got by without it, but I certainly carry extra ammo today. It's no feather in a hunter's cap to head into the field short of ammo. You never know when you might need that extra fodder.

I needed some recently, and not because of bad shooting, either. I was hunting a remote part of central Arizona with a friend. We found an old road and decided to take it into the outback to seek our deer-hunting fortunes. When things looked right, we got out of the truck, and I took the right-hand ridge while my friend took the left one. This was steep, rugged terrain, by the way.

We were to meet back at the vehicle at dark, or within a half hour after the light left. All of the area was good hunting, we believed, so there was no need to come back very late. We felt it was advisable to hunt in a circle back to the vehicle. Besides, it was Thanksgiving Day and we had a turkey in the oven back at the trailer. I puffed my way down out of the rough country just 15 minutes past the arrival of full dark, expecting to find my friend waiting by the rig. He wasn't there. He wasn't there an hour later, either, or an hour and a half later.

Finally, I got worried, and to make a long story a short one, it was my signal shots and his return shots which got us back together. He had gone a little too far in his excitement to locate a deer, and had missed the road on his way back out of the mountains in the dark. He was in some pretty rocky landscape and could easily have broken a leg or twisted an ankle up there. Those extra rounds that we carried came in very handy. Never be ashamed to carry some extra ammo. The turkey back in the oven? My two sons were also on the trip; they got back to the trailer and saved our Thanksgiving bird.

Stuffing a bunch of rounds into a pocket is all right, I suppose, but it's better to use some sort of container for extra ammo. The first holder that comes to mind is the cartridge pouch. I have a couple of these, and they work out well. They slip on the belt, but I carry mine within my pack. My usual hunting outfit consists of the packframe with daypack looped over the upper struts, and my extra ammo is within that pack. My favorite 30-30 holds but three rounds in the magazine, so I do pack a couple of extras in a shirt pocket for fast retrieval, but my main supply of extra rounds is in the pack encased in an ammo pouch.

Federal ammunition comes with a built-in ammo carrier, by the way, a plastic container that fits on the belt quite well. I've used this method of carrying extra ammo, and it works fine. The only thing to watch for is that an ammo carrier located on the belt can press into your belly or side if not positioned correctly.

I like the cartridge pouch or ammo wallet better than a big belt loaded down with ammo. But to each his own. Those ammo belts remind me of the bandeleros worn by Pancho Villa's men in Mexico. I suppose they were fine for that application, but a simple pouch with perhaps 10 to 14 extra rounds seems better for our purposes today.

Hammer Extension

I mention this little item because some of the buyers of modern Angle-Eject 30-

Uncle Mike's hammer extension allows the hammer to be eared back easily when a scope is mounted on the Model 94.

30s will put scopes on those firearms. The hammer extension makes it easy to ear the hammer back when the scope is low-mounted on the rifle. It is merely a piece of metal that attaches to the hammer spur, but it's worth its weight in gold when a hunter wants to get off a shot and must cock the hammer back. This inexpensive item can make scope-sighted Model 94s a lot easier to use.

Stocks

I'll list these as accessories because they don't seem to fit well elsewhere. Many Model 94 lovers want to upgrade their favorite rifles without going full custom. One way to do this is with a new stock. Two-piece stocks are the only proper ones for remodeling the 94, and several different ones are available to the shooter. Bishop company offers such a stock, as does Reinhart Fajen.

There is one point concerning these stocks which cannot be said about the one-piece stocks found on modern bolt-action firearms. The latter require professional fitting—the action must be bedded with great care in order to prevent the stock from splitting later at the recoil lug or along the tang. Furthermore, the barrel channel must be cut just right. I'm

Accoutrements for the Model 94

not going to suggest that a Model 94 stock can be ill-fitted — it can't if the shooter expects good results. But I can fit a 94 stock myself if it is pre-inletted, and I won't try that with a Model 70, Model 700 or any other bolt-action rifle stock.

A careful 94 owner may well do a fine job of fitting a new stock to his 30-30. Mistakes can be made, of course, and sloppy work will not improve the 94. Better to leave the original stock in place if careful, patient work is not going to rule. But the 94 stock can be renewed by the shooter if he so desires.

Stock finishing is no problem, either. Good instructions come with most finishing kits, and they need only be followed. I like to sand the stock until the wood is truly smooth, using steel wool to create a sheen before any finish of any sort even touches the wood. When the wood is smooth, and filled if necessary (and it will probably be necessary), then the finish is applied. If a real oil is to be used, I begin with pure, boiled, inedible linseed oil first, applying it warm with the fingers. It penetrates well. After at least a full day of drying time, the stock is gently sanded. Some whiskers may rise up from the application of the linseed oil. Then more linseed oil is applied, with heavy handrubbing.

When I've applied five or six coats of linseed oil and handrubbed the wood as much as patience and time will allow, I set the stock aside for a month or so. Then comes the final finish. I may use a treated linseed oil here, such as Tru-Oil. Follow directions. The finish will look great. If it is too shiny, rub a little Rottenstone on it to cut the glare.

Never rush a stock job. Do this work when there is no need to hurry. In my neck of the woods, this means wintertime. Although I get out 12 months of the year, winter days do tend to invite a person to sit by the fire and finish a stock. Lots of sanding and preparation of the wood before any finish is applied makes the difference between a smooth surface and a bumpy one. If the wood is porous, wet it with a splash of hot water, which will raise the whiskers. Do this in between periods of sanding the raw wood. Let the wet stock dry, and then sand again. This will get much of the sapwood out of the grain.

The Moses Stick

This is an option I would never be without, but many hunters won't bother with it. It's called the Moses Stick because it reminds many users of the staffs mentioned in the Bible. I use the stalk of an *agave*, a cactus plant, to make my sticks. This stalk is terribly light in weight and amazingly strong. I insert a rubber crutch bumper on the bottom of the stick and wrap tanned deerskin or pigskin around the upper third of the staff. The crutch bumper makes the stick quiet for walking, and the leather makes a good handle. Atop the staff, under the tanned leather, I place a foam-rubber pad that serves as my binocular rest.

The staff is for walking, of course. It's a case of arm-power aiding leg-power, and it's especially great for backpacking because it helps the hiker maintain his balance. It's also a fantastic binocular rest. Shaky pictures don't show a hunter much. The hunter with a Moses Stick can stand up and rest his glasses atop the staff for a good, steady view.

The staff can be used for a rifle rest, too. I have made some good shots where I could not kneel, sit or achieve the prone

The top end of the Moses Stick is covered with soft, tanned hide. Here the author uses the stick to steady the little Model 94 Trapper 30-30.

position. I used the walking staff as a rifle rest and was able to put the bullets on target. I have used the staff to signal friends in the field—putting a hat on the staff and holding it high. The hat can be seen a very long distance away. At night, the staff can be used as a probe to reveal obstacles in the path.

I consider the Moses Stick a part of my hunting gear and an accessory to my special 30-30 outings where a steady shot can make a big difference in game-taking.

The Knife

Somehow it seems appropriate to match a nice basic hunting knife with the nice basic Model 94 30-30. There are many such knives, and I own more than one. One is a handmade knife which is very plain, simple and useful, and recently I have come upon another simple knife I like very much. The Mora model, made in Sweden, is small, yet not ridiculously so, and it is easily sharpened. I can

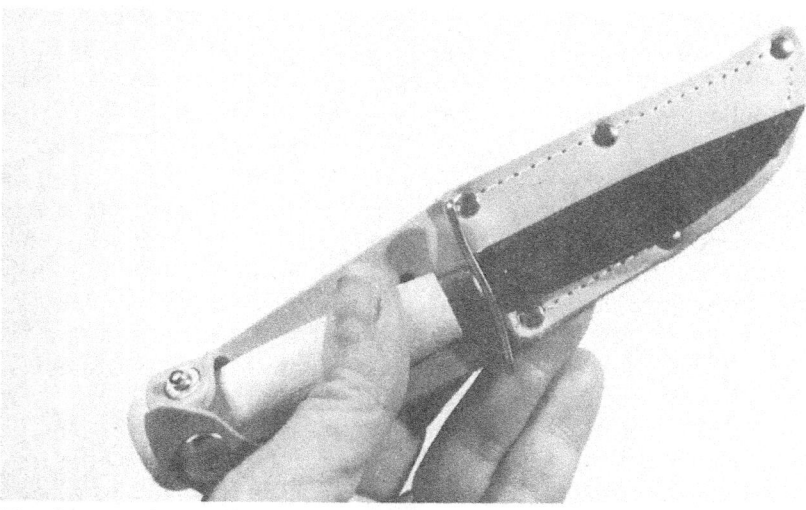

The plain, simple, yet effective Mora knife from the Gutmann Company is one of the author's choices as a companion blade for the Model 94 Winchester.

put a razor edge on the Mora in a few moments, and that edge will last through field-dressing a deer and longer. It also touches up nicely. In the field, a small, diamond-impregnated steel will put an edge on this knife with a few swipes. The knife is designed in a simple blade shape, with a straight line that allows me to dress a deer and later skin it out, all with a knife weighing but a few ounces. The Mora comes with a sheath and is available from the Gutmann Company.

Parts

Since there are so many Model 94s around, and since they have been around since 1895, it only stands to reason that owners need parts from time to time. Obsolete parts would create a problem, except for the fact that we have dealers who supply these little items for us. For example, Walter H. Lodewick, 2816 N.E. Halsey, Portland, OR 97232 is a supplier of obsolete Winchester parts, as is Tommy Munsch of Prior Lake, MN 55372. When

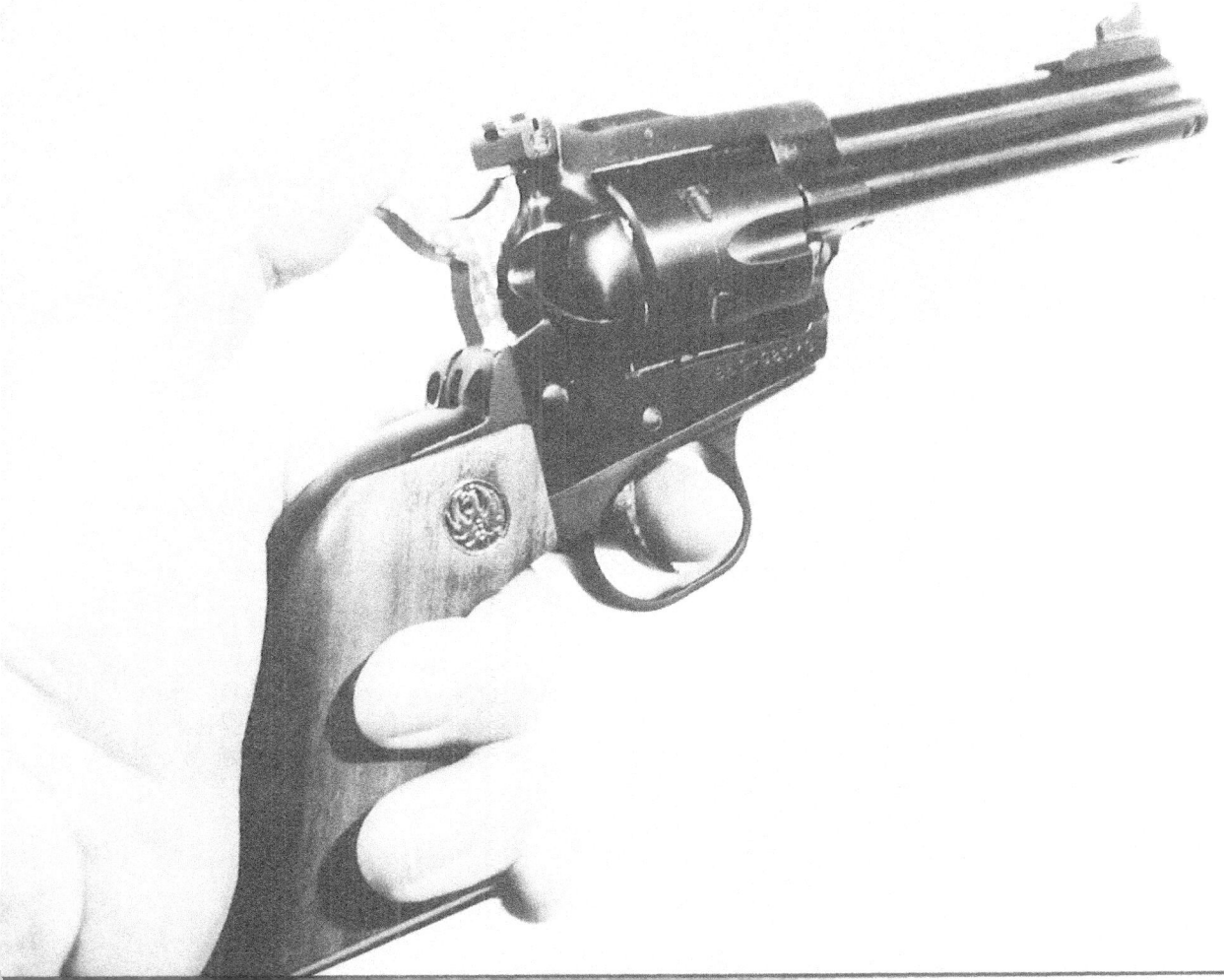

The author favors a Ruger sidearm as a companion piece for the Model 94 Winchester. The western single-action style revolver is of the same general time period as the Model 94 general style. One of the author's favored calibers is the 32 Magnum, useful for small game and modest-sized wild animals. It will fire the 32 S&W, 32 S&W Long and 32 Magnum round, the last having about the authority of the 38 Special.

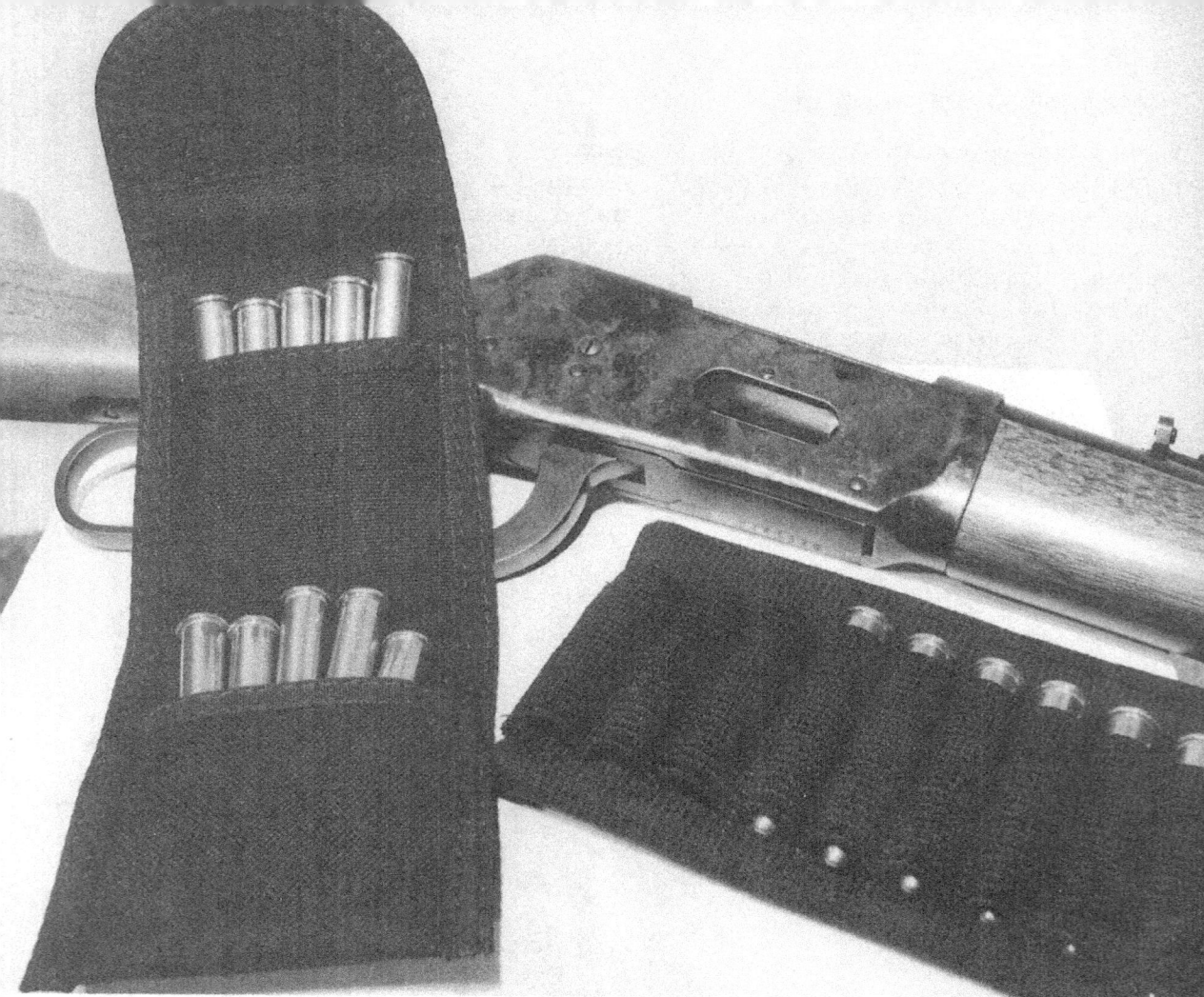

Ammo carriers are important to outdoorsmen who head into the primitive places. A good one is Uncle Mike's Sidekick Folding Rifle Cartridge Carrier, on the left. It holds 10 30-30 rounds and folds into a small belt-carry unit. It's made of quiet Cordura® nylon with a Velcro® closure.

my Storey Conversion custom was going together, I was happy to have such suppliers, especially for my button magazine and curved buttplate.

The Sidearm

A sidekick for the Model 94 should probably be a six-shooter. As it turns out, I have two handguns which mate up with the 30-30 when I go hunting; one is a sixgun, the other a pistol. The pistol first. It's a 22 semi-automatic, the Ruger Model Mark II Target with bull barrel. I carry an extra clip for it in the outback, where I use the gun for obtaining small edibles. It could also serve as a signal gun, I suppose, thus saving my 30-30 ammo for bigger things, but I have yet to use it in this capacity.

Accoutrements for the Model 94

What I really wanted in a sidearm to match my 30-30 was an original Colt Bisley sixgun in 32-20 caliber. In a way, I'm lucky I never located one, because what I ended up with is more practical. I acquired a Ruger Single-Six in 32 Magnum caliber. I chose the 4⅝-inch barrel on this light sixshooter. It's a really fine piece because it is accurate and wears sights which allow the shooter to take advantage of this accuracy.

The 32 Magnum round, at the moment, is loaded with a 95-grain bullet or a speedy 85-grain jacketed hollow-point bullet. What's more, I can also use 32 S&W ammo in my Ruger 32 Magnum, as well as 32 S&W Long ammo. This option is excellent. These loads are mild, and a hunter in the backcountry can carry the 32 Magnum with a lead bullet 32 S&W or 32 S&W Long as the first shot out, with a hotter 32 Magnum round as follow-up. Small game can be harvested with the light load, and the 32 Magnum can be used if heavier-duty work is necessary.

Federal offers an ammo holder right in the cartridge box. Also note the Winchester belt buckle from the Gutmann Company.

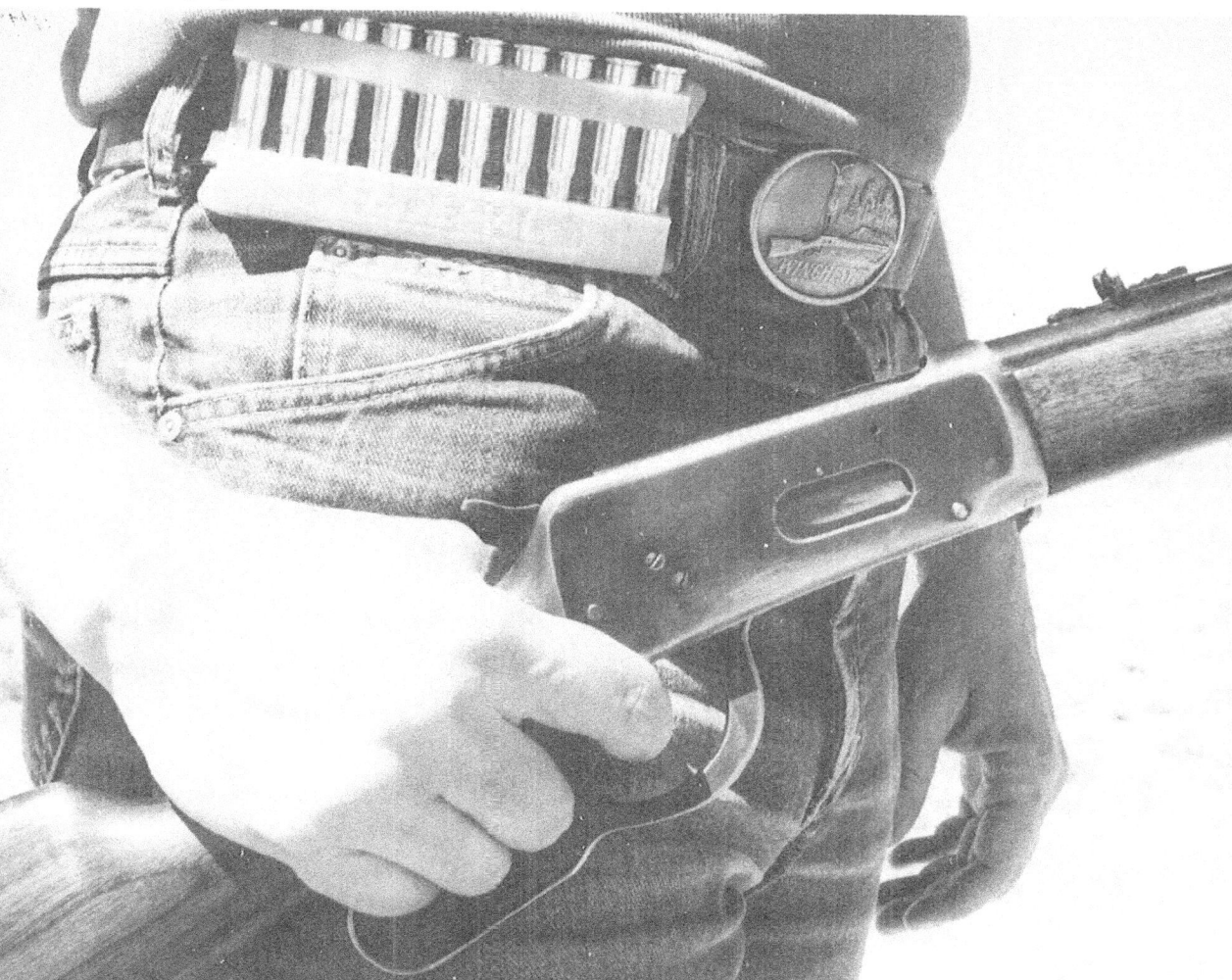

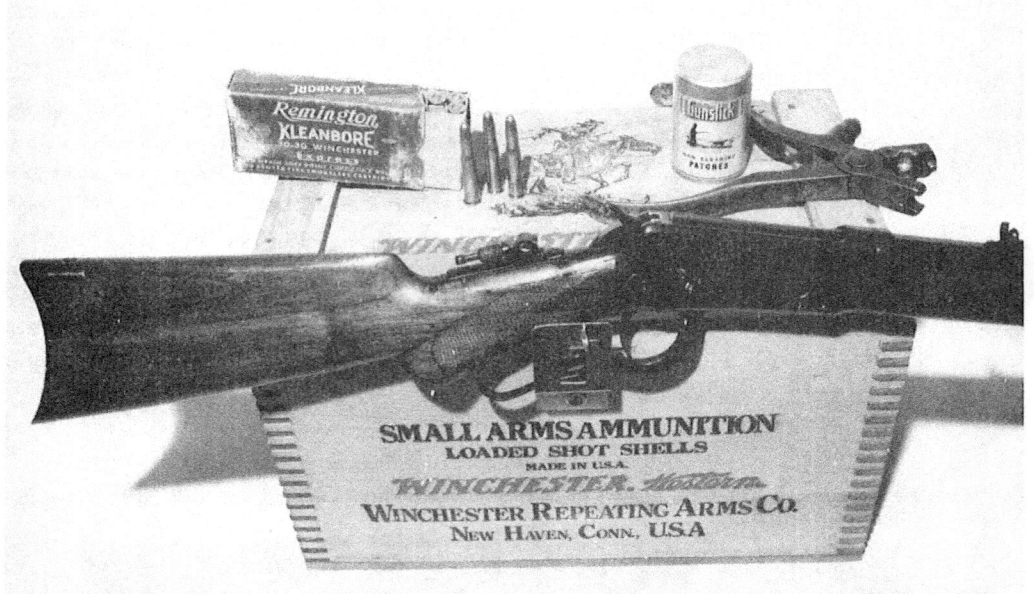

Many little items enhance the Model 94 rifle, such as this ammunition box from Winchester.

There are various kinds of Winchester belt buckles. This one is available from the United States Repeating Arms Company.

Accoutrements for the Model 94

The Ruger Single-Six in 32 Magnum is not much larger than the same revolver in 22 rimfire chambering, and yet the 32 Magnum round is much more powerful than either the 22 rimfire or the 22 rimfire Magnum load. In fact, where allowed by law, the 32 Magnum could probably put an animal the size of a javelina in the bag with one well-placed shot at close range. When I had originally wanted that nice 32-20 as companion to my 30-30 rifle, I had no idea I'd get 32-20 ballistics in a handgun which could also fire a much more powerful round as well, and with excellent target-type sights.

Boxes and Gadgets

The 30-30 round is so famous that it has given us a few collectable items in addition to the standard shooting accoutrements. For example, I have a key ring which has an unloaded 30-30 round as the fob. The 94 is honored in many ways. I have a special tanned leather case made for the 94 with a big "Winchester" logo on the side, and I also own a belt buckle honoring Winchester and the Model 94. Winchester has offered an ammo box, too. Though it is not specifically Model 94 oriented, it's still old-time in nature, and I have mine loaded down with 30-30 gear and a couple boxes of ammo.

The Model 94 would not be a complete shooting iron without all the little things that attend it. I have made a specific list of such hardware for my own 94, and I've found that each item is not only useful but also rewarding in a non-utilitarian way. Of course, you'll want to outfit yourself personally for your own 30-30 hunting style.

15

Maintaining Your Model 94

The Model 94 Winchester is about as rugged as a hunk of railroad track, but even a railroad track needs some maintenance. The special problems inherent in taking care of the 94 are basically two. First, it is impossible to clean the Model 94 lever-action rifle from the breech. It must be cleaned from the muzzle. That problem will be discussed here. Second, I have already admitted that the design of the 94, while foolproof, is not simple. A devotee of the 94 knows that it takes special care and attention to clean and lubricate the workings.

Damage to the crown of the muzzle can result in lost accuracy. The best solution is to have a professional gunsmith recut the crown. The precious rifling at the muzzle is directly responsible for accuracy levels. I have conducted a few tests in which rifle muzzles were deliberately scratched and knicked, and accuracy provably suffered. Therefore, cleaning from the muzzle requires great care in order to maintain the sharp edges of the lands in that area.

Here are some ideas to help you clean the 94 in a manner which will preserve the integrity of the muzzle's crown. The first step is to purchase a pull-through cleaning wire. This is no problem. The fine Outers Pocket Pak has one of these devices in it as standard equipment. This compact little kit, coupled with an old toothbrush and some Q-Tip swabs, along with some good chemicals, are all you need to maintain the 94.

The Outers Pocket Pak contains a couple of bore brushes. These are the Phosphor Bronze Bore Brushes, for which Outers is known. They do not scratch the bore, but they do remove fouling nicely.

There is also the Swivel Cleaning Cable with Handle—the pull-through bore-cleaning wire. It's compactly set into the Pocket Pak with removable handle. By the way, this cable is covered with a smooth plastic. It will not wear the muzzle down.

There are also two cleaning tips in the kit. One is the right size for the 30-30. They are slotted and are used to hold the cleaning patch. An adaptor allows the larger cleaning tip to be used as well as a smaller one. Because of this, the kit is good for calibers of 24 (6mm) on up to at least 8mm.

There is also an 8 x 8-inch silicone cloth impregnated with preservative chemicals. I use it all the time to remove fingerprints from the metalwork of my 94s. A third problem with the 94 is the two-piece stock, which forces the user to handle the metal receiver quite a bit. Fingerprints there can cause a problem. To go on, the kit also contains a bottle of cleaning solvent and a batch of cleaning patches. When my patches were used up, I bought some new, soft, flannel cloth and cut some more, putting them in the kit. All these items are contained in a plastic container about 4 x 6 inches in size. The pack opens up to about 6 x 8 inches.

I recommend this type of kit for the Model 94. I add a small tube of Gunslick as well as a few Q-Tip swabs to the kit—they will fit—and I carry this unit into the field as well as using it at home. The kit's compactness allows it to go anywhere. It's especially useful on backpack trips. I'm not an ambassador for Outers, and if the shooter has a pull-through unit he uses, fine. But the Pocket Pak seems to be just right for the maintenance of the Model 94.

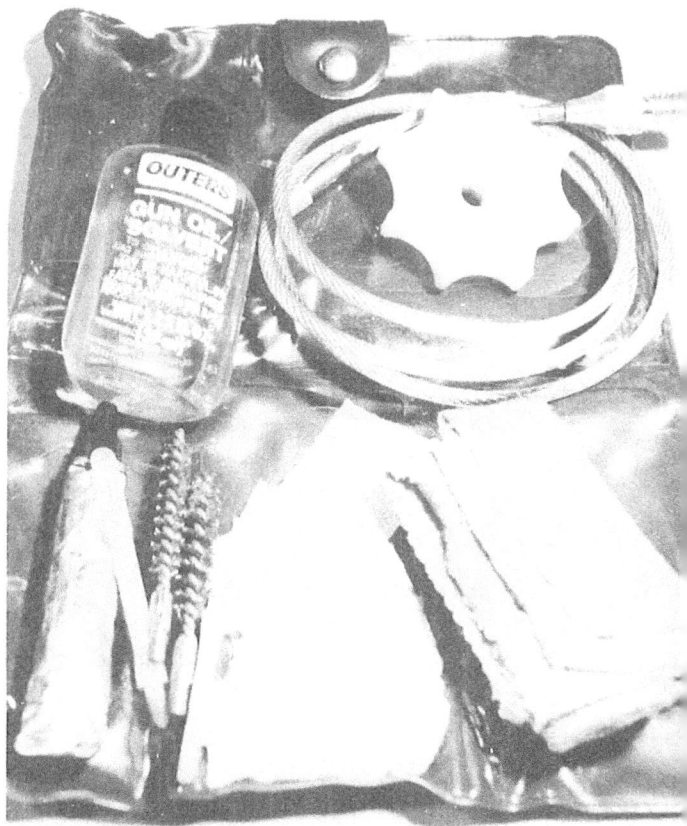

Fadala likes this little pull-through cleaning cable in the Outers Pocket Pak. This compact kit is all a Model 94 owner needs to keep the bore clean in the field.

Damage to any gun comes in many forms. Basically, the enemy is ferric oxide, good old rust. Rust is formed when metal and moisture get married to each other. Fingerprints don't do the metalwork any good, either. I suspect there are acids in the body oils deposited on our firearms, and I have actually seen a fingerprint etched into the receiver of a rifle. That is why I wipe my 94s down after every handling. The silicone cloth is good for that, or the shooter may wish to use a spray such as good old WD-40, applied lightly with a clean cloth. Blood, by the way, is ruinous of steel. I have seen blood take the blue off by the time a gun

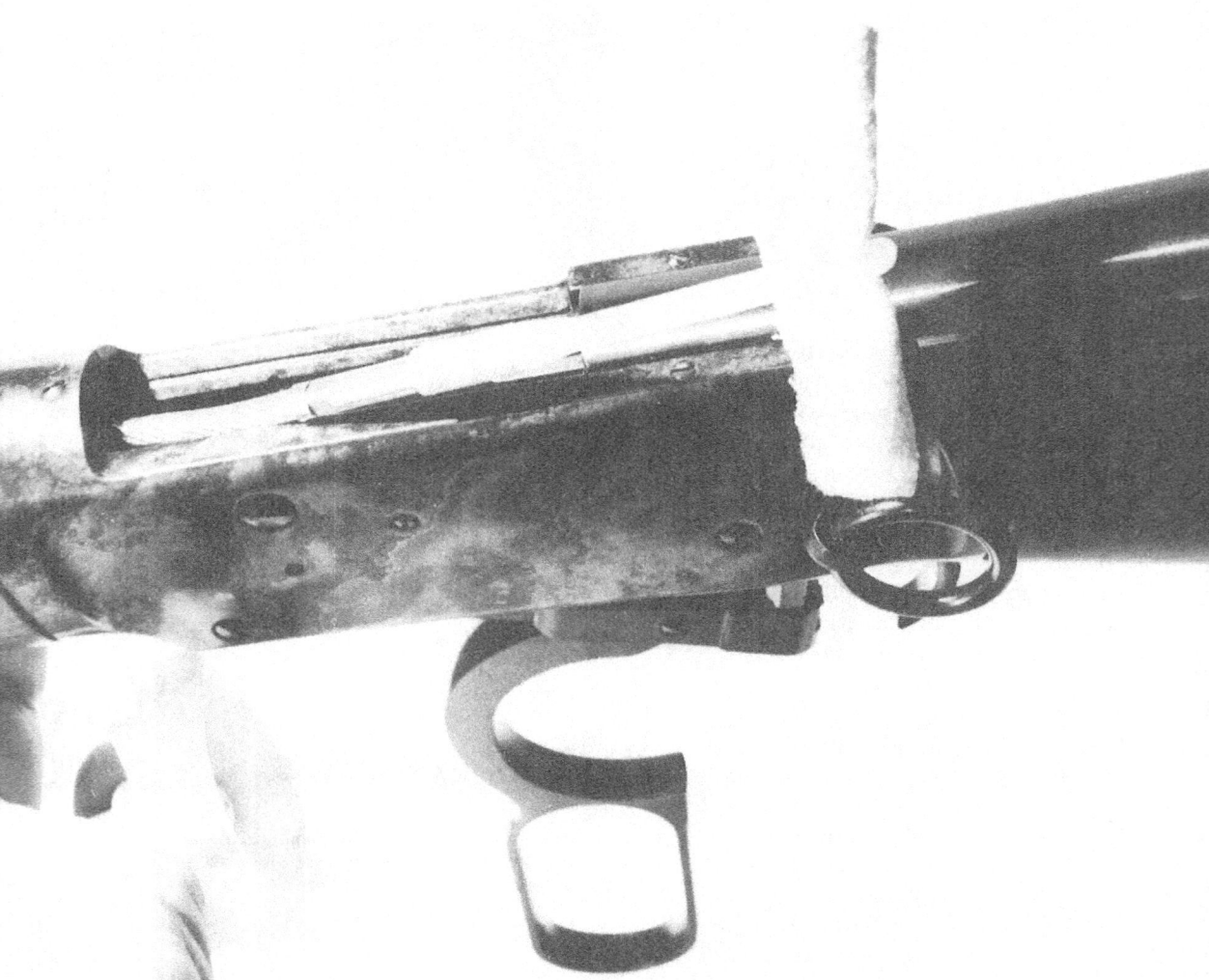

The cleaning cable is inserted from the muzzle, and the tip protrudes through the action, as shown here. A cleaning patch is inserted through the slot as illustrated.

reached home. Avoid contact with blood by making it a habit to put Old Betsy safely away from the downed game before you start field-dressing procedures. Perspiration is also a culprit, as is humidity in the air, rain, snow or any other form of moisture.

Before I go into a step-by-step cleaning procedure for the 94, let's talk briefly about modern gun-cleaning chemicals. My previously mentioned kit contains but two chemicals: Gunslick, a grease, and the Outers Gun Oil/Solvent. However, I use several other chemicals in home care. Gun-cleaning chemicals fall into three categories. There is the solvent, used to remove fouling. Lubes reduce friction. And third, the preservative class of chemical are designed mainly to safeguard the metal from moisture.

Solvents such as Hoppe's Number Nine have been used for years to remove powder residue and even some leading. The solvent softens fouling so that a cleaning patch can pick up the mess. Most lubes have in the past been greases. But today we have silicone chemicals and all sorts of sprays which cling to the metal and give a slicker surface, thereby reducing friction and allowing smoother operation with less wear. This is very important for the Model 94, because it does have some moving parts which we want to preserve from wear. Chemical preservatives have come a long way, too. I use a lot of Accragard, a special oil designed to wed with the steel and stay put. It's highly sophisticated stuff, and it seems expensive until you use it. A bottle lasts a long time because Accragard goes a long way. There is also a good spray from Outers called TR-3, and it seems to have some cleaning properties as well as preserving virtues. I use a lot of it. It comes in a spray can and is easily applied. Modern ammo is non-corrosive, but the dangers of rust are still present, so an anti-rust agent such as Accragard helps a lot in saving our firearms.

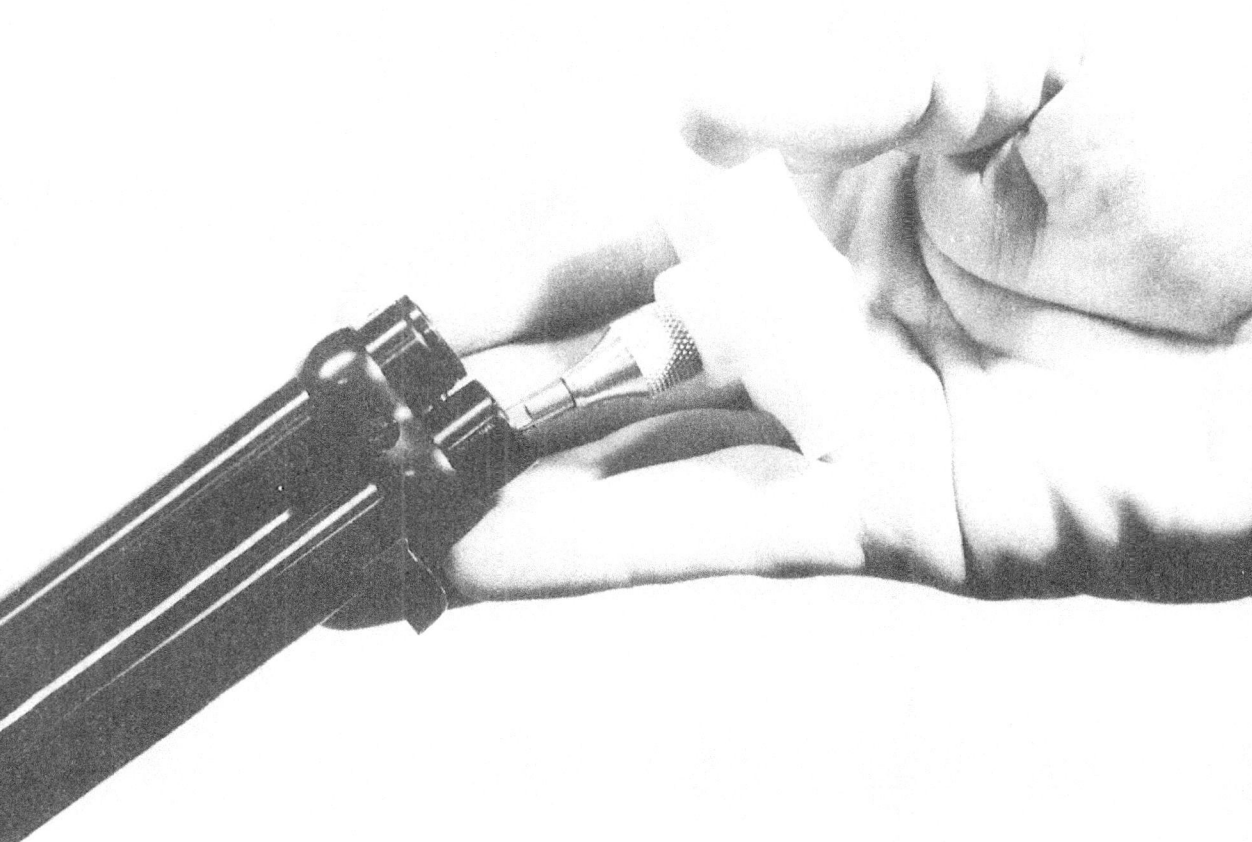

The pull-through Outers cleaning cable has a removable handle. The cleaning patch is pulled through the bore with this handle.

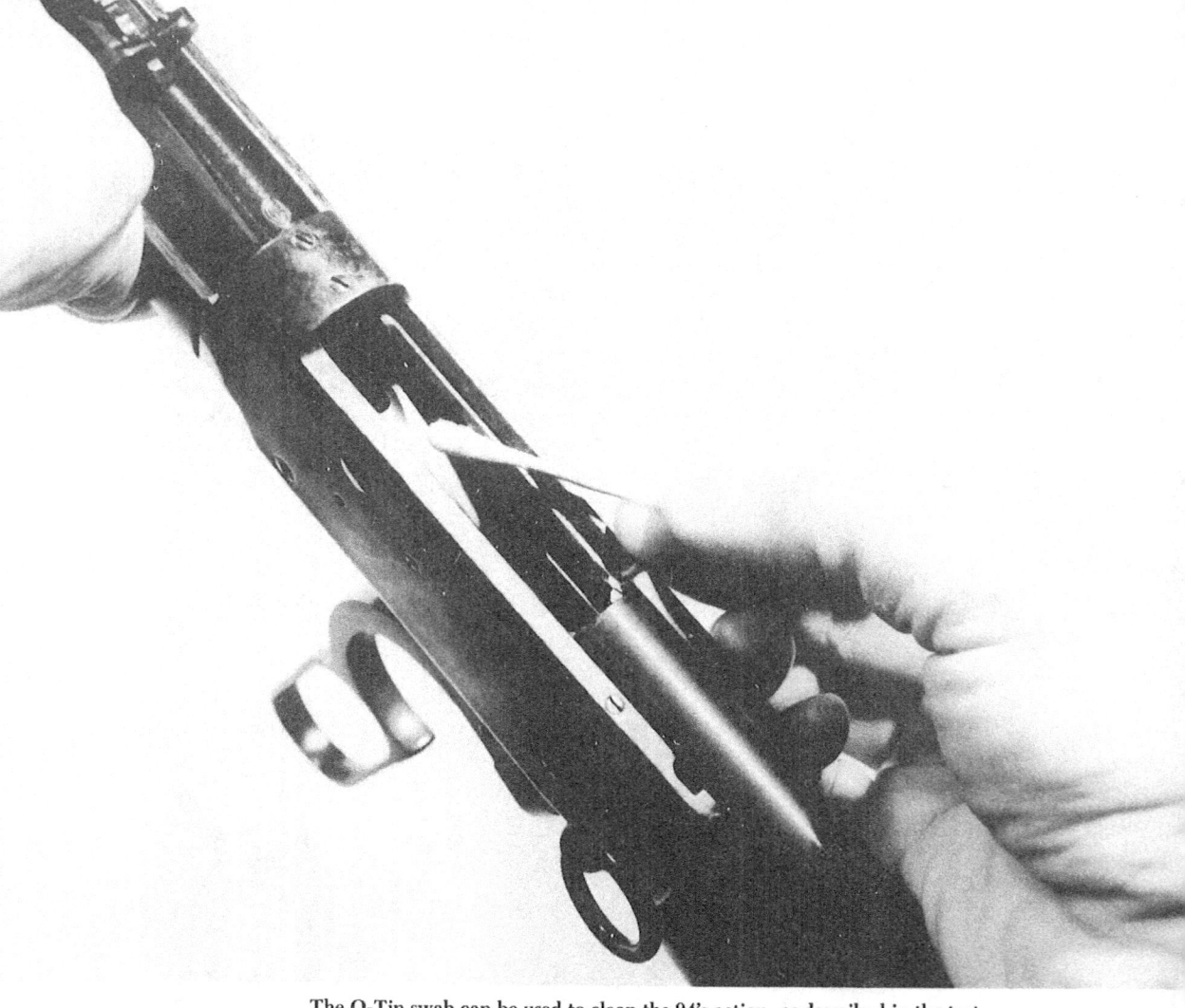

The Q-Tip swab can be used to clean the 94's action, as described in the text.

Steps in Cleaning the Model 94

1. Make absolutely sure that the firearm is completely unloaded. This is an obvious step, but is vital to safety.

2. Using the pull-through type of cleaning cable, insert the correct tip and gently thread the tip through the muzzle and out into the action of the 94. Then slip the cleaning patch through the slot in the cleaning tip, saturate the patch with solvent and pull it through.

3. After a few swipes with the solvent-soaked patch, run a dry patch through the bore. If the patch comes out dark, you may have to go back to a solvent-soaked patch or the bristle brush.

4. After softening up the fouling and running a drying patch or two through the bore, you can use a bristle brush to remove stubborn residue and fouling from the bullet jacket. Lead deposits may also exist in the bore. The bristle brush is attached after the cable is inserted into the muzzle and out through the chamber

into the action. The cable is pulled through with bristle brush attached. After the brush is run through a few times, a clean patch follows. This patch will tell the tale. If it is pretty dark with fouling, it's wise to apply a light dab of solvent and run the solvent patch through the bore, followed by another drying patch. This should do the job. The last drying patches should come out relatively clean.

I do not use the brush every cleaning session. I use it only occasionally, or following a target session in which cast bullets have been fired. I doubt that continued use of the bristle brush will cause any measurable bore wear, but it's simply not necessary to use a brush after every little shooting session.

5. The bore is now clean. I use Accragard, TR-3 or a similar chemical agent at this point, lightly dabbed on a clean patch and run through the bore a couple of swipes. This puts a fine film of protective chemical in the bore. Rust in the bore eventually causes pitting. An anti-rust agent may be the difference between a barrel free of pits for life and one that looks like a bad road.

6. Now is the time to clean the action.

A toothbrush may be helpful in scrubbing hard-to-reach spots within the action of the Model 94.

Many excellent solvents are available for cleaning the Model 94 or any other modern firearm. One is Outers Nitro Solvent.

With a small toothbrush, solvent-soaked if the rifle is really dirty, scrub the inner action. To get into the cracks and crevices, use a Q-Tip swab soaked with solvent. The gunk will be cleared up in no time. Pipe cleaners and solvent can also serve to clean hard-to-reach places in the action.

7. Dry that action. Q-Tip swabs work pretty well here. All the fouling loosened up by the solvent needs to be wiped away. The action should be free of powder residue at this point and ready for anti-rust chemicals.

8. Using a Q-Tip swab or pipe cleaner, dab a little bit of Accragard, TR-3 or similar agent on those parts of the action which have been freed of residue. A light coating of Gunslick will aid in lubrication of moving parts. I always carry a bit of Gunslick with me and apply a very light film to all moving parts in the action.

9. Wipe the gun down. Remember that fingerprints, humidity and any other moisture producer can damage the metal. Since handling of the gun is about at an end here, the metal can be wiped down. And wiping the wood with a clean dry cloth is a good idea, too. The rifle is now free of dirt inside and out, and the metal is coated with a light film of oil to prevent rust. Remember, the wiping cloth is impregnated with a touch of TR-3, Accragard or some other anti-rust agent. So the wipe-down is for rust prevention as well as for cleaning.

10. If the wood is dirty, it can be wiped off with a clean cloth dabbed with pure, boiled, inedible linseed oil. This will shine up the wood fairly well. Do not leave a noticeable coating of linseed oil on the wood. The oil is used here to soften up any clinging dirt and foreign materials—this is not an oil application as such.

About once a year or following any trip, especially a backpack hunt on which my 94 may have taken strain, I do some field stripping—mainly, the removal of the trigger guard/finger lever and the breech bolt assemblies. You may also break the 94 down further for inspection and cleaning. If you do this, be sure to use well-fitted screwdrivers so as to prevent stripping of the screw and bolt heads. This extra cleanup measure is only necessary once or twice a year.

Before the next shooting session, any trace of oil should be removed from the bore. There are two big reasons for this.

Maintaining Your Model 94

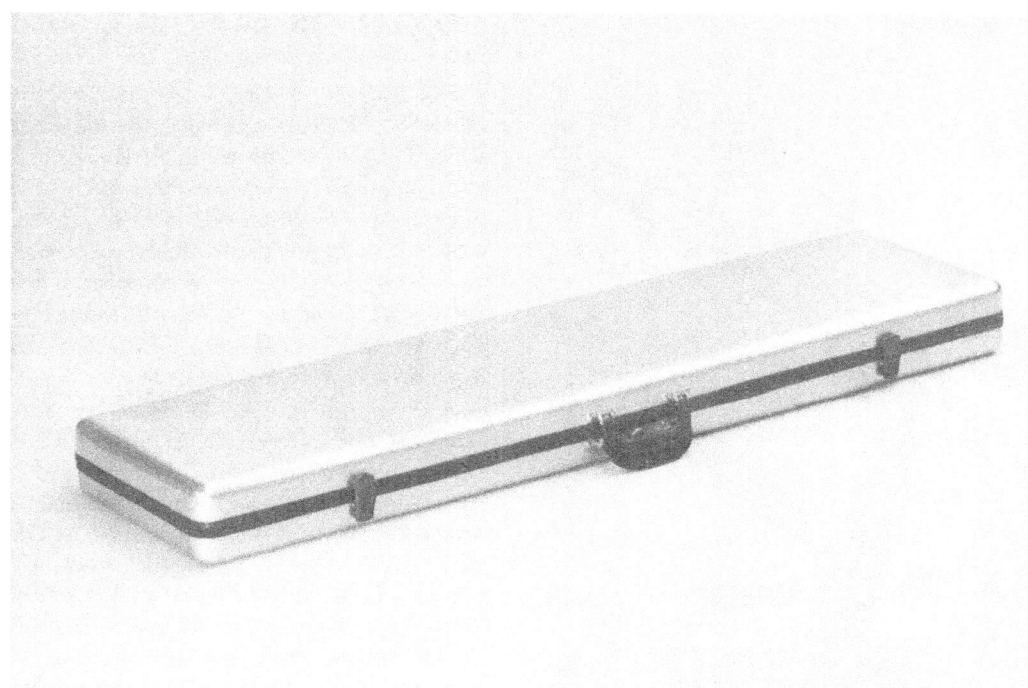

A metal gun case—this one is from Outers—is preferred for air travel, as well as when the rifle is to be loaded into the back of a truck for a long hunting trip. Although the Model 94 is rugged, sights can get knocked out of alignment. This sort of gun case can prevent the problem.

First, an oily bore will not shoot to the same point of impact as a dry bore. Sight in with a dry bore. Always shoot with a dry bore, never an oily one. I have seen bullets fly off target by a few inches at 100 yards when fired from an oily bore. Second, an oily bore could be damaged through firing. So it's important, before any shoot, to run the cleaning cable down the bore, insert one dry patch on the slotted jag and then mop out the bore with a couple of swipes. That's all that is necessary.

I have an excellent handmade bore light which was given to me by Admiral R. J. Schneider, an esteemed friend. Admiral Schneider made this unit so tiny that it will drop into a 17 caliber air rifle bore as well as a larger caliber. A bore light is also available from gunstores, by the way. It is useful for inspection from time to time to determine if there is any lingering lead fouling, bullet jacket metal or, heaven forbid, rust. The bore light allows a visual inspection of any type of firearm, but it is especially useful on the 94 since its design prevents the inspector from holding the bore up to the light and looking down it.

Storing the cleaned 94 is another important aspect of your maintenance schedule. If the rifle is to be stored for any length of time, it's wise to apply extra anti-rust protection to the bore via the

Don't plug the barrel with anything. Some shooters insist that the rifle be stored muzzle-down for drainage of excess oils. Since my 94s see use all year long, I simply store them in their hard gun cases in the horizontal position. Never store the rifle in any sort of plastic, which may capture and hold moisture. I realize that some firearms come from the factory in a plastic wrap, but generally they are totally saturated with grease, so it's a little different story.

A dehumidifier may be desirable. The "Golden Rod" electronic dehumidifier is said to work quite well. It removes moisture from the air, and it comes in various wattages, the best one determined by the size of the area in which the guns are stored. Those little moisture-attracting pellets are also useful for gathering up excess wetness from the atmosphere. At any rate, the idea is to keep the old 94 dry.

Most of what has been said here applies universally to cleaning and caring for guns. But the Model 94 requires a little special attention, for the reasons stated earlier—especially the inability to clean it from the breech and the exposed metal parts. Many a 94 has become a trusted companion on the backtrail, and like any good friend, it should be cared for through a good maintenance schedule such as the one outlined here. In that way, when the 94 is called upon, she'll respond the way you want her to.

The Kolpin 007 Gun Boot is both a hard gun case and a saddle scabbard. Although made for a scope-sighted rifle, it will accept the Model 94. And the new Angle-Eject 94 may well wear a scope, making the 007 a good case for it.

chemicals mentioned above. Also, it's not a bad idea to wipe the exterior metal and the action down with rust preventative. Then store the rifle in a dry place.

16

The 94 Goes to the Movies

Around 1894 two interesting phenomena were getting under way. The 1894 rifle would be available in blackpowder rounds, to be followed in 1895 by smokeless powder rounds in a new nickel steel barrel and stronger action, and the silent western movie was being made by the Edison Company. "The Great Train Robbery," a western film of 1903, would be a classic, as would "Ramona," a W. D. Griffith movie of 1910. A certain western attitude was being built in these movies, and something else, too — the Model 94 Winchester. While the 94 may not have dominated the silent films, it did go on to appear in most westerns made right up to the present day.

Some shooters believe that part of the continued popularity of the 94 stems from its image as a cowboy rifle, an image promoted by the western movie. I don't believe that. But it's great fun to watch the older films and try to spot 94s. A shooter can see some interesting 94 Winchesters that way.

The western promoted the West. The good guy was usually a fellow raised out West, while the bad guy was an eastern dude. Mostly, the "code of the West" was honored, and the image of the western hero was one of a gun-toting but righteous man. A couple of big names in the old westerns were William S. Hart and Tom Mix. Mix actually came first, according to my source, a fine work entitled *Western Films* by Brian Garfield, published in 1982 by Rawson Associates of New York and well worth buying.

Firearms have always been abused by Hollywood. The 94 is no exception. Cowboys are shown with 94s during the days of the great buffalo herds, and I watched

Although John Wayne often carried a Model 92 rather than the Model 94, the movie audience was often treated to America's lever-action repeater. Here is Wayne from the movie "The Searchers." — *Courtesy of Replica Products.*

one western hero pump about 30 rounds through a 94 without reloading. But the western film did attempt to depict real characters from our historical West, though these fellows, and a few ladies, were seldom shown with biographical correctness. There was Billy the Kid. Paul Newman did him as the left-handed gun. Actually, Billy was right-handed, but a backward-printed photo made him appear to be a southpaw. Wyatt Earp was overdone at the cinema. William Cody was, too. Wild Bill Hickok, Jesse James, The Daltons and Pat Garrett — all were portrayed on the silver screen long after they had departed to Boot Hill.

And the Model 94 Winchester was much in evidence in most films portraying these hardy characters, including quite a few classics. Each moviegoer will pick his own favorites, and the real experts may condemn my choices, but I have never picked my toothpaste or my films because some critic told me to. I like "The Shootist," "High Plains Drifter," "Ox-Bow Incident" and "Red River." I also like "High Noon" and "The 3:10 to Yuma." "Shane" was good, and the old "Stagecoach" film was real entertainment.

The Model 94 fan may wish to look at the western film as a symbol of the firearm he enjoys. I enjoy glancing at the "B" westerns these days. Presently there are lots of them on TV, especially on weekends. The "B" film was generally made hastily and on a low budget and was rented at a flat rate to theaters. Garfield says it was washed up by late 1954. But in the meanwhile, hundreds were made, and quite a number of big stars were in them. Garfield says that the "B" western centered around one of three plots — clearing the hero's name, rescuing a distressed maiden or avenging the murder of a father or brother.

There really wasn't much serious shooting up of either good or bad guys. There was plenty of outlandish shooting, however, and lots of stunts — stunt men often made the film what it was in terms of adventure. There were Buck Jones and Tim McCoy, pretty good cowhands in real life. And there was Marion Michael Morrison, a football star who got his start in the movies as a prop man, more or less. This fellow ended up making dozens of "B" westerns, such as "Range Feud" in

In the famous western film "Stagecoach," a young John Wayne rolls a cigarette in frontier style. Note the hoop lever of his rifle. — *Courtesy of Replica Products.*

A current Model 94 is again made with the 16-inch barrel and the hoop finger lever. Here is John Wayne with such a rifle in the movie "True Grit." — *Courtesy of Replica Products.*

1931 and "Lawless Range" in 1935. Only he wasn't called Marion any longer — he was John Wayne.

Gary Cooper was in on it, too. So were Tex Ritter and Rex Allen and Randolph Scott, and Hopalong Cassidy, Gene Autrey, Roy Rogers and the Lone Ranger. The talkies came along, and that did not harm the western film one bit. You could hear those guns now, as well as seeing the smoke from the blackpowder cartridges. Some pretty fine westerns came along. These were definitely "A" films, not cheaply made or rushed, and certainly not sold lightly at the theaters.

"The Treasure of the Sierra Madre," a 1948 film, starred Humphrey Bogart. "Red River" had John Wayne up front, as did the much later "Shootist." Gregory Peck was "The Gunfighter" in 1950. Alan

A forerunner of the Model 94 Winchester was the popular 1873 model. Jimmy Stewart poses with one here in the movie "Winchester 73." — *Courtesy of Replica Products.*

elderly lady riding in a covered wagon, and you know Old Betsy is a Model 94 Winchester. I saw this in "The Pioneer Trail," a 1938 movie with Jack Luden. I realize there's more corn in some of these westerns than in a field of Iowa's best crop, but there is also entertainment. "South of the Rio Grande," a 1932 film, shows Buck Jones about to be hammered by a 94 in the hands of "Peedro," a desper-

The western movie has given the non-shooter a definite image of the rifle used by the cowboy. Here is John Wayne from the famous "Hondo" movie. — *Courtesy of Replica Products.*

Ladd was the hero of "Shane" in 1953. Sometimes realism took over, as in "The Wild Bunch," a 1969 western put together by Sam Peckinpah. Some viewers thought this last film contained a bit too much realism, in fact.

Television got in on the western, too — did it ever! There were "Rawhide" and "Bonanza," "Gunsmoke" and "Wagon Train" and "Lawman." "The Virginian" was big, and so was "Big Valley." "The Rifleman" series starred Paul Fix as Sheriff Micah Torrance. Paul had been in many "B" westerns long before this TV series.

"Hand me up Old Betsy," says Ma, an

ado, and Errol Flynn carries a Model 94 on a sling in "Northern Pursuit," a 1943 film.

Glenn Ford rides through "The Day of the Evil Gun," a 1968 movie in which Paul Fix has a small part. We see the ever-present 94 resting in a saddle scabbard, but an intrepid Indian manages to lasso the rifle from its leather home. Lots of old 94s saw action in this one. Much earlier, Paul Fix starred in a 1935 film, called "The Westerner," with Tim McCoy the hero.

Thus, while the Winchester Model 94 was making history in the hands of American hunters, ranchers, farmers and outdoorsmen, it also played a prominent role in most of the western films of our land. I certainly would never buy a hunting rifle because I saw a particular model in a movie. And I don't think that the western film had an awful lot to do with the success of the 94, though I could be wrong as rain at a picnic. I do think that some influence was exerted by the fact that our big western heroes used the Model 94. But I submit that the Model 94 was selected on its real-life merits, not its movie image.

All the same, the 94 lives on in films as it lives on off the screen—the most famous rifle in American history. Many other types of firearms were depicted in the movies, but the one which dominates this book also dominated the silver screen. I sort of enjoy that fact. And I think other Model 94 shooters feel the same.

17

The Model 94 in Your Life

Those shooters who insist on having the biggest and fastest and most up-to-date calibers won't want to bother with our little hunter's gem, the Model 94, or with its mundane round, the 30-30. In fact, those boys will look down their noses at us when you and I enter the hunting camp toting our little lever-action rifles. They'll snicker as they hold up their rounds — Coke-bottle-sized in comparison with our moderate 30s — and they will quote yards and yards of ballistic data.

In one such camp, a fellow approached me and began a friendly conversation. "What are you shootin'?" he asked politely, and when I told him, he laughed and said something about the extinction of the dinosaur. He wanted to know if I hadn't heard about the newer rounds, the ones "that would really get the job done."

I remained a gentleman to the end of the hunt and never said much about the fact that my buck made his look like a sausage with four legs.

The Model 94 and the 30-30 are not for everyone. We all know that. And what's more, I don't see the 94 as a take-over rifle. In other words, my 94s are hardly the only firearms I own. I have no intention of trading away my fine 6.5mm custom or my 7mm custom and turning to the 30-30 exclusively. The 94 has a place, but it's not necessarily a place that fills the gun cabinet. Not at all. However, the old 94 does some things mighty well, and for many reasons the little lever gun has gained one heck of a following. Readers who already have a 94 and know why they own it may not find this chapter very enlightening, but I think it's worthwhile to talk about the 94 in your life —

even if you own one now and especially if you don't.

I got back into the 30-30 because it stimulated my interests. It always sounds haughty to say that you wanted an added challenge, but in fact, millions of people have turned back to more basic tools in order to achieve a certain added spice that is not available with high-technology tools. I found, as stated earlier, that the 30-30 is a middle-ground rifle for me, fitting nicely between my muzzleloaders and my scope-sighted long-range rifles. After living with the 30-30 again, I learned that part of its reward came through the extra challenge, which I expected, but another part of it came through the things the little 30 can do so well, maybe better than any other round or rifle.

The Working Rifle

I think of the 94 as a working rifle — no frills, no bows, no lace. Even my custom 30-30 gets out there and *works*. It brings in the bacon, and if it did not, all the nostalgia in the world, including old western movies, could never get me to keep it. She's a slab-sided tool, the 94, an American tradition in getting things done. The 94 is compact, and I don't mean just short or narrow — its flat sides and no-bolt figure let it fit into a lot of tight places, such as the saddle scabbard, from which it exits about as slick as a greased roller skate. She's a fast-handling piece, ready to get with the action. In short, the 94, even the prettier ones, are meant for labor. And I think many hunters have added a 94 to the battery for this reason.

Here's a portrait of a "working rifle," the little Model 94 carbine — no frills, no ribbons, no bows. Just rugged action.

Even in the longer rifle style, the 94 is a flat-sided, easy-carrying piece, a companion. Dale Storey poses with a Model 94 with 26-inch barrel.

The Handmate Rifle

The 94 is also a companion, close by, like a good dog, ready to help out. It's a sidekick, a partner. And like a good partner, it can be counted on all the time. I've never had a 94 lie to me by failing to function when I needed it. Ranchers, farmers, brush/woods hunters, meat-seekers, all who are willing to work hard in the outdoors, find their 94s as reliable as gravity and just about as ubiquitous. The handmate rifle is always there when you need it. Ken Warner said in *Handloader's Digest Bullet & Powder Update*, a DBI product from about 1980, "If someone isn't counting already, we're going to lose track of how many million 30-30 rifles have been and will be built. It's fashionable to downgrade the cartridge and the principal rifle models that use it, but such critics have lost sight of the central fact: This cartridge and the guns that shoot it are tools that worked then and work now." That's the handmate aspect of the 94.

Survival Rifle

I was asked once by a magazine interested in matters of survival which rifle I would choose if I were turned loose in the backcountry and had to make a living off the land. I thought it over and decided that it would be my 6.5mm custom because it's so blasted deadly. It shoots a 140-grain bullet at well over 3,000 fps, and it's a very reliable bolt-action rifle with a fine scope sight. That's what I'd use if I were having to "make meat" in a survival situation.

I haven't changed my mind. But I have had moments when I swayed from that decision, and when I have swayed, it has always been in the direction of the 94 and the 30-30. If any rifle will take it in the outback, it's the 94; and the 30-30, when used as a hunting round where the hunter does some work, is plenty capable of meat-getting. I don't think the ideal survival rifle exists at the moment, but if you want to think about one, maybe the 94 should be on the list.

Backcountry Rifle

I use the 30-30 in the backwoods, up in the mountains and out on the plains. I

The Model 94 In Your Life

The Model 94 collector has many models to choose from. This photo shows a longer-barreled 94 rifle on the left, a saddle-ring carbine in the center and an octagon-barreled Model 94 carbine on the right.

use it because it's easy to carry and because it works so hard for me. Of course, I also like that challenge spoken of earlier. I'm a sportsman, not a professional hunter. I hunt hard and I use what I harvest, but getting game doesn't mean survival for me. Nonetheless, the little 30 has given me many hours of joyful shooting and hunting in the out-of-the-way places. I think it fits in fine for the hunter who wants to experience the joys of the lonesome places.

Collectors like the little things, such as this grip cap on the semi-pistol grip Model 94 rifle.

Extra Gun

A spare rifle is always a handy thing to have. I contend that an older 94, one with real character — maybe with a few gouges in the wood and nicks in the metal — might be ideal as the extra rifle in camp, the one which goes into service when the hunter's main rifle is knocked out of commission. That older 94 might also make a good loaner, for those whose friends need to borrow a rifle now and then. This does not seem a romantic or even honorable use for the old gal, but it's a practical one.

The Collector

Quite a few collectors have 94s in their holdings. A Winchester collector, of course, simply must have this most famous of all models in the lineup. Most of us don't collect guns. I don't. But my natural love for old things got me to looking for a vintage Model 94, and I found it at the Elmira Gun Works in Elmira, New York. It was made in about 1899, and somebody had done a professional refinish — a facelift if you will. It had been reblued, and the wood had been refinished. That was all right with me. The refurbishing probably reduced its collector value, but I did not want to collect that 94 anyway — I wanted to hunt with it.

The barrel was 26 inches long, octagonal in shape, and the rifle was a takedown model. These are not supposed to be terribly accurate, but I found that it outshot my 1955 Model 94 handily at 100 yards from the bench. It came with a full magazine, semi-pistol grip and I-style checkering. And it wore a tang sight. The action was still as tight as a ranch fence after the rainy season.

Soon I was hunting with that original 1894 rifle and enjoying the experience very much. It's a graceful rifle, slim and nice-handling, and I learned from it that the handiness of the 94 style does not come only with the short barrel of the carbine. This rifle was very neat and portable—its slenderness made it that way, I think. So I packed that 1894 into the field, and I'm still packing it. A season ago, it brought down a nice antelope on the plains.

Therefore, another aspect of owning a 94 is for the sake of show and preservation, but the collector may well find that his rifle is much more than a collector's rifle after all, such as my reworked Model 1894 30-30. I use it faithfully, even though, as I write these words, the piece is about 86 years old.

The Custom

Although there were many different Model 94 styles—from half-magazine to full-magazine to semi-pistol grip and straight grip, checkered and plain, rifle and carbine of varying barrel lengths—there is nothing as unique and personal as a custom. And a respectable number of customs have been built around the Model 94 action.

I wanted a custom 94 because of a desire to have a unique lever-action rifle built around the "old cowboy gun," as a friend of mine calls his 94 model. I was not after more power than was available

A custom Model 94, such as this Storey Conversion, can turn into a beautiful piece. Note the presentation-grade walnut stocks.

in 30-30. I went with the 30-30 Improved for the case design, using standard 30-30 loading data in the cartridge, data straight from the manuals.

I have described the Storey Conversion elsewhere and won't backtrack over that trail, but I do need to say a few words about the custom 30-30 in your life because I did run into a few snags before I got together with Dale Storey to build my own custom 94. First, I encountered some very high quotes for rebarreling an older 94 with an octagon barrel. In fact, quite a bit of the work I originally priced in my initial investigation seemed high.

It became clear that the best way to end up with a custom was to find an action and have an entire rifle built on it to my desires. I wanted the beauty I knew would be inherent in a custom built around the sleek action of the Model 94, and I got it. Special presentation walnut wood was no giveaway in price, and I asked for some checkering, too, but all in all, the rifle turned out to be a good buy. I say this to encourage the shooter interested in a custom 94 to do some shopping first.

Next, I suggest that you and your potential gunmaker sit down over a cup of coffee and talk about the actual project. I wanted accuracy as well as good looks, and Storey came up with the answer in extra close tolerances and a fine barrel. I did not want to change the character of the old Model 94, either. I just wanted a special, personal piece which was still a 94 through and through, and I got just that.

Finally, I think there should be an agreement, an understanding, between the buyer and the gunmaker. Before closing the bargain, each person should fully understand the other's expectations, and I'd go so far as to have the whole deal written up in a contract — at least a good estimate. In this manner, both smith and shooter know just what the deal is.

No, the 94 is not for everyone. But there's a 94 in the future for quite a number of American sportsmen, just as there has been a 94 in the past for a great number of outdoorsmen. The 94s in my life have given much, and in return have needed just some decent maintenance and a feeding of good ammo, plus a little consideration by way of stalking in for the medium-range shot instead of calling on the old gal to shoot from hill to hill. For these few demands, she has provided a lot of good game in the freezer and plenty of faithful service. That's why there's a 94 in my life.

18

Commemorative 94s

This is not a history book. It is a shooting book, and it has been dedicated to the Model 94 Winchester shooter whose major interest lies in getting the most from his Model 94 30-30. However, if we are going to talk about Model 94s, we must mention the commemoratives which have been manufactured over the years. Winchester has been interested in milestone 94s and special Model 94s for a very long time, and that trend continues today in the United States Repeating Arms Company, current Winchester 94 purveyors.

Winchester built a large number of Model 94s, most of them in 30-30 caliber, with collection in mind. To be sure, a great many of these firearms were not collected but rather used in the field. Bill Howe, owner of Timberlane Sports in Casper, Wyoming, told me the tale of one Winchester 94 commemorative which was picked up in a previously fired condition, so Bill used the rifle to bag some big game. Such occurrences are not rare apparently — in my own circle of hunting friends and acquaintances are several who either had bagged game with a commemorative 94 or knew someone who had. Mostly, however, the commemorative has been for keeping, not so much for shooting. This chapter will emphasize the visual aspects, presenting a selection of 94 commemoratives in few words and allowing the pictures to say most of it.

If there is a trend in Winchester's commemorative models, it is that most of these rifles honor some phase of Americana. Things American rule here. For example, the bald eagle, symbol of our country, is exalted in one commemorative. Another honors Oliver F. Winchester, for rather obvious reasons; after all,

185

The NRA Centennial rifle.

this man's name was to become famous through the Model 94 Winchester, as American a firearm as was ever made.

Examples of Model 94 Commemoratives

Winchester National Rifle Association (NRA) Centennial Rifle

This commemorative is one of the most interesting of the lot. It's a Model 94 Winchester, all right, but it's a companion piece to the Centennial Musket and is very much like a Model 64 Winchester rifle, which had a 24-inch barrel and was labeled as a special deer-hunting firearm. The Winchester NRA Centennial rifle also wears a 24 inch barrel. It is a half-magazine rifle and has a unique pistol grip. You would have to call it a semi-pistol grip, in fact, as the finger lever is all but straight on this Model 94, though it is slightly contoured.

The NRA Centennial is a 30-30 and wears traditional sights—a hooded front sight on a ramp and an open rear sight with an elevator bar. The rifle has built-in sling swivels, which suggests that someone thought it might be carried into the field as well as admired in the gun room. An NRA seal, set into the right-hand side of the buttstock, is struck on a special silver-colored medallion.

The metalwork is deep blue (almost black), and the receiver is inscribed with modest engraving. I have never fired this model, but it could be an accurate one in terms of the barrel/magazine union. There are no barrel bands. The fore-end cap has two screws in it, and the end of the magazine tube is held in via a retainer which in turn is dovetailed into the lower barrel. There is a magazine plug screw which pins the end of the magazine tube to the stock in the standard Model 94 fashion, and on a shooting NRA Centennial, you might enhance accuracy by ensuring that this little screw is not too tight.

Chief Crazy Horse Commemorative

In keeping with tradition, the Chief Crazy Horse model symbolizes a famous American hero, Chief Crazy Horse of the Sioux Nation. He was one of the best leaders of his people, and this model was unanimously approved by the 11 Tribal Chairmen of the United Sioux Tribes of South Dakota. In fact, a special ceremony was held at the SHOT (Shooting, Hunting and Outdoor Trade) Show in

Commemorative 94s

The Chief Crazy Horse Commemorative.

Dallas, where a royalty payment from the sale of these rifles was presented by U.S. Repeating Arms to the United Sioux Tribes of South Dakota for the benefit of the Sioux people.

This very special commemorative is a Model 94 Winchester; however, the chambering is for the 38-55 Winchester cartridge, which is a good choice because the Model 94 was originally chambered for the 38-55 blackpowder round. Today a handloader can create fine deer-hunting rounds with the 38-55, by the way.

Chief Crazy Horse led the Sioux in the 1870s. Incidentally, the Congress of that time had all but decided to abandon the western half of what was to become the United States of America because of the superior fighting ability of these and other Plains Indian warriors. The Chief Crazy Horse commemorative wears a barrel of 24 inches. Weight is about 6.75 pounds. Magazine capacity is seven rounds. Uniquely, it sports a series of brass tacks embedded in the buttstock and forestock. Brass tacks were of Indian design and could be found on trade muskets, plains rifles and other firearms used by the Plains Indians of untamed America.

The receiver, gold-filled, is engraved with a portrait and a buffalo-hunting scene. A medallion in the stock is in the logo of the United Sioux Tribes, and the names of all 11 tribes are engraved on the receiver in both Lakota Sioux and English. The barrel is inscribed "Chief Crazy Horse," and the buttplate is crescent-shaped (rifle style). For the first time in the Winchester commorative series, a

The Model 94 "Antlered Game" Commemorative.

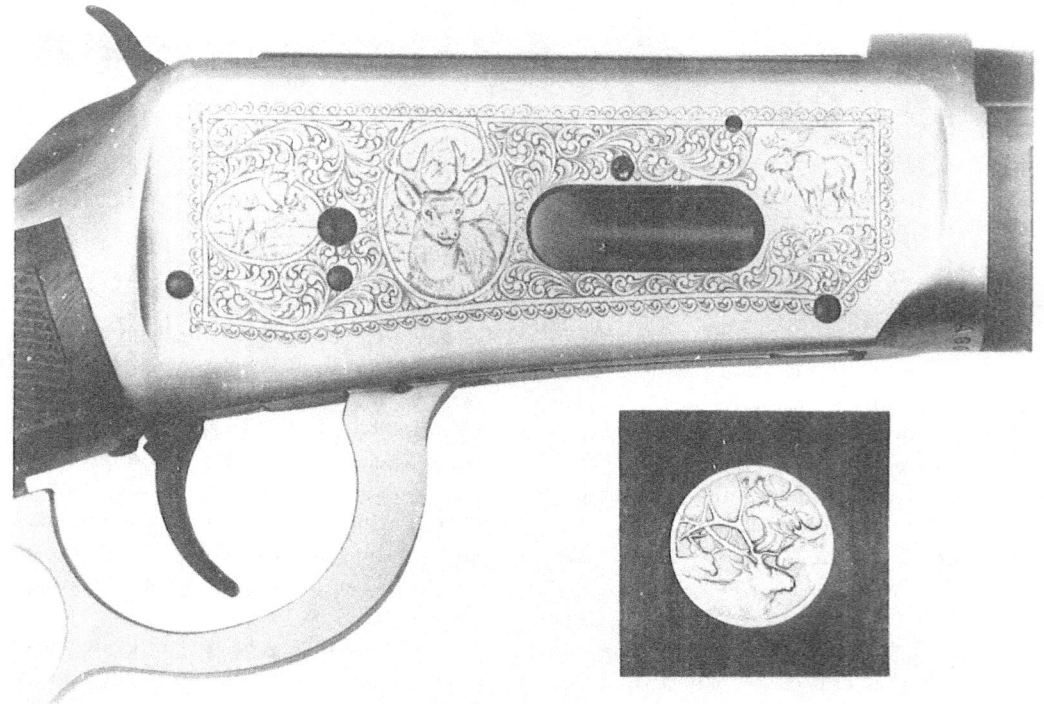

Close-up of Model 94 "Antlered Game" Commemorative.

case-hardened antique finish was used on forearm cap and receiver. Only 19,999 Chief Crazy Horse commemorative rifles were made, all consecutively numbered.

Antlered Game Model 94 Carbine

Although most of the 94s in commemorative style deal with American heroes or history, this 30-30 honors American antlered game—elk, moose, deer and caribou, the four species found on our continent and harvested with the Model 94 rifle and carbine for many years. The images of these four animals are engraved on the receiver of the rifle, which has a gold-plated finish with the antique look.

The metal finish of this rifle is satin-blue. The wood is semi-fancy walnut featuring fine cut checkering. Embedded in the buttstock is a gold-colored medallion showing in bas relief an elk, a moose, a deer and a caribou. The words "Antlered Game" are inscribed in gold-colored letters deeply into the blued and polished 20-inch barrel. The finger lever is gold-plated, as are the tang and twin barrel bands, which match the receiver. Again, the run was just 19,999 units.

Commemorative 94s

John Wayne Commemorative.

John Wayne Commemorative Model 94

Following the passing of the famous movie actor, United States Repeating Arms Company brought out this little carbine. It is the Model 94 Winchester, and it wears the 20-inch carbine barrel. In the right buttstock is embedded a medallion bearing the likeness and name of John Wayne, and the words "John Wayne Commemorative" appear on the barrel near the open rear sight.

A rifle-style, curved buttplate is used, and the barrel band up front is placed forward of the front sight, which is the same style used on the very early Model 94 carbines. The John Wayne Commemorative comes with a hoop-style finger lever (just like the Rifleman's on TV), and it is chambered for 32-40 caliber. Special collector's ammo was available in 32-40 for this model. By the way, the 32-40 is another original blackpowder round found in the lineup way back in the late 19th century.

The receiver of this rifle is engraved. A mounted horseman adorns the right-hand side of the receiver toward the hammer, along with another rider and some cattle. Scrollwork adorns the edges of the scene. John Wayne used a Model 94 Winchester in many of his movies, and even those moviegoers and TV watchers who are not shooters no doubt recognize the rifle.

Winchester-Colt Commemorative Set

This beautiful offering is one part of a two-part set that includes a Colt Peacemaker and a Winchester Model 94, both

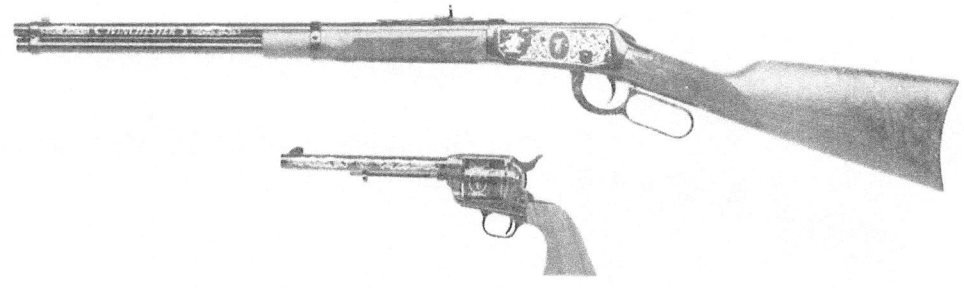
Winchester-Colt Commemorative Set.

chambered in caliber 44-40, another old-time blackpowder round which has lived into the present day in smokeless form. A total of only 4,440 sets (44-40 influence) were made, the serial numbers running from 1WC through 4440WC.

The Colt Peacemaker is the single-action Army revolver famous in the West. The backstrap bears the signature of "Col Sam Colt" as copied from his own hand, this in engraved gold. A "WC" monogram is etched into the left side of the cylinder. The left side of the barrel bears the words "Serpentine Colt." The right side of the cylinder is emblazoned with the Rampant Colt trademark. And the right side of the barrel is marked with the Colt horse. Scrollwork adorns the gun, and the frame is of case-hardened color. A rear sight is formed by a notch in the topstrap, and the barleycorn front sight is used.

The carbine wears the standard 20-inch barrel. The magazine holds 11 rounds. The famous Horse and Rider trademark is found on the left-hand side of the receiver, in gold, and so is the WC marking as on the Colt. Scrollwork is abundant on the receiver, both sides. On its right-hand side is a likeness of Oliver F. Winchester, founder of Winchester Arms.

The Winchester name appears on the barrel in the "lightning" style, along with ample scrollwork. The right-hand side of the barrel bears a detailed and impressive rendering of the original Winchester factory. An Oliver F. Winchester signature, in gold, adorns the tang of this Model 94. The crescent-shaped buttplate is used, and select-grade American walnut makes up forestock and buttstock. The wood is checkered. The metalwork bears a high-luster blue.

Winchester Legendary Frontiersman Model 94

Here is a fine-looking Model 94 Winchester in 38-55 caliber honoring the pioneers who opened the vast western half of the United States of America. This model was the first commemorative to be chambered in other than 30-30 Winchester caliber. The medallion embedded in the right buttstock depicts a buckskin-clad frontiersman in hand-to-hand combat with an American Indian. This medallion is of nickel-silver composition. Only 19,999 copies were made.

There were many other fine commemorative models. The first major production Winchester commemoratives were the Centennial 66s, actually, but they

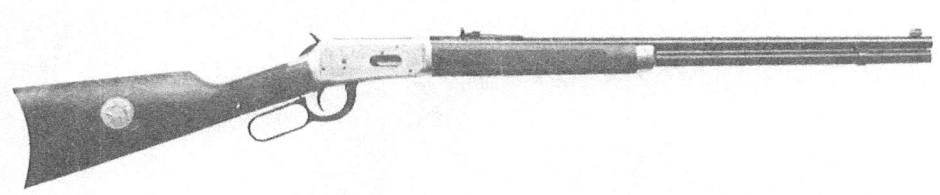

Legendary Frontiersman Commemorative Model 94.

Winchester Centennial Model 66 Carbine.

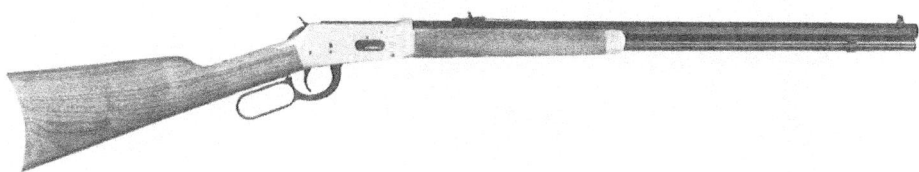

Winchester Centennial Model 66 Rifle.

Wells Fargo Commemorative.

were 30-30s, and the plural is used because a carbine and a rifle were offered to the shooting public. A Wells Fargo commemorative was offered in tribute to that agency of the Old West, and again it was the famous Model 94 in carbine form. The medallion, embedded in the right buttstock, depicted a stagecoach scene with "1852–1977" printed below the scene. The stock's wrist was checkered, as was the forearm. Typical barrel bands were used, but the foremost band is located behind the front sight, in more modern fashion.

The right-hand receiver shows a scene of a typical western town, as well as "W.F. & CO.," plus scroll, plus "1852" on one side and "1977" on the other. A non-

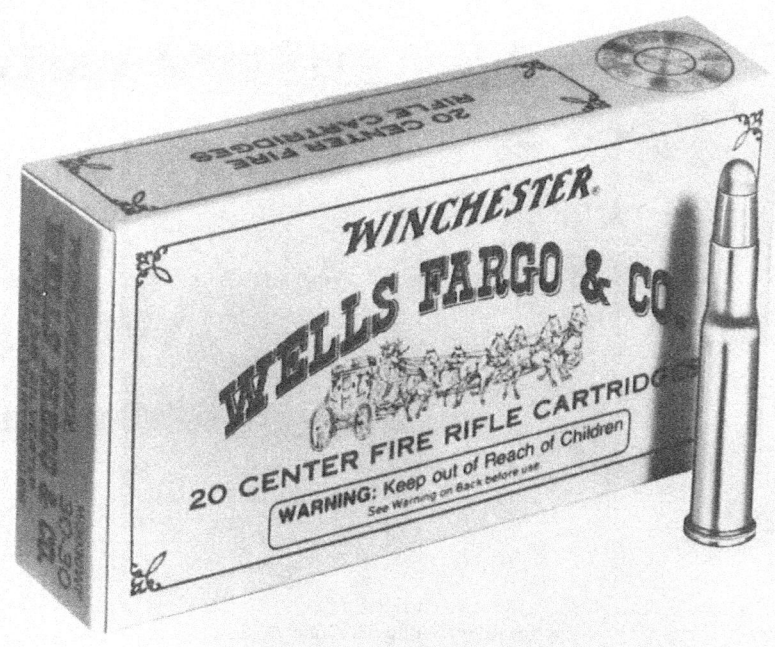

Wells Fargo ammo.

hooded front sight (post) is traditional on this model, and the open rear sight is semi-buckhorn with the usual elevator bar. One unique addition to this commemorative is specially boxed ammunition to go with it. This ammo was in the standard 20-round box, but it said "Wells Fargo & CO" on the face of the box. The rounds were 150-grain Silvertips.

There was the Oliver F. Winchester model, a Model 94 rifle without barrel bands, in 38-55 caliber. The scrolled receiver bore the lettering "W.R.A.," Winchester Repeating Arms, as well as a rifleman making an offhand shot and other figures. There was also an American Bald Eagle Commemorative, a Winchester Model 94 in the Big Bore model, caliber 375 Winchester. This carbine with 20-inch barrel commemorated the bald ea-

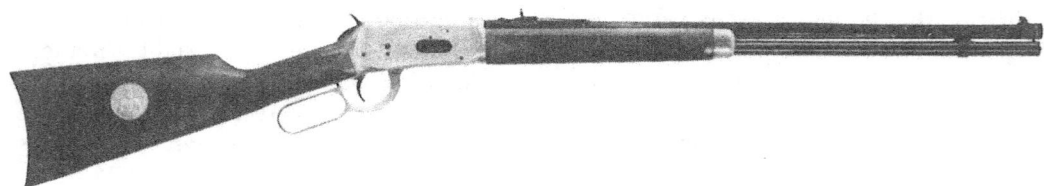

Oliver F. Winchester Commemorative.

Commemorative 94s

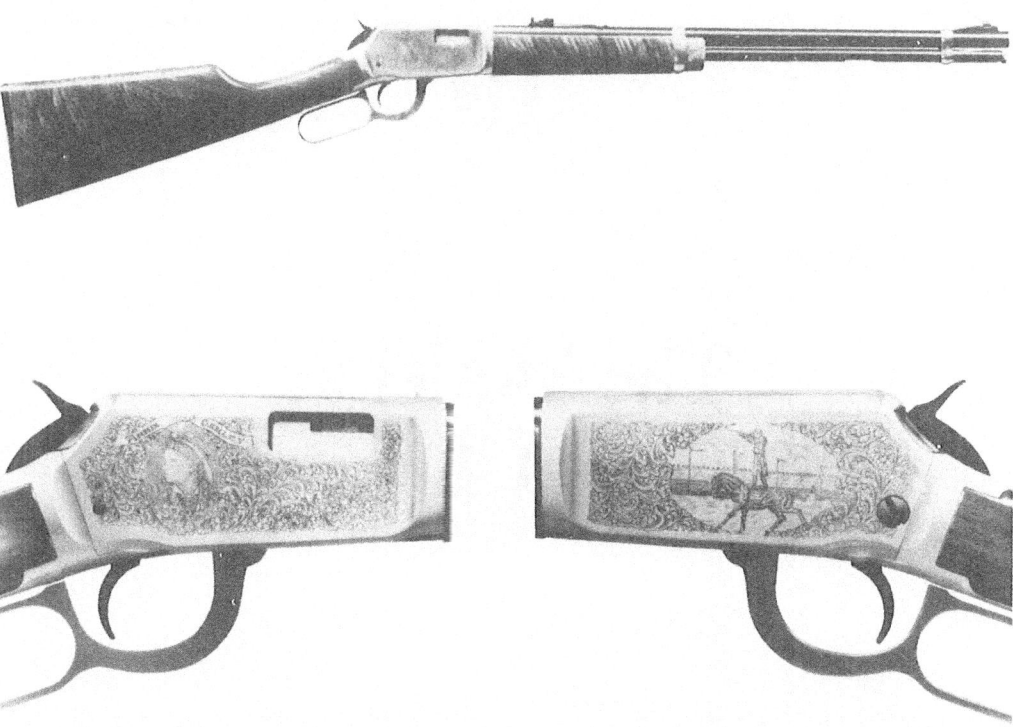

Annie Oakley Commemorative Model 9422.

gle's 200 years as America's symbol. Only 3000 units were made.

We also have the Bicentennial Carbine 76 commemorative, caliber 30-30, Model 94, and the Annie Oakley Commemorative, which was not a Model 94 but rather its little brother, the Model 9422 XTR in take-down form. Annie Oakley, the famous shooter who was so popular in the Buffalo Bill Wild West Show, was known for her remarkable shooting talents. This decorative rifle has gold receiver, gold barrel bands and gold finger lever. These antique gold-plated features and the roll-engraved receiver make the little rifle stand out. Only 6,000 were made.

The Model 94 Winchester's fame is further etched into the scene of American shooting by its many commemorative models, most of them in 30-30 caliber. Collectors all over the world have added these rifles to their holdings. Most of them will not be fired. They will simply be kept and admired, for they make note of some unique event or personage in this country's history.

19

The Model 94 Today and Tomorrow

The top eject Model 94 is yesterday. The Angle-Eject Model 94 is both today and tomorrow. However, when you have five million of anything around, it's highly unlikely that the old will be totally eclipsed by the new for a very long time to come. A great many down-to-earth, skilled hunters are still going to grab their old-style 94s when it comes time to put venison in the pot, and they'll drop those deer with the same round they've been using for years, the 30-30 Winchester.

The recent goal of the manufacturers of the Winchester Model 94 has been to leave its character intact—why tamper too much with a winner?—while at the same time changing the model internally so that it does a few things better than the older 94. The United States Repeating Arms Company has managed to do this. The current Model 94s still handle well, are built very well of the best materials available and yet bear a couple of features which, technically speaking, go ahead of the older 94.

Today's 94 is an Angle-Eject, not only in name but also in function. The cases whiz off to the side instead of straight up in the air. The only major benefit is that this arrangement accommodates scope-mounting, but it can be quite a plus factor for the hunter who desires the compactness of the 94 but also wants the superior aiming qualities of a scope sight. What's more, the scope mounts *low* on the new 94, very low, meaning the rifle is fast and the stock need not be given a super high comb.

The other modern feature of the new 94 involves the strength of the action. My own tests showed me right away that the newer 94s were stronger of action than

The Model 94 Today and Tomorrow

The Model 94 of today is the Angle-Eject. It tosses the spent case out to the side, not straight up, as did the original 94.

the older ones. I have learned since that the Angle-Eject and Big Bore Model 94s are supposed to be operable in the 50,000-psi (pounds per square inch) range. The older 94s were more at home in the 38,000- to 40,000-psi domain. This has changed the Model 94 in one big way—now it will handle more powerful rounds. Part of this chapter will deal with those cartridges.

A somewhat better trigger pull is another feature of the new Model 94. The pull seems a bit crisper to me, compared with that of a factory model from bygone days. There is also a rebounding hammer, so half-cock notches are a thing of the past. The safety features of the new 94 differ slightly from the older models, although I found the old-style 94 to be a very safe firearm. Of course, shooter responsibility is always the big factor in safety.

The standard Model 94 Winchester of today looks very much like the original 94 of 1895. The new Angle-Eject Carbine has the familiar straight-grip stock, the hooded front sight, the forward barrel band behind the front sight, a standard rear sight with elevator bar and an exposed hammer. There is a slice of metal missing at the ejection port, however, which quickly shows that this little full-magazine 94 is the Angle-Eject. There are many other minor differences, and a 94 fan can spot a pre-1964 94, a post-1964 94 and a new Angle-Eject from about 40 paces.

There is also a Model 94 Angle-Eject

Here is the Model 94 Angle-Eject in the Trapper model, a 16-inch barrel being its strong point. It's a good one for close-in shooting.

The Wrangler II is another Angle-Eject 16-inch-barrel Model 94.

Trapper model which wears a full tubular magazine, but that magazine rests under a barrel a mere 16 inches long. The Model 94 Wrangler II Angle-Eject also wears a 16-inch barrel, and it has the over-sized hoop-style finger lever. The 94 XTR Angle-Eject Rifle differs from the carbine in barrel length, obviously, but also in caliber, for this 24-inch rifle is chambered for the 7-30 Waters round. Also, it's a rifle in respect to the barrel bands—there is only one, at the fore-end; no barrel band exists near the front sight as on the carbine.

The Winchester Angle-Eject in the Big Bore model is a horse of a slightly different hue. This outfit has the heavy receiver, beefed up at the rear. And it's chambered for the more powerful rounds now available in the Model 94 Winchester. This is a carbine, for the barrel length is 20 inches. In an attempt to raise the comb of the stock a little, the Big Bore now wears a Monte Carlo stock, which

The Big Bore is distinguished by its heavy receiver. Note standard open sight. Calibers such as the 307 Winchester, 356 Winchester and 375 Winchester make this model a fairly powerful one, though author's 30-30 handloads are quite close to the 307 Winchester in punch.

The Model 94 Today and Tomorrow

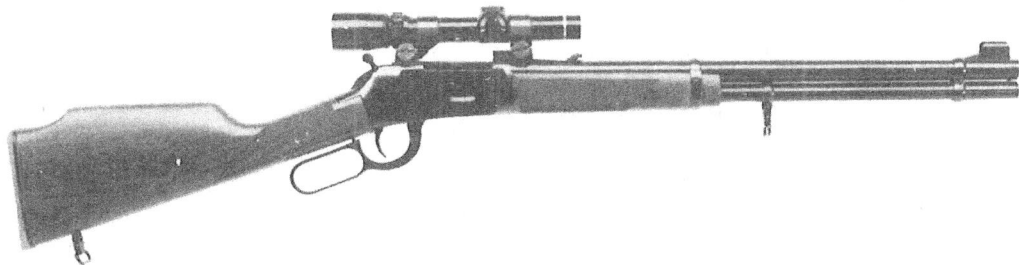

The big difference in today's Angle-Eject over yesterday's top-eject is the low-mounting of a scope sight. Cases kick out to the side, allowing normal scope use. Author does not care for Monte-Carlo type stock, especially on a "cowboy gun."

fits its overall appearance about like a sunbonnet fits a heavyweight boxer. I've fired this rifle, however, and the recoil is fairly straight-line, and you can see into the scope sight well from this comb height. I just wish that USRA had gone to the higher comb without the useless Monte Carlo cutaway at the heel of the stock.

The Big Bore is a hunting instrument right down to its sling swivels, which are pre-attached at the factory. The Big Bore wears a recoil pad as standard equipment. The low mounting of the scope here, plus a sling, plus the heavier rounds, put the Model 94 Winchester of today quite easily into the realm of larger-than-deer game. There is no doubt that a big 7mm Magnum in a bolt-action rifle would still be ahead of the 94 for elk in long-range shooting; however, under most elk-hunting circumstances this wouldn't be true. Up close, even out to 150 yards or so, the 94 in 356 Winchester will surely handle an elk about as well as a 7mm Magnum.

To summarize, the new Model 94 is a standard carbine which is meant to do the work always expected of the lever-action, fast-action rifle, or carbine if you must. It is chambered up in the famous 30-30 round, which is still a fine deer

The 356 Winchester, right, is compared with a 30-30 Winchester.

number, and also 44 Remington Magnum. More on the calibers in a moment. The little Trapper Model 94 or Model 94 Wrangler II, both with 16-inch barrels, will be the brushmasters, fast as a rattler and totally reliable. The little Trapper is available in 30-30 caliber and also in 45 Colt, while the Wrangler is outfitted in the 38-55 round for use of a heavier bullet up close.

Then there is a longer-barreled Model 94 in the 7-30 Waters round. This is a sleek, light rifle, very reminiscent of the original Model 94 rifles. Its 24-inch barrel is extremely slim, and in fact the magazine tube is slightly larger in diameter than the barrel on the 7-30 model. I should also point out that with the standard Model 94 Winchester there is a sister XTR version, in 30-30 only as this is written, and with finer wood, checkering and other minor cosmetic additions.

The Big Bore is the heavy-duty member of the 94 team. Obviously, it's the calibers which make it so, for it comes in 307 Winchester, 356 Winchester and 375 Winchester. I hasten to point out that these offerings are current as this book is composed; additions and deletions are always possible with the Model 94 and any other firearm.

Perhaps more important to the modern Model 94 enthusiast are the rounds for it. Here, too, some changes are probably in store for the future. For example, as good as the 38-55 round is, I wonder if Model 94 fans will take to it. They used to love the 38-55 back in "the old days," but even then the 30-30 sounded its death knell. Only the huge number of 38-55s around kept the ammo production going after the 30-30 had rung the bell on it. Years went by without a 38-55 rifle produced at all. Here is a rundown on the rounds now chambered up in Model 94s.

30-30 Winchester

We are not going to talk much about this one since it's a major topic of this work. Let it suffice to say that the 30-30 is far from dead; it isn't even a little sick. It doesn't have a chance of dropping by the wayside in the next few decades. It still works and works well, and is still just right for modest-range deer hunting, in spite of the hotshot rounds which are standing in the wings waiting to take over center stage. While some folks chat idly about the archaic 30-30, the boys who make ammo for the round keep right on doing so, and improving it where they can.

Very recently, for example, Federal brought out a Premium load for the 30-30. It's the already-mentioned 170-grain Nosler Partition bullet at standard 30-30 velocities. The term Premium, though a trademark of Federal, is also a very honest statement about the ammo. It is premium fodder. Winchester still has the famous and excellent Silvertip bullet loaded up for the 30-30, and Remington has its fine Core-Lokt in both soft-point and hollow-point designs, while the Hornady Company offers its Interlock bullet in Frontier factory form. The 30-30 round is still viable.

44 Remington Magnum

I have nothing at all against the 44 Remington Magnum round. It's my favorite big-bore handgun number, in fact, and for close work on deer-sized game it proves itself powerful and adequate. That it will whip the 30-30, even from the long barrel, is false, however. Choose the 44 Magnum for two reasons. First, the round is short. The Model 94 lever-action Carbine with a 20-inch barrel will hold

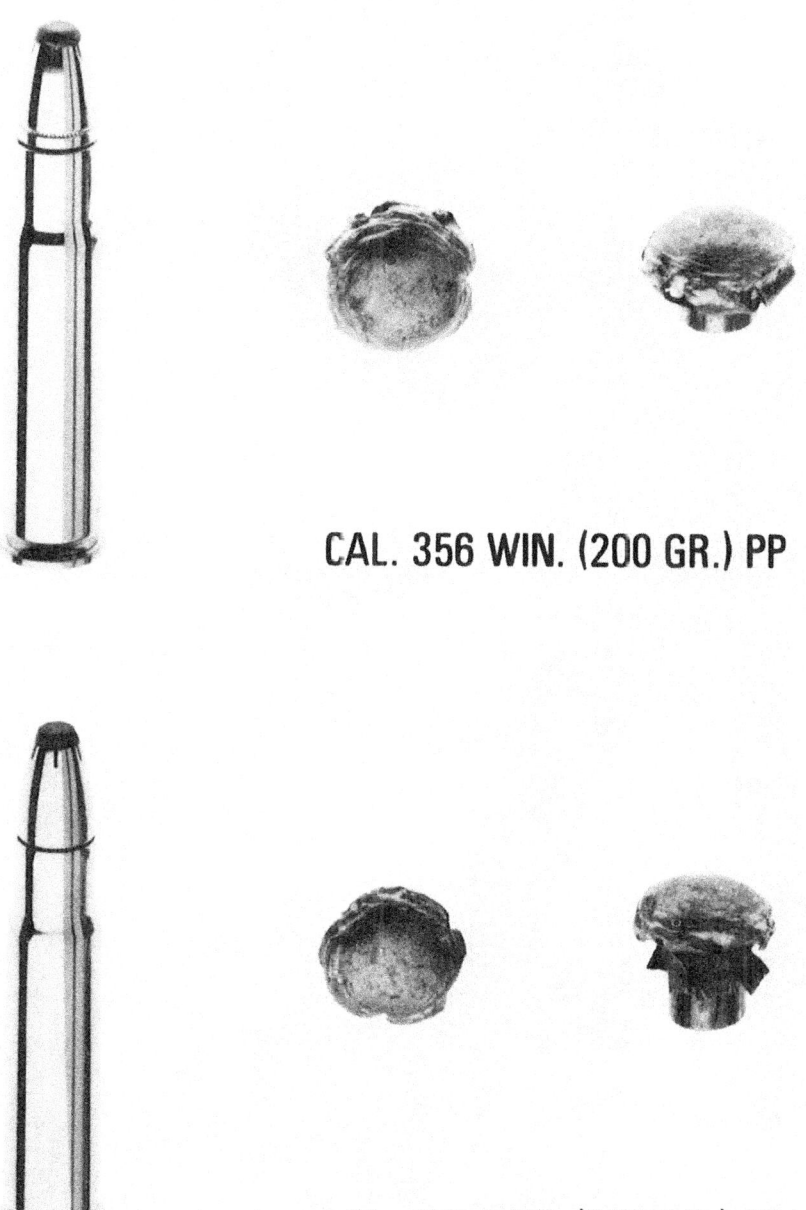

The 356 Winchester is a powerhouse round chambered in the new Big Bore Model 94.

Author shoots the sleek Model 94 7-30 Waters rifle. Note slim lines, 24-inch barrel.

11 44 Magnum rounds in the magazine. That's lots of shooting at one loading. The second point favoring the 44 Magnum is that it will also use a 44 S&W Special round, giving the chambering a bit more versatility, for this load is milder than the 44 Magnum. Ammo for the 44 Magnum is very good, and muzzle energy is high, but the 30-30's is higher.

45 Colt

This round is reserved for the 16-inch-barrel Model 94, and it has a place. Again, I don't know if the buyer will take to the 45 Colt as a chambering in the Model 94 Winchester, but it is a very nice round for deer and wild boar and such at *close* range. Is it better than the 44 Magnum? No. Is it better than the 30-30? No. But the 45 Colt offers a very light-recoiling round for the close-range hunter, and it comes in a 16-inch-barreled, close-range rifle, so it fits the challenge well. Also, the owner of a 45 Colt-chambered revolver will have that often-sought advantage of being able to use the 45 Colt in both rifle and handgun.

7-30 Waters

This is a very interesting round. It is basically the 30-30 necked down to accept 7mm bullets, and it was created by the well-known ballistician and writer, Ken Waters. Ken wanted a light-kicking caliber for the Model 94, and the 7-30 Waters is just that. Is it more powerful than the 30-30 round? Not really. My own 30-30 handloads certainly surpass it, but that was never the point in the first place. The 307 Winchester is more powerful than the 30-30. Waters wasn't trying to beat the 30-30 in punch; he wanted a

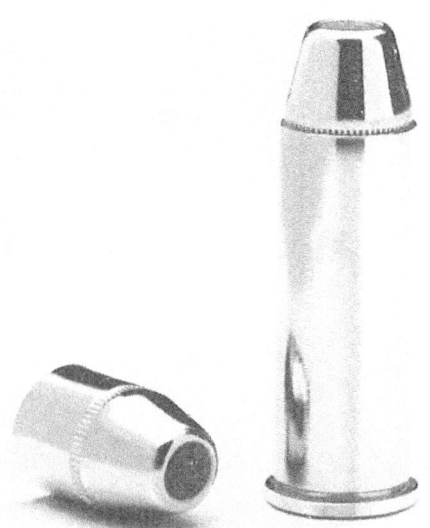

The Model 94 is chambered for the 44 Magnum round. This allows 44 Magnum handgun fans to use the same ammo in rifle and sidearm.

bit more flatness in trajectory and that nice light "kick."

The chart with this chapter shows the 7-30 Waters round as driving a 120-grain bullet at 2,700 feet per second muzzle velocity. Federal Cartridge Corporation factory-loads the 7-30 Waters with a 120-grain boat-tail bullet, soft-point. Incidentally, the round underwent some changes before it hit the street, and it's not simply a 30-30 necked down to 7mm. Its shoulder is thrust forward, and case capacity is a bit greater than its parent round. But does the 7-30 actually push the 120-grain bullet out at 2,700 feet per second? No. The bullet leaves the muzzle at 2,750 feet per second, over my own chronograph screens and according to Ken Waters' tests as well. So the 7-30 does what it was invented to do. It fires flat enough for 200-yard shooting, maybe a bit more, and it has adequate authority for deer-sized game with light recoil.

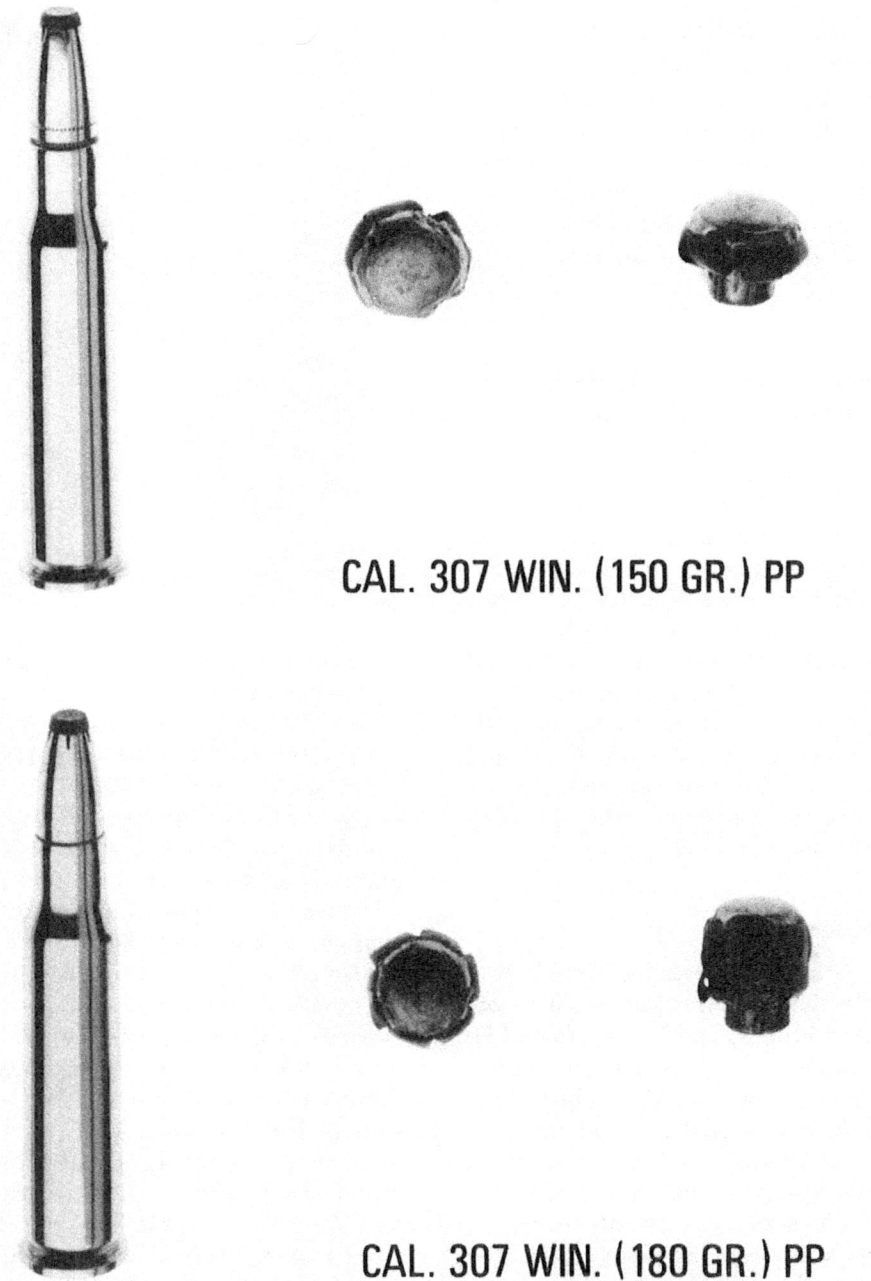

CAL. 307 WIN. (150 GR.) PP

CAL. 307 WIN. (180 GR.) PP

The 307 Winchester is very much like the 308 Winchester in muzzle velocity and energy, though the 308 does remain ahead of the 307 in all departments.

The Model 94 Today and Tomorrow

307 Winchester

The idea here was to produce a 308 Winchester cartridge suitable for the Model 94. Since the new Angle-Eject is said to be capable of handling 50,000-psi pressures, perhaps the 308 Winchester would have worked through the new action, but the engineers felt more comfortable with a round just a bit milder. The 307 will push a 180-grain bullet from a 20-inch barrel at 2,375 feet per second. Handloaders easily get about 2,400 fps. That's a good punch. Obviously, the shooter who has larger game in mind for his Model 94 would want to consider the 307 Winchester chambering, or the 356 or 375 rounds. A 150-grain bullet from the 307 Winchester leaves the muzzle at about 2,600 feet per second, same as my 30-30 Improved, from a 24-inch barrel.

356 Winchester

The goal with this one was a round very similar to the excellent 358 Winchester, but suited for the new Model 94 Angle-Eject action. A factory load with a 250-grain bullet earned a muzzle velocity of about 2,025 feet per second, but the current load listed is with the 200-grain bullet at about 2,350 feet per second. In my mind, a good strike on an animal the size of an elk at modest range with this 35 caliber 200-grain bullet would be meat in the larder. It's a strong cartridge, though behind the 358 Winchester.

375 Winchester

This 38 caliber cartridge is very much like the 38-55 round, but the case is stronger and the consequent muzzle velocity and energy are also better than with the 38-55 Winchester. This is a pow-

The 375 Winchester is a beefed-up 38-55 round. Here it is compared with the standard 30-30 Winchester on the right.

erful number up close, that's for sure. Its 200-grain bullet leaves the muzzle at about 2,100 feet per second, factory fodder, and the 250-grain bullet moves out at about 1,850 feet per second. With a bullet of good mass and large caliber, the 375 Winchester cartridge is plenty large enough for bigger-than-deer animals at close range.

Just for comparison purposes, a look at the 358 Winchester round is in order. From a 22-inch barrel, with a 200-grain bullet, a muzzle velocity of 2,500 feet per second was achieved. The same 358 out of the same barrel gained about 2,300 feet per second with a 250-grain bullet, so the 356 Winchester is not quite on par with the 358 round, but out of the little 94, the 356 makes a strong package—a combination of punch with ease of handling and ease of packing.

Today's Angle-Eject standard model with a scope sight.

All of the above data were taken from chronographed velocities. Factory figures will differ very slightly from these. However, for hunting purposes, the information listed below, courtesy of United States Repeating Arms (Winchester), is perfectly accurate. The differences are to be expected, as no two rifles produce identical velocities, and there are always minor variations in test machinery as well.

In 1983, USRA's lineup had the 444 Marlin round chambered in the Model 94 Angle-Eject carbine. The 1985 lineup did not show that round. What's the future for both the Model 94 and its calibers? There have certainly been some changes along the way from 1895 to 1985. The first two smokeless sporting cartridges offered to American shooters were the 30-30 and the 25-35. The 25-35 has been gracing the boneyard for quite some time

The Winchester Limited Edition II comes in 30-30 caliber.

The Model 94 Today and Tomorrow

now, though ammo can still be purchased for it thanks to the large number of 94s previously made in that round. Of course, the 30-30 marches near the front of the band.

The 32 Winchester Special saw a chambering in a Model 94 Wrangler with its 16-inch barrel, but the 32 Winchester Special is not a hot number these days and is highly unlikely to turn the heads of shooters in the future. It's a decent round—certainly a 30-30 factory-wise. But it does nothing that the 30-30 won't do as well. I like the 7-30 Waters very much. It's a light-kicker, plenty accurate in its handsome 24-inch-barrel Model 94 rifle, and it will do well on deer at modest range. Federal Cartridge Company has been pleased with 7-30 Waters sales. Will it put the skids under the 30-30? I doubt it. A 30-30 in the woods on deer is so good that its reputation will carry it along for at least a while longer, in spite of the excellent 7-30 round.

What about the 375 Winchester round? I loaded up a batch of 375 Winchester cases using the fine 220-grain Hornady bullet, and I truly like this short-range buster. Will it outdo the 356 Winchester, however? Let's take a look. With a 200-grain bullet, the 375 Winchester at a starting velocity of about 2,100 feet per second earns a muzzle energy of 1,959 foot-pounds. The 356

This fancy Wrangler comes in 38-55 caliber.

Ballistics

Comparison of Winchester Model 94 Cartridges

Caliber	Barrel Length Inches	Bullet Wt. Grs.	Velocity In Feet Per Second			Energy In Foot Pounds			Height Of Trajectory (Inches)*		
			Muzzle	100	200	Muzzle	100	200	50 Yds.	100 Yds.	200 Yds.
7-30 Waters	24	120	2700	2300	1930	1940	1405	990	+0.1	0	−7.3
30-30 Win.	20	125	2510	2030	1600	1747	1142	709	+0.2	0	−9.2
30-30 Win.	20	150	2330	1960	1620	1806	1278	873	+0.2	0	−9.8
30-30 Win.	20	170	2160	1860	1580	1759	1305	941	+0.3	0	−10.3
307 Win.	20	150	2680	2249	1860	2393	1685	1153	+0.3	0	−6.1
356 Win.	20	200	2400	2058	1747	2559	1881	1356	+0.4	0	−7.4
375 Win.	20	250	1870	1620	1401	1942	1457	1090	+0.7	0	−9.9
44 Rem. Mag.	20	240	1760	1362	1094	1650	988	638	Not Applicable		
45 Colt	16	255	1000	887	807	566	446	369	Not Applicable		

*0 = Line of sight. All values calculated by computer.

Courtesy of USRA (Winchester)

Author's note:
My own 30-30 custom with 24-inch barrel gains 2,600 fps MV with a 150-grain bullet when using 37.0 grains to 37.5 grains of H-335 rifle powder. This data, given for comparison, is especially interesting when matched with data for the factory 307 Winchester Remember, however, that this velocity is from a 24-inch barrel, while the 307 muzzle velocity is from a 20-inch barrel.

Winchester pushes its 200-grain bullet at about 2,350 feet per second for a muzzle energy of 2,453 foot-pounds. Handload a 220-grain Hornady bullet in the 375 Winchester, and you can get 2,200 feet per second for a muzzle energy of 2,335 foot-pounds.

Since both rounds are for comparatively close-range shooting, I see little difference between them in terms of actual harvesting of big game. The 200-grain 35 caliber bullet has a better sectional density than the 200-grain 38 caliber bullet, so carry-up would be in favor of the former. Penetration might be, too, to some degree. If I had a 375 Winchester, I'd keep it. If I were just buying a big-bore Model 94 and choosing between the 356 and the 375, I would probably go with the 356, but the race would be a near photo finish.

Quite a few gun gurus have seen in their crystal balls the death of the Model 94 Winchester, but the view has always been pretty clouded. These fellows forget that the deer hunter has done a pretty good job with the handy Model 94 for a long time and he intends to hang onto it until shown a much better way to go.

Calibers? There is no doubt in my mind that the 307 Winchester round is better than the 30-30 in ballistic punch. The question is one of need. For my purposes, using the Model 94, the 30-30 will suffice almost all the time. If I decide to shoot farther than I do now, or if my hunting with the Model 94 takes in regular elk and moose forays, I'll go with the 307 load or the 356.

Economy still plays a part in Model 94 sales, and USRA knows this. The introduction of a Ranger Model 94 in 30-30 proves it. This one is a standard 94 indeed, quite serviceable and made of top-rated materials, but it costs less than the other 94s. At this time it is offered in 30-30 caliber.

If I had a crystal ball, I imagine my picture would be as hazy as a rainy day at the seashore. But I'll take a guess that the 94 will stay around for a long while yet, and a number of 30-30s will be sold. It hardly matters. Five million 94s, most of them 30-30s, will not fade into oblivion before the setting of the sun.

20

A Year of Modern Hunting with My 94

The soft glow of the lantern looked like a distant lighthouse beacon in a dark sea. Two hours before midnight, my shoulders sagging under the weight of the boned venison on my packframe, I looked down upon my campsite. Before leaving camp in the pre-light of dawn, I had struck a bargain with my partner. He had to return to town at midday. "Would you flick the Quiklite lantern on?" I asked him. "And just set it about as low as it'll go. The fuel cartridge is new. It'll last until I get back tonight."

I knew what I was in for. The deer were hanging in the dense cover by day, venturing out to feed only in late afternoon. If I wanted a buck, the best way was to get up into the higher country and stick it out until dusk.

I unshouldered the load and moved the meat into a spot that would be hidden from the first rays of morning sun. And then I lit the fire sticks which I had built into a teepee. The little flat receiver of the 30-30 mirrored the long, yellow fingers of fire that seemed to reach up into the darkness. Then I plunked down on a heavy horsehide blanket to wait for coals as the oak fire grew. The heat began to search through the fibers of my hunting coat, and it felt good.

Presently, I snaked some hot coals from the fire and made my dinner. The main course was thick-sliced venison loin with Lemon & Pepper condiment, fried quickly in hot bacon fat. I heated homemade flour tortillas over the coals, and perked a pot of coffee as well. The fresh venison was good. The day's hunt had been good, and the harvest swift. I had spotted the buck as it fed below a rimrock cliff, my binoculars revealing a piece of grass-covered earth there which failed to camouflage the animal. All I had to do was keep the wind in my favor and stay to the high ground. One 170-grain Core-Lokt bullet in the shoulder blades took the buck.

I had elected to spend 1984 with the Model 94 Winchester 30-30 as my exclusive hunting tool. The season of 1983 had brought the decision. It was a good season, and I took some nice game with a muzzleloader and a few good heads with a fast-stepping, modern, bolt-action, scope-sighted rifle, hunting three states. Only two game animals had fallen to my old 1894 rifle, both antelope — one a buck, the other a doe.

"Next year," I said, "I'm going to hunt with my old cowboy rifles." I had three 30-30s in hand, and I intended to use them. I also intended to coax a couple members of my hunting family into using a 30-30, too, for at least one or two harvests. And that is what happened. Nineteen-Eighty-Four with the 1894 would be for real.

The 94 Meets a Pronghorn

The entire country presented itself to me as if it were an optical illusion. Badlands, some call it. The earth is parched in some places, and in others it is just plain dry as a wad of sunbaked cotton. White rocks form miniature cliffs in some places. The murky little ponds here and there in this terrain offer temporary resting places to many ducks and some geese during the year. And it's not impossible to find a few cottontail rabbits here and there, wonderful white-meat edibles. Sage hens that look like little turkeys abound in some parts of the region.

A few mule deer live here, too. And badgers and coyotes and bobcats. And the pronghorn antelope. Furthering the illusion of a lifeless terrain, the vegetation appears to be less succulent than it might be for forage. But it is this vast sagebrush domain which allows the antelope to thrive in high windswept places approaching and even surpassing 7,000 feet above sea level. It is the sagebrush — and there are many kinds, some as high as your head — which gives the antelope a staple diet, even in winter, for sagebrush is superb winter food, not only for pronghorns but also for deer, elk, moose and other game.

I was carrying the Storey Conversion. It was loaded with only two rounds. Both were in the magazine. Both were 150-grain Speer Mag-Tip bullets pushed by 37.5 grains of H-335 for nearly 2,600-feet-per-second muzzle velocity out of the 24-inch barrel of the custom 30-30 Improved. Around my neck were my favorite binoculars, the superior 8x42 Bausch & Lomb Elites, and they were the real hunter's eyes on this trip. With them I located herds of pronghorns so far off that they were otherwise invisible in the mirage rising from the plains. I found the herds and then got close enough to inspect the group for that special antelope buck I wanted, a buck which might go 15 inches, maybe more, with enough horn massiveness to make him a trophy.

When I was near the vehicle, my spotting scope was also used to help judge heads. But I spent a lot of time on foot here, in a place between two major roads. There were several linear miles and hundreds of square miles of broken terrain between these two roads, terrain seldom entered by humans, for few antelope chasers leave the trails to wander afoot in these little hidden pockets and dry washes.

I had enough gear along to stay overnight if I desired, but that was not in the game plan. The plan was simple. Hunt in the roadless area all day. Enjoy lunch out there. Look a lot. Walk a lot. Find a good buck. Stalk him and harvest the trophy with, I hoped, one shot from the 30-30. There was some challenge in that — a middle challenge, as I've called it, somewhere between the muzzleloader and the flat-shooting rifle.

Many bucks were located. Many were passed up. One was truly a fine specimen, but I couldn't get 30-30 close to him. My time had run out. On the last day of the hunt, I decided that anything in the 14-inch range would be good enough, and I found him. I was on the crest of a hill, searching with my binoculars, when I located a lone buck antelope, easily seen as a good one, but just as easily recognized as a 14-inch-class animal, not my ideal but certainly a harvest to be proud of.

I could get closer only by backtracking along the ridge and then sliding over to another ridge, which would put me above the feeding animal and, I hoped, within 30-30 range. I kept low as I approached the crest of the new hill. I had no spotting scope with me, but as I lay prone on the ridge, my binoculars showed me all I needed to see. He was indeed a buck in the 13½- to 14-inch range, and his was an interesting head — good cutters (prongs) and a curious-looking flatness to the horn beyond the prong. He was a good buck, a mature animal.

There really was no place for me to go from there. If I dropped down from the hill, I'd be as exposed as a newborn baby. If I tried to go down and around, I would have to show myself at the bottom of the hill on the flatlands. How far away was the buck? More than a decade of annual plains hunting in the area had schooled me to judge range fairly well, but nobody can be sure of exact distances on those deceptive prairies. Maybe 200 yards. Maybe 225 yards, not farther, I agreed with myself.

The fine-bead front sight seemed to fairly cover the chest area of the buck. I held right on. The prone position was good for glassing, but not for shooting, because it gave me a faceful of short grass and sagebrush. So I eased to a sitting position when the buck put his head down and away from me in order to feed. But he was slightly quartered away from me now. I squeezed the trigger and fired. Whack! There was plenty of steam left when the bullet got there, and I had my 1984 pronghorn buck with my 30-30.

Good luck perched on my shoulder all the way. Unknown to me, there was an old road in the bottom of the draw, a road I could not see from on high. Not only did I have a pretty good antelope, I also had a road on which to retrieve him. I patted the metal packframe as I set it down in order to get my cutlery kit out of the pack. "Not going to need you today," I said out loud, and the lazy part of me sighed in relief.

The same 30-30 was back on the plains a little later in the season. My brother Nick Fadala and his hunting partner Dennis Stogsdill had come to Wyoming to hunt. I had told them that I had a big surprise for them, a special rifle to share, and that they need not bring their own guns. They didn't. Actually, part of the surprise was mine, because when I showed them the fancy Model 94 they were going to use, a 30-30 Improved but loaded with standard 30-30 powder charges, they both got excited and said they'd rather use that rifle than a bolt-action job, at least for that season.

Dennis got his buck at less than 50 yards. One shot. He had a hill between himself and the animal, and it was no trick to use that hill for the approach. He popped over the hill, surprised the buck at close range and fired one shot at the running animal. The harvest was instantaneous. Dennis and Nick went on to take another buck and a couple of does each with additional antelope tags. And I had a very interesting harvest myself. Two of my three Wyoming antelope tags were filled — one additional tag remained.

An old doe antelope gave me a chase that actually proved more challenging than my buck had been. She slipped along a ridgeline, keeping a nice distance between us. I would close in, or so I thought, but when I poked my head over the rise, the animal would be a few hundred yards farther from me. At last I cut in front of her far enough ahead so that she might come to me. But she did not. Instead, the old gal turned at an angle and now stood on the edge of a flat plateau.

I sat and wrapped up in the carrying strap to get a steady stance. The $1/16$-inch bead covered a lot of the animal, for she was well over 200 yards away from me. But I had faith that the 150-grain bullet would do the trick. At the crack of the rifle, the gray old-timer disappeared. But I had heard the strike. No animal was ever harvested quicker than this one.

My son John also used the 30-30 that season, and so did my son Bill. We each had our three antelope tags — the buck tag and two "additionals" — and a couple of extra depredation permits as well. So

the 30-30 got a workout, and it performed supremely out of both the custom rifle and the old original rifle. Including our visitors' harvests, the 30-30s accounted for a dozen pronghorns in 1984. In 1985, the custom 30-30 would be at it again, too, back on the windy flats.

The 30-30 Meets a Mule Deer

The hardest person to convince was my wife. She had seen me take game cleanly with the 30-30 for a long time, but she wanted no part of a rifle that wore a lever and failed to wear a scope sight. "You go ahead and use that thing," she told me, "and I'll stick with my 6mm/222!" She did take her fine 6mm/222 Frank Wells rifle along, but she didn't get to use it.

"Wouldn't you like the extra challenge?" I coaxed. "We can get close. You won't have to shoot at over 100 yards." I meant what I said. Really, I did. But the best laid plans of mice and men. . . . Usually, Nancy is the first to find deer because she is so patient with binoculars. She finds them both bedded and feeding, and often very far away. When she and I are glassing for deer together, I get lazy because I have so much faith in her ability to locate buckskin with optics.

But I happened to spot these deer — three bucks in a bunch. Rut was still a couple of weeks away, but the bucks were in with a handful of does, and all were working around on a high ridge about 7,000 feet above sea level. We puffed up toward the animals, trying to stay out of sight, but the country was too open. They saw us. And they quickly climbed another big hill just like the one we had negotiated.

What took them a few moments to accomplish would take us quite a while, but one significant fact gave us hope. At the very top of the hill, the only mature buck in the group made a left-hand turn. There was a chance that this buck, maybe the entire herd, would move along the other side of that hill and we could cut 'em off. That's how it worked, too, but the herd had not stayed on the slope of the second hill. It had crossed over to another little hill, and the range was now close to 200 yards. The little 30-30 had done fine so far on 200-yard shots, I assured Nancy. Besides, it was loaded with a 165-grain bullet at about 2,400 feet per second from the 24-inch barrel.

Nancy is a very good shot, but she took the buck a bit far back and needed a second thump to put him away. However, true to every harvest that little rifle has made, the bullet penetrated fully, leaving an exit hole and doing plenty of damage to tissue. What a nice buck he was, too, with a mature though not outstanding rack — a four-pointer we'd call him in the West, an eight-pointer back East, four points to the side in other words.

The buck had been taken at the edge of the pine-tree forest of the high country, and I had to backpack it down to the vehicle below, after cutting the deer in half where loins meet ribs. I could not lift the entire animal by myself. We spent the remainder of that day packing the fine meat back to the rig. And I had an opportunity to get a buck for myself before the packing was finished, for Nancy, who is always glassing, found two bucks bedded on a high ridge. But I had my duty cut out for me, which was to get the meat home, so those bucks were left to grow even larger than they were. Lucky for them I didn't turn that little 30-30 loose because my confidence in that rifle had soared over the course of the season, topping off a feeling which had been growing for close to 30 years of hunting.

The 30-30 Meets a Whitetail

My buck tag remained open. I try to hunt in more than one state annually to increase my experiences, but my own state allows me two deer — a buck and an additional antlerless deer. My son John and I had our additional tags along in a place frequented by mule deer. We had studied the flats where we knew a good number of deer fed in late afternoon. We found a big mule deer doe all alone, and the stalk made for a rather easy shot. My additional deer tag was filled, I was sure, and the freezer would have more venison in it. The 30-30 had worked so admirably over the years on deer that I never even considered losing that doe, but when I walked to the spot where she had been standing, she was not there.

Nothing. No sign at all. I looked for a long while, as did my son, and finally it was John's willingness to walk right to the edge of a little river which saved the day. He found the big animal. It had run about 50 yards, which was about 50 yards farther than anything else did that fine season. I had loaded a hard 165-grain bullet, not my usual choice, and it was just too much in jacket thickness. It punched a 30 caliber hole going in and a 30 caliber hole going out. The heavy-jacketed bullet, from a company now defunct, would have been fine on larger game, but was wrong for the mule deer. I went back to the 165 Speer, 165 Hornady and other bullets after that experience. Thanks to my son, the deer was not lost and I had learned a lesson.

When the whitetail season opened, it found me along another riverbottom.

This time, a 170-grain Speer bullet was in use. The day was chameleon in nature, the color of the sky changing whimsically. Never have I seen the weather more fickle. One minute, clear heavens. The next minute, tiny ice particles whirled on a wind uncommon among the big trees of that bottomland. My time was limited, and I decided that my goal would be another 30-30 harvest, this one for meat only (I always put meat first, but I also have a definite interest in a good mature head).

Moving as silently as possible along a fast-running creek, I managed to close on a small buck and take him. Again, there was no bullet recovery—the bullet exited the target, as usual. The 170-grain Speer bullet had exhibited its usual performance—deep penetration with little loss in mass. Another surefire 30-30 harvest.

The 94 Meets a Javelina

The San Carlos Apache Indian Reservation in Arizona possesses some of the most interesting hunting terrain I have ever been privileged to enjoy. One of the leaders of the Reservation, Charles Aday, had told me that if I couldn't get a javelina there, I probably couldn't get one anywhere. I had taken a large number of these little peccaries in the past, several with a 30-30, but I wanted the little pigs to comprise another leg of my 1984 season, so I put my hat in the ring for the 1984 San Carlos Apache Reservation javelina (pronounced *have-ah-leena*) hunt.

The term javelina has become a part of the language of American hunters, but its derivation is Spanish, from a root word meaning spear or tusk. A more universal name for the little porker is peccary. He's

The 30-30 devotee puts the *hunt* back into his hunting. Here the author checks for sign during a javelina hunt.

not really a pig, but he's close enough that we simply refer to a chase for him as a "pig hunt." He's a little character, about 25 to 35 pounds dressed out and seldom over 50 pounds on the hoof, though much larger ones have been recorded from time to time.

The peccary is not the greatest challenge in the world, and some hunters look down their noses at him because he wouldn't make a bump on a big Russian boar of the forests. That is all right with me. I find the javelina interesting. He occupies some unique hunting terrain, and if he's so blasted easy to hunt, how come a 10 to 15 percent success rate is about all Arizona boasts annually on these little porkies?

The big secret to hunting pigs is finding them. And if that sounds redundant, so be it. It's true anyway. The javelina is small and close to the ground, and though he appears almost black against his environment, this slow-moving creature is anything but easy to see when he's a canyon away and three-fourths hidden by the vegetation he likes to eat, such as prickly pear cacti.

I own no stock in any optical company, so when I try to sell the reader, especially the 30-30 fan, on binoculars, it's only because I believe in them. And I firmly believe in getting the best ones you can afford. The glasses are valuable in much hunting, but I can attest to the fact that at least 75 percent of my javelina have been located with this optical aid.

The javelina is special, too, because the hunt is in the springtime. Without black bears, I'd have no big-game springtime hunt at all if it weren't for the peccary, and the blackie is quite a springtime challenge without dogs and horses. So is the little hog, but a foothunter can do all right if he goes where there are sufficient numbers of these fellows, and if he looks for them harder than he'd search for a priceless pearl dropped into a haystack.

The wonderful Indian Reservation is much more than the interesting San Carlos Lake, which blesses the land there. But a hunter does have to apply himself in order to get into the truly exciting areas. The roads are numbered, and a pretty good reservation map is available. That's how we got around the place without getting lost. That's also how we found the better areas.

But it isn't how we found the javelina. I like to think I'm a reasonably good peccary hunter. I try to find 'em with my glasses, and I look where they ought to be, where the food is. Prior to a pig hunt, or during the first few hours of the hunt if I cannot pre-scout, I'll look for javelina food. The sure way to a pig harvest is through his stomach. And it is easy to spot javelina chewings. The porkers are not dainty eaters.

You'll see neat little bites taken from prickly pear pads, looking like a child's unfinished apple. Sometimes the pigs dig for wild onions, tubers which grow in javelina habitat, and the result is pockmarked ground that looks like a series of miniature bomb craters. The javelina also eat *agave*-type plants, and the cactus leaves are often scattered about. In short, spotting a javelina supermarket is not too difficult.

But I found something else that led me to my 1984 hog. Water. My partner and I located a little waterhole, and everywhere around that cool oasis in the high desert were the telltale tracks of *el coche*, as the people of Mexico sometimes call the peccary. These little heart-shaped tracks are quickly recognized for what they are, because they are too small and shaped wrong to be deer tracks.

I also found javelina scat about 50 yards from the waterhole. I'm told that the wild peccary will not soil his immediate bedding area. Maybe so. I've never found scat in their bedding grounds. With this sign to go on, we decided to expand our search, using the waterhole as a focal point for our wanderings. The immediate area was loaded with the food the pigs like best.

An afternoon later, we were back near the waterhole, about 300 yards from it, when I spotted a dark form in the brush. This time, one of the few such occur-

Javelina are not hard to hunt, some say, but if so, why are the success ratios for hunters so low? The little pigs are small, their environment is large and so they are hard to locate. The author uses binoculars as his main hunting tool for peccaries.

rences in my pig hunting, my naked eye spotted the hog before my binoculared eye found 'em. The pig did not look like a pig when I first saw him — which convinced me he was a pig. Often, I've seen burned-out *sotos* in the distance and deemed them worthy of stalking because I *knew* those round, black cacti were hogs. It's a humbling experience to discover your error.

But here indeed was a hog, motionless — they love to do that, just stand there without moving a hair on their bristly little bodies. He waited. I waited. And then I knew the truth — it was a hog, all right, but only about half grown. When you see one pig, there are almost surely more of the same around. I waited, and a larger one did indeed materialize from the brush.

I was well above the hog. He stopped, his Mr. Magoo eyes searching around for whatever it was that bothered him, and I had time to plant a single 150-grain Speer Mag-Tip bullet into the shoulder area. That was that. The hog did not twitch once. Another clean harvest for the 30-30. This time I thought I might find a bullet. No, the hog did not stop the bullet, but from the angle of the shot, I figured I could dig it up. No luck. Hardpan earth either hid the hole or had forced the bullet to skid away.

I think the 30-30 is just right for javelina. They are generally a close-range game animal. They can be stalked. Sure, get the wind wrong and the herd can take off as if the animals had been scorched with a blowtorch. But when the wind is in your favor, you can slip in very close for a clean and quick dispatch.

Springtime in the Southwest is generally a very beautiful time, and a time of good weather, though I must admit that I have been snowed on during javelina hunts. The porkers are up early, and they like to forage about much of the day. They run in bands, so they can definitely be spotted if the hunter will take to the seat of his pants, get the glasses steady and then search, not just gaze, for the quarry. Look for sign. And stay with it. Even where sign is abundant, the smallish peccary can be hard to locate.

The 30-30 and the Gobbler

I found out that it was legal to hunt with a full metal jacket bullet where I wanted to take a wild turkey gobbler, so I went to my loading bench and cranked up the RCBS press, putting out a few rounds which carried a 110-grain, round-nose, full metal jacket bullet backed up by a mere 16.0 grains of No. MP5744 Accurate Powder from the Accurate Arms Company.

The wild turkey is not intelligent, but he might as well be. He's harder to hunt than deer in many locales, but in fact a turkey's brain is tiny — the term birdbrain arose from the fact that avians, including Ben Franklin's favorite, the wild turkey, are not smart enough to go to college or hold public office. They evade hunters, though, because, first of all, they are small for their habitat. A wild turkey in the woods and riverbottoms where I hunt is proportionally about like a grain of sand on the beach. He is swallowed up in the vastness of it all. Furthermore, though a wild turkey won't outsmart us, he will "out-instinct" us. He simply has it all going for him. If he sees, hears or perhaps smells anything which does not fit into his normal routine picture, his instinct tells him to beat it out of there.

I know the bird can see and hear wonderfully. I doubt that sense of smell does much for him, but I stand to be corrected on this. So the hunter of the wild turkey has simply got to keep quiet, and he'd better not show himself if he wants to get close to that bird. Calling can bring a turkey gobbler in, and this tactic allows the hunter to hunker down, remain still and thereby also remain invisible to the bird.

I've also located the birds with binoculars, then stalked so that, in the last phase of the chase, the flock came to me instead of my continuing to head for the flock. That's how I got my 30-30 bird in '84. The spring hunt was under way. The gobblers were gobbling and the hens were answering, but the toms were not foolish enough to come in to my calls—which must have sounded like a ruptured rooster to them, for at one point I saw a big tom making haste to depart the county after I scraped on my slate with the chalk. I thought it sounded very romantic, but the turkey must have heard it otherwise.

Then I got up on a ridge, one of my favorite ways to hunt turkeys in the riverbottoms. The glasses went to work, optically weeding through bits of country below like a mama monkey grooming its baby. The flock I saw may have consisted of 20 birds. I really couldn't count its members. But I could see where it was going. The group was heading right along the creek, pecking around and being so noisy that when I did stalk the birds I could hear them long before I could see them.

The wind was all wrong, so if wild turkeys do use their olfactory ability to detect hunters, these birds did a poor job of it. I used a fallen log as a hideout. I pulled my hat down low so my eyes would not give me away in case a bird looked in my direction. I'm sure birds did see me, but I think all they saw was a lump—my hat—on top of a log with a twig—the gun barrel—sticking out from the lump.

Then, there he was. Twenty yards. I shot for the pinion area, where wings join body because I wasn't brave enough to go for the head. Actually, no more than a few ounces of meat were lost. The flock fled into the thick foliage along the creek so quickly that within a few seconds nothing was visible or audible to prove that a wild turkey had ever been along that path. But there was proof of at least one—he lay harvested for our dinner table.

Small-Game Edibles

A number of small-game animals were dropped by my 30-30s in 1984. In Arizona, on the fine Apache Indian Reservation at San Carlos, the tassel-eared squirrel was mine with the 30-30 and hard 130-grain Speer bullets loaded way down. On a scouting trip in the winter, a search for deer on the wintering grounds, we ate cottontail rabbit harvested with light loads from the old Model 94, and I bagged a few more bunnies on a late antelope depredation hunt, again slipping the mild rounds into the chamber in place of longer-range cartridges.

A few varmints were also bagged with the 30-30—quite a few in fact. There were a couple of coyotes as well as some prairie dogs and other rodents. And though the range was quite limited when compared with the distances traversed by a true varmint rifle, the easy-to-pack 94 was all right under the circumstances.

All in all, the year 1984, in which I set

the long-range rifle aside, was a good one. All the game taken by my 94s, by myself or other hunters, was dropped in such a fashion that the shooter could be proud. We did not shoot beyond the range of our 30-30s; and though we did use fine factory ammo for much shooting, it was handloaded rounds which accounted for the 200-yard work.

I unashamedly uncased 30-30s in a few hunting camps where my partners at first turned their noses up, but whistled a different tune by the end of the safari. And I had several shooters tell me they were going to use their own dust-covered 94s from time to time when they wanted to reach that middle-ground challenge between the truly basic hunting tools and the modern long-range rifles.

I found the 94 to be a specialized tool. I found it to be far more versatile than I had thought before studying and using the rifle and its round as a main instrument of the harvest. I also found it to be an expert's firearm, but one easily mastered at the same time. In other words, any dedicated hunter can turn expert with the little 30 if he truly wants to. No special talent is required, just desire and maybe a few drops of patience.

All in all, I learned that H.V. Allen Jr. was right in his assessment of the 30-30 in his long-ago article for *The American Rifleman* magazine of February, 1948. Allen had hunted exclusively with his 94 for a year, too, and had taken much game over the years with the 30-30, just as I have. He concluded on page 26 of his piece:

> For some few years prior to and ever since the war [WW II], I have been reading articles in the various sporting magazines to the effect that the .30-30 is obsolete, lacks killing power, range, velocity, accuracy, has too high a trajectory — in the common parlance of the streets is just "no damned good." Gentlemen, all I can say (strictly a personal opinion again) is "Don't you believe it!" There's a lot more to the successful killing of game than stepping into your favorite sporting goods store and, after parting with two or three hundred skins of filthy lucre, stepping out with the latest rip-snorting, flat-shooting, long-range, high-speed

Tied to the Moses Stick, a small tripod will be used to help steady the glasses used to find game.

pompoms. Sure, I like 'em — wish I had the time and money to see and own a lot more of them.

I am not defending the .30-30, gentlemen, for the gun needs no defense. Let it stand on its record. The next time you gather round the camp fire and notice one of those little ugly-looking '94s that some dope hasn't any better sense than to use in this day and age of super-duper hand-controlled combustion chambers, don't stick your nose in the air as though you suddenly smelled a polecat. The chances are that little gun can and will shoot far truer on a running deer than you can hold it as long as you stay within its effective range, which admittedly is limited. Something my Dad told me when I was just a wee button has always stuck in my mind and seems applicable in the case of Little Eva [Allen's 30-30]. It was: "Trust in God, but keep your powder dry, son. Beware of the man with only one gun, for he knows its capabilities and limitations, and in knowing them he has reduced those limitations and increased those capabilities."

The Model 94 30-30 is an American tradition. The old gal was around when spats and knickers were fashionable, and she was there through a couple of world wars and a couple of "police actions," and she might just be in the deer coverts when the first interplanetary spaceship run becomes fact. That the 94 won't do what some of the bolt-action jobs will do is factual. But that's like comparing an off-road vehicle with a limousine. What one will do, the other may not do very well at all. The 94 has its place. That place is with the shooter who is willing to get closer, who likes the added challenge, who may not consider himself an expert but is probably a lot better outdoorsman than he thinks he is and who believes that placing his bullet for a clean harvest is linked with his personal honor. He also doesn't really mind at all when somebody chides him about his "cowboy gun," for he's learned to make that flat-sided little cowboy gun do a great big job in first-class style. He's learned how to handle it, what sort of ammo to use under various circumstances, how to handload special rounds for special tasks and how to put the bullet on the mark. The old 30-30 reminds me of the American hunter himself — reliable, steady and true.

Index

Accragard, 167
Accuracy
  bullets and, 54-55
  handloading and, 42-43
  of powders, 42
  reloading and, 42
  of 30-30s, 22-23, 135-39
  of 30-30 Improved, 63
  underloads and, 42
American Bald Eagle Commemorative, 192-93
Ammunition
  ballistics for 30-30 factory, 35-36
  cost of, 30
  holders for, 154-55
  how to choose, 37
  importance of clean, 63
  standard deviations and, 25-26
  for the 30-30 Improved, 57
  See also Bullets
Angle-Eject
  Big Bore, 196-97
  features of, 194-95
  rounds for, 198, 201, 203-7
  Trapper model of the, 195-96, 198
  Wrangler II, 196, 198
  XTR, 196
Annie Oakley Commemorative, 193
Antelope. *See* Pronghorn antelope
Antlered Game Model 94 Carbine, 188

Bait, use of, 125-26
Barrels, accuracy and design of, 137
Beads and sights, 68
Bear, hunting of, 120-29
  attacks on man, 123
  bullet types for, 127
  history of, 121-25
  how to locate bears, 127
  use of bait in the, 125-26
  use of dogs in the, 125
Bicentennial Carbine 76 Commemorative, 193

Big Bore, 196-97
Big game, 112-19
  bear hunting, 120-29
  bullet types for, 117-19
  elk hunting, 115-16
  moose hunting, 114-15
  successive shots and, 117
  where to aim, 116-17
Binoculars
  used in antelope hunting, 109
  used in deer hunting, 101-2
Bolt thrust and 30-30 Improved, 63
Bore light, 171
Bullets
  accuracy chart for, 54-55
  ballistics for 30-30 factory, 35-36
  bear hunting and types of, 127
  big game and types of, 117-19
  blowing up of, 44-45
  cast, 47, 80-81, 89, 91
  cost of, 30
  difference between pointed and flat-nosed, 45-46
  handloading and, 41-43
  for hunting antelope, 106-7
  100-grain Half-Jacket design, 49
  100-grain round-nose, 74
  100-grain Speer Half-Jacket, 54-55
  110-grain, 32, 49-50
  110-grain Hornady Round Nose, 55
  112-grain (CAST, No. 2 Alloy), 53
  125-grain, 32
  125-grain flat-nose, 32, 50
  125-grain Hollow Point, 36
  125-grain Sierra Flat Nose, 55
  130-grain flat-nose, 50-51
  130-grain Speer Flat Point, 55
  130-grain spitzer, 75
  150-grain, 51
  150-grain Hornady Interlock, 107, 117
  150-grain Hornady Round Nose, 55

Index

150-grain Interlock Round-Nose, 35
150-grain soft-point Hi-Shok, 36
150-grain soft-point Winchester, 35
150-grain Speer Mag-Tip, 107, 117
150-grain spitzer, 75
150- versus 170-grain, 28
160-grain, 32
165-grain, 32, 51–52
165-grain Hornady BT, 55
165-grain spire-point, 76
170-grain, 52, 117
170-grain Core-Lokt soft point, 36, 117
170-grain flat-nose, 76–77
170-grain full metal jacket, 30, 32
170-grain Interlock Flat Point, 36
170-grain Nosler, 117, 127
170-grain Sierra Flat Nose, 55
170-grain Silvertip, Winchester, 35, 117
170-grain soft-point Hi-Shok, 36
170-grain soft-point Winchester, 35
180-grain, 52, 117
180-grain (CAST, No. 2 Alloy), 53
190-grain, 53
190-grain round-nose, 77
190-grain Winchester Silvertip, 55, 117
pointed, 44–47
seating of, 48
shock waves and, 26–27
small game and types of, 80–82
soft-point, 28, 30
for 30-30s, 17, 28–30, 32–34
trajectories and, 74–77
varmints and types of, 89–92

Cartridges, comparison of Winchester Model 94, 206
Case cling, 63
Cases
    for guns, 154
    maintenance of, 48
    stretching of, 62
    of the 30-30 Improved, 62
Cast bullets
    for small game, 80–81
    for 30-30s, 47
    for varmints, 89, 91
Centennial 66s, 190–91
Charging of cases, 48
Chief Crazy Horse Commemorative, 186–88
Cleaning
    of blood, 165–66
    for cases, 48
    of fingerprints, 165
    gun cleaning chemicals, 166–67
    kits for, 164–65
    of rust, 167
    of sights, 68
    steps in, 168–72
    wire, 164

Commemoratives, 185–93
    American Bald Eagle Commemorative, 192–93
    Annie Oakley Commemorative, 193
    Antlered Game Model 94 Carbine, 188
    Bicentennial Carbine 76 Commemorative, 193
    Chief Crazy Horse Commemorative, 186–88
    John Wayne Commemorative Model 94, 189
    Oliver F. Winchester Commemorative, 192
    Wells Fargo Commemorative, 191–92
    Winchester-Colt Commemorative set, 189–90
    Winchester Legendary Frontiersman Model 94, 190–93
    Winchester National Rifle Association (NRA) Centennial rifle, 186
Creep in triggers, 135
Crimping, 48–49

Daypack gear, 110–11
Deer, hunting of, 94–103
    binoculars and, 101–2
    brush/woods, 98–101
    drives and, 100
    field position and, 99, 101
    mule, 211–12
    open country methods of, 101–3
    power of the 30-30 and, 97–98
    sight-in and, 98
    stand hunting, 100
    stillhunting, 98–99, 101
    use of sights, 96–97
    use of slings on rifles, 96
    use of smoke bags, 100–101
    whitetail, 212–13
Deer rifles, 95–96
Dehumidifier, use of, 172
Dogs, use of, 125
Drives and deer hunting, 100

Elk hunting, 115–16
Europe, the 7.62x51R in, 12

Federal Cartridge Company, ammunition of, 36, 90–91, 117
Field position, importance of, 99, 101
Field stripping, 170
Fore-end band, 134–35
44 Remington Magnum, 198, 201, 206
45 Colt, 201, 206
Frontier Cartridge Company, ammunition of, 35–36, 117
Full metal jacket bullets
    for small game, 80, 81
    for varmints, 91
Furbearing varmints, hunting of, 88–89

Game. *See* Big game; Small game
Gas checks and cast bullets, 80, 81
Gun cases, 154
Gun cleaning chemicals, 166–67

Gun racks, 154
Gunslick, 166

Hammer extension, 155-56
Handloading
　accuracy and, 42-43
　big game and, 40
　bullet selection and, 41-42
　examples of handloads, 49-54
　problems with, 43
　procedures for, 47-49
　variations in, 43
　versatility of, 38-41
Handloads
　hot and mild, 91
　tuning and, 133
Hoppe's Number Nine, 166-67

Iron sights, open, 66-67, 68

Jaguar, hunting of, 88
Javelina, hunting of, 213-14, 216
John Wayne Commemorative Model 94, 189

Knives, use of, 158-59

Lubes, use of, 167

Magazine/front band, 134
Magazine plug screws, 133-34
Mexico, 30-30 in, 12, 118
Micrometer receiver sights, 70
Model 55, 20
Model 64, 20
Model 85, 20-21
Model 94 30-30. *See* 30-30, Model 94
Moose hunting, 114-15
Moses stick, 157-58
Mountain lion hunting, 88
Movies, Model 94 in, 173-77
Muzzle velocity. *See* Velocity

Nickel Steel, 19

Oliver F. Winchester Commemorative, 192
Open country methods of deer hunting, 101-3
Open iron sights, 66-67, 68
Outers Pocket Pak, 164-65

Parts for the 30-30, how to obtain, 159-60
Peccary, hunting of, 213-14, 216
Peep sights, 67, 68, 70, 136
Plinking rounds, loading of, 42
Powder, selecting the right, 42
Power in early 30-30s, 19
Practice, importance of, 146-49
Primers, 48
Pronghorn antelope
　binoculars and, 109
　habits of, 107-9
　hunting of, 57, 104-11, 209-11
　loads for, 106-7
　spotting scopes and, 109-10

Rabbit, hunting of, 83
Rate of twist and bullets, 41-42
Receiver sights, 67
Recoil in early 30-30s, 17-18
Reloading
　accuracy and, 42
　of the 30-30 Improved, 62
　See also Handloading
Remington Accellerator load, 90
Remington Arms Company, ammunition of, 36, 90
Resizing of cases, 48
Rust, protection against, 167

Safety measures, 145-46
Savage models, 21
Scabbards, 152-54
Scope sights, 70
7-30 Waters rifle, 201, 206
Shadowgraphs, use of, 26
Shock waves, 26-27
Sidearms, 160-61, 163
Sighting/Site-in
　procedures for, 68-71
　small game and, 79-80
　trajectories and, 70-77
Sights
　beads and, 68
　deer hunting and, 96-97
　effects of dirt on, 68
　micrometer receiver, 70
　open iron, 66-67, 68
　peep, 67, 68, 70, 136
　receiver, 67
　scope, 70
　speed and, 67
　tang, 67
　telescopic, 67
　tuning of, 132-33
Slings, use of, 96, 150-52
Small game, 78-84
　bullet types for, 80-82
　hunting of, 217-19
　hunting of rabbit, 83
　hunting of turkey, 82-83, 216-17
　sighting of, 79-80
Smoke bags, 100-101
Smokeless powder in 30-30s, 17, 18
Smokescreen, lack of a, 19
Snapshooting, 141
Soft-nose bullets for small game, 81-82
Soft-point bullets, 28, 30
Solvents, use of, 166-67
Spotting scopes and pronghorn antelope, 109-10
Squib load, 79

Index

Stand hunting, 100
Stillhunting, 98–99, 101
Stocks, 156–57
Storey, Dale, 57, 135
Storing the 30-30, 171–72

Tang sights, 67
Telescopic sights, 67
25-35 model, description of, 20
30 caliber Winchester Center Fire (WCF), 15
  origin of name, 16, 17
30-30, Model 94
  accuracy and, 22–23, 135–39
  in America, 15–24
  as a backcountry rifle, 180–81
  for collectors, 182–83
  commemoratives, 185–93
  comparison of cartridges, 206
  converting to the 30-30 Improved, 64
  custom, 183–84
  in Europe, 12
  future of the, 198
  how to handle the, 140–49
  in Mexico, 12, 118
  numbers manufactured, 20
  reliability of the, 180
  as a survival rifle, 180
  uses for the, 12
  as a working rifle, 179
30-30 Improved
  accuracy and, 63
  advantages of, 57–58, 62
  ammunition for, 57
  cases of, 62
  costs of, 57, 64
  neck stretch and, 62
  reloading of, 62
  velocities and, 59–60, 62, 63–64
32 ACP (Automatic Colt Pistol), 80
32 Winchester Special, 20, 29, 205
307 Winchester, 203, 206
356 Winchester, 203, 206

375 Winchester, 203, 206
Trajectory
  of early 30-30s, 17
  sighting and, 70–77
Trapper model of the Angle-Eject, 195–96, 198
Triggers, 131–32
Trimming of cases, 43
TR-3, 167
Tuning of the 30-30
  fore-end band, 134-35
  handloads and, 133
  magazine/front band, 134
  magazine plug screws, 133–34
  sights, 132–33
  triggers, 131–32
Turkey, hunting of, 82–83, 216–17

Underloads and accuracy, 42

Varmint rifles, 86, 93
Varmints
  advantages of using a 30-30 on, 86–87, 89
  bullet types for hunting, 89–92
  furbearing, 88–89
  types of animals listed as, 85–86, 87–89
Velocity
  in early 30-30s, 17
  of pointed versus flat-nosed bullets, 45–46
  of the 30-30 Improved, 59–60, 62, 63–64

Waters, Ken, 201
Weights, of 30-30s, 13, 140
Wells Fargo Commemorative, 191–92
Winchester, ammunition of, 35
Winchester-Colt Commemorative set, 189–90
Winchester Legendary Frontiersman Model 94, 190–93
Winchester Model 1894, description of, 19
  See also under model number, e.g., Model 55
Winchester National Rifle Association (NRA) Centennial rifle, 186
Wrangler II, 196, 198

www.ingramcontent.com/pod-product-compliance
Lightning Source LLC
Chambersburg PA
CBHW060532010526

44107CB00059B/2621